THE
REAL ESTATE
AGENT
PLANNER

THIS BOOK BELONGS TO

_____

Don't
wish for it.

Work for it.

MONTH

MONTH:

This Months Goals

COMMISSION TOTAL

GOAL: ACTUAL:

CLOSINGS

GOAL: ACTUAL:

NEW LISTINGS

GOAL: ACTUAL:

#NEW CONTACTS

GOAL: ACTUAL:

APPOINTMENTS SET

GOAL: ACTUAL:

NEW SELLER PROSPECTS

GOAL: ACTUAL:

NEW BUYER PROSPECTS

GOAL: ACTUAL:

. . . .

GOAL: ACTUAL:

. . . .

GOAL: ACTUAL:

. . . .

GOAL: ACTUAL:

Monday	Tuesday	Wednesday	Thursday
☐	☐	☐	☐
☐	☐	☐	☐
☐	☐	☐	☐
☐	☐	☐	☐
☐	☐	☐	☐

THIS MONTHS MAIN GOALS

☐ . . . .

☐ . . . .

☐ . . . .

☐ . . . .

☐ . . . .

Friday	Saturday	Sunday

ACTIONS TO TAKE

- ☐ ....
- ☐ ....
- ☐ ....
- ☐ ....
- ☐ ....
- ☐ ....

BUSINESS EXPENSES

MLS FEES	....	CLIENT GIFTS	....
OFFICE FEES	....	LUNCHES	....
DUES / FEES	....	COFFEE	....
OFFICE SUPPLIES	....	SIGNAGE	....
TRAVEL MILEAGE	....	MAILERS	....
SUBSCRIPTIONS	....	FUEL	....
PARKING FEES	....	MISC.	....
ONLINE MARKETING	....	MISC.	....

NOTES

....
....
....
....
....
....

WHAT POSITIVE HABITS DO I WANT TO NURTURE THIS MONTH?

- ☐ ....
- ☐ ....
- ☐ ....
- ☐ ....
- ☐ ....

DATES / / - / /

MON

TUE

WED

THU

FRI

SAT

SUN

WORD OF THE WEEK

. . . .

THIS WEEKS TOP PRIORITIES

☐ . . . .
☐ . . . .
☐ . . . .
☐ . . . .
☐ . . . .

TO - DO

☐ . . . .
☐ . . . .
☐ . . . .
☐ . . . .
☐ . . . .
☐ . . . .
☐ . . . .
☐ . . . .
☐ . . . .
☐ . . . .

HABIT / RITUAL TRACKER

	M	T	W	T	F	S	S
. . . .							
. . . .							
. . . .							
. . . .							
. . . .							
. . . .							
. . . .							

STAYING FOCUSED ON YOUR GOALS

- ☐ REVIEW WEEKLY GOALS
- ☐ REVIEW MONTHLY GOALS
- ☐ REVIEW 6-MONTH GOALS

THIS WEEKS NUMBERS

NEW LISTINGS	. . . .
CLOSINGS	. . . .
COMMISSIONS	. . . .
CONTRACTS ACCEPTED	. . . .
SHOWINGS	. . . .
CALLS MADE	. . . .
NEW LEADS	. . . .
APPOINTMENTS SET	. . . .
SOCIAL MEDIA POSTS	. . . .
OTHER:	. . . .
OTHER:	. . . .

NOTES

WHAT ACTIONS DO I NEED TO TAKE THIS WEEK IN ORDER TO MOVE THE NEEDLE FORWARD?

WHAT ARE MY MAIN GOALS THIS WEEK?

HOW WILL I CELEBRATE MY WINS THIS WEEK?

IS THERE ANYTHING I'VE BEEN AVOIDING THAT NEEDS TO BE COMPLETED OR STARTED THIS WEEK?

WHAT MIGHT TRIP ME UP THIS WEEK AND MOVE ME OFF COURSE? HOW CAN I AVOID THESE PITFALLS?

Monday
/

Tuesday
/

Wednesday
/

TOP 3 PRIORITIES

. . . .
. . . .
. . . .

DAILY GRATITUDE

. . . .
. . . .
. . . .
. . . .
. . . .

TO-DO

☐ . . . .
☐ . . . .
☐ . . . .
☐ . . . .
☐ . . . .

TIME BLOCKING

6
7
8
9
10
11
12
1
2
3
4
5
6
7
8
9

TOP 3 PRIORITIES

. . . .
. . . .
. . . .

DAILY GRATITUDE

. . . .
. . . .
. . . .
. . . .
. . . .

TO-DO

☐ . . . .
☐ . . . .
☐ . . . .
☐ . . . .
☐ . . . .

TIME BLOCKING

6
7
8
9
10
11
12
1
2
3
4
5
6
7
8
9

TOP 3 PRIORITIES

. . . .
. . . .
. . . .

DAILY GRATITUDE

. . . .
. . . .
. . . .
. . . .
. . . .

TO-DO

☐ . . . .
☐ . . . .
☐ . . . .
☐ . . . .
☐ . . . .

TIME BLOCKING

6
7
8
9
10
11
12
1
2
3
4
5
6
7
8
9

Thursday
/

Friday
/

Weekend
/

TOP 3 PRIORITIES
....
....
....

DAILY GRATITUDE
....
....
....
....
....

TO-DO
☐ ....
☐ ....
☐ ....
☐ ....
☐ ....

TIME BLOCKING
6
7
8
9
10
11
12
1
2
3
4
5
6
7
8
9

TOP 3 PRIORITIES
....
....
....

DAILY GRATITUDE
....
....
....
....
....

TO-DO .
☐ ....
☐ ....
☐ ....
☐ ....
☐ ....

TIME BLOCKING
6
7
8
9
10
11
12
1
2
3
4
5
6
7
8
9

TOP 3 PRIORITIES
....
....
....

DAILY GRATITUDE
....
....
....
....
....

TO-DO
☐ ....
☐ ....
☐ ....
☐ ....
☐ ....

NOTES
....
....
....
....
....
....
....
....
....
....
....
....
....
....

DATES / / - / /

MON

TUE

WED

THU

FRI

SAT

SUN

WORD OF THE WEEK

. . . .

THIS WEEKS TOP PRIORITIES

☐ . . . .
☐ . . . .
☐ . . . .
☐ . . . .
☐ . . . .

TO - DO

☐ . . . .
☐ . . . .
☐ . . . .
☐ . . . .
☐ . . . .
☐ . . . .
☐ . . . .
☐ . . . .
☐ . . . .
☐ . . . .

HABIT / RITUAL TRACKER

M T W T F S S

STAYING FOCUSED ON YOUR GOALS

- ☐ REVIEW WEEKLY GOALS
- ☐ REVIEW MONTHLY GOALS
- ☐ REVIEW 6-MONTH GOALS

THIS WEEKS NUMBERS

NEW LISTINGS	. . . .
CLOSINGS	. . . .
COMMISSIONS	. . . .
CONTRACTS ACCEPTED	. . . .
SHOWINGS	. . . .
CALLS MADE	. . . .
NEW LEADS	. . . .
APPOINTMENTS SET	. . . .
SOCIAL MEDIA POSTS	. . . .
OTHER:	. . . .
OTHER:	. . . .

NOTES

WHAT ACTIONS DO I NEED TO TAKE THIS WEEK IN ORDER TO MOVE THE NEEDLE FORWARD?

WHAT ARE MY MAIN GOALS THIS WEEK?

HOW WILL I CELEBRATE MY WINS THIS WEEK?

IS THERE ANYTHING I'VE BEEN AVOIDING THAT NEEDS TO BE COMPLETED OR STARTED THIS WEEK?

WHAT MIGHT TRIP ME UP THIS WEEK AND MOVE ME OFF COURSE? HOW CAN I AVOID THESE PITFALLS?

Monday	Tuesday	Wednesday
/	/	/

TOP 3 PRIORITIES

. . . .

. . . .

. . . .

DAILY GRATITUDE

. . . .

. . . .

. . . .

. . . .

TO-DO

☐ . . . .

☐ . . . .

☐ . . . .

☐ . . . .

☐ . . . .

TIME BLOCKING

	Monday	Tuesday	Wednesday
6			
7			
8			
9			
10			
11			
12			
1			
2			
3			
4			
5			
6			
7			
8			
9			

TOP 3 PRIORITIES (Tuesday)

DAILY GRATITUDE (Tuesday)

TO-DO (Tuesday)

TIME BLOCKING (Tuesday)

TOP 3 PRIORITIES (Wednesday)

DAILY GRATITUDE (Wednesday)

TO-DO (Wednesday)

TIME BLOCKING (Wednesday)

Thursday
/

Friday
/

Weekend
/

TOP 3 PRIORITIES

. . . .
. . . .
. . . .

DAILY GRATITUDE

. . . .
. . . .
. . . .
. . . .
. . . .

TO-DO

☐ . . . .
☐ . . . .
☐ . . . .
☐ . . . .
☐ . . . .

TIME BLOCKING

6
7
8
9
10
11
12
1
2
3
4
5
6
7
8
9

TOP 3 PRIORITIES

. . . .
. . . .
. . . .

DAILY GRATITUDE

. . . .
. . . .
. . . .
. . . .
. . . .

TO-DO

☐ . . . .
☐ . . . .
☐ . . . .
☐ . . . .
☐ . . . .

TIME BLOCKING

6
7
8
9
10
11
12
1
2
3
4
5
6
7
8
9

TOP 3 PRIORITIES

. . . .
. . . .
. . . .

DAILY GRATITUDE

. . . .
. . . .
. . . .
. . . .

TO-DO

☐ . . . .
☐ . . . .
☐ . . . .
☐ . . . .
☐

NOTES

. . . .
. . . .
. . . .
. . . .
. . . .
. . . .
. . . .
. . . .
. . . .
. . . .
. . . .
. . . .
. . . .
. . . .

DATES / / - / /

MON

TUE

WED

THU

FRI

SAT

SUN

WORD OF THE WEEK

. . . .

THIS WEEKS TOP PRIORITIES

☐ . . . .
☐ . . . .
☐ . . . .
☐ . . . .
☐ . . . .

TO - DO

☐ . . . .
☐ . . . .
☐ . . . .
☐ . . . .
☐ . . . .
☐ . . . .
☐ . . . .
☐ . . . .
☐ . . . .
☐ . . . .

HABIT / RITUAL TRACKER

M T W T F S S

. . . .
. . . .
. . . .
. . . .
. . . .
. . . .
. . . .

STAYING FOCUSED ON YOUR GOALS

- ☐ REVIEW WEEKLY GOALS
- ☐ REVIEW MONTHLY GOALS
- ☐ REVIEW 6-MONTH GOALS

THIS WEEKS NUMBERS

NEW LISTINGS	. . . .
CLOSINGS	. . . .
COMMISSIONS	. . . .
CONTRACTS ACCEPTED	. . . .
SHOWINGS	. . . .
CALLS MADE	. . . .
NEW LEADS	. . . .
APPOINTMENTS SET	. . . .
SOCIAL MEDIA POSTS	. . . .
OTHER:	. . . .
OTHER:	. . . .

NOTES

WHAT ACTIONS DO I NEED TO TAKE THIS WEEK IN ORDER TO MOVE THE NEEDLE FORWARD?

WHAT ARE MY MAIN GOALS THIS WEEK?

HOW WILL I CELEBRATE MY WINS THIS WEEK?

IS THERE ANYTHING I'VE BEEN AVOIDING THAT NEEDS TO BE COMPLETED OR STARTED THIS WEEK?

WHAT MIGHT TRIP ME UP THIS WEEK AND MOVE ME OFF COURSE? HOW CAN I AVOID THESE PITFALLS?

Monday

/

TOP 3 PRIORITIES

. . . .

. . . .

. . . .

DAILY GRATITUDE

. . . .

. . . .

. . . .

. . . .

TO-DO

☐ . . . .

☐ . . . .

☐ . . . .

☐ . . . .

☐ . . . .

TIME BLOCKING

6

7

8

9

10

11

12

1

2

3

4

5

6

7

8

9

Tuesday

/

TOP 3 PRIORITIES

. . . .

. . . .

. . . .

DAILY GRATITUDE

. . . .

. . . .

. . . .

. . . .

TO-DO

☐ . . . .

☐ . . . .

☐ . . . .

☐ . . . .

☐ . . . .

TIME BLOCKING

6

7

8

9

10

11

12

1

2

3

4

5

6

7

8

9

Wednesday

/

TOP 3 PRIORITIES

. . . .

. . . .

. . . .

DAILY GRATITUDE

. . . .

. . . .

. . . .

. . . .

TO-DO

☐ . . . .

☐ . . . .

☐ . . . .

☐ . . . .

☐ . . . .

TIME BLOCKING

6

7

8

9

10

11

12

1

2

3

4

5

6

7

8

9

Thursday
/

TOP 3 PRIORITIES
· ·
· ·
· ·

DAILY GRATITUDE
· ·
· ·
· ·
· ·
· ·

TO-DO
- [ ] ·
- [ ] ·
- [ ] ·
- [ ] ·
- [ ]

TIME BLOCKING
6
7
8
9
10
11
12
1
2
3
4
5
6
7
8
9

Friday
/

TOP 3 PRIORITIES
· ·
· ·
· ·

DAILY GRATITUDE
· ·
· ·
· ·
· ·
· ·

TO-DO
- [ ] ·
- [ ] ·
- [ ] ·
- [ ] ·
- [ ]

TIME BLOCKING
6
7
8
9
10
11
12
1
2
3
4
5
6
7
8
9

Weekend
/

TOP 3 PRIORITIES
· ·
· ·
· ·

DAILY GRATITUDE
· ·
· ·
· ·
· ·

TO-DO
- [ ]
- [ ]
- [ ]
- [ ]
- [ ]

NOTES
· ·
· ·
· ·
· ·
· ·
· ·
· ·
· ·
· ·
· ·
· ·

DATES / / - / /

WORD OF THE WEEK

....

THIS WEEKS TOP PRIORITIES

☐ ....
☐ ....
☐ ....
☐ ....
☐ ....

MON

TUE

WED

THU

FRI

SAT

SUN

TO - DO

☐ ....
☐ ....
☐ ....
☐ ....
☐ ....
☐ ....
☐ ....
☐ ....
☐ ....
☐ ....

HABIT / RITUAL TRACKER

	M	T	W	T	F	S	S
....							
....							
....							
....							
....							
....							
....							

STAYING FOCUSED ON YOUR GOALS

- ☐ REVIEW WEEKLY GOALS
- ☐ REVIEW MONTHLY GOALS
- ☐ REVIEW 6-MONTH GOALS

THIS WEEKS NUMBERS

NEW LISTINGS	. . . .
CLOSINGS	. . . .
COMMISSIONS	. . . .
CONTRACTS ACCEPTED	. . . .
SHOWINGS	. . . .
CALLS MADE	. . . .
NEW LEADS	. . . .
APPOINTMENTS SET	. . . .
SOCIAL MEDIA POSTS	. . . .
OTHER:	. . . .
OTHER:	. . . .

NOTES

WHAT ACTIONS DO I NEED TO TAKE THIS WEEK IN ORDER TO MOVE THE NEEDLE FORWARD?

WHAT ARE MY MAIN GOALS THIS WEEK?

HOW WILL I CELEBRATE MY WINS THIS WEEK?

IS THERE ANYTHING I'VE BEEN AVOIDING THAT NEEDS TO BE COMPLETED OR STARTED THIS WEEK?

WHAT MIGHT TRIP ME UP THIS WEEK AND MOVE ME OFF COURSE? HOW CAN I AVOID THESE PITFALLS?

Monday	Tuesday	Wednesday
/	/	/

TOP 3 PRIORITIES (Monday)

. . . .

. . . .

. . . .

DAILY GRATITUDE

. . . .

. . . .

. . . .

. . . .

TO-DO

☐ . . . .

☐ . . . .

☐ . . . .

☐ . . . .

☐ . . . .

TIME BLOCKING

6

7

8

9

10

11

12

1

2

3

4

5

6

7

8

9

TOP 3 PRIORITIES (Tuesday)

. . . .

. . . .

. . . .

DAILY GRATITUDE

. . . .

. . . .

. . . .

. . . .

TO-DO

☐ . . . .

☐ . . . .

☐ . . . .

☐ . . . .

☐ . . . .

TIME BLOCKING

6

7

8

9

10

11

12

1

2

3

4

5

6

7

8

9

TOP 3 PRIORITIES (Wednesday)

. . . .

. . . .

. . . .

DAILY GRATITUDE

. . . .

. . . .

. . . .

. . . .

TO-DO

☐ . . . .

☐ . . . .

☐ . . . .

☐ . . . .

☐ . . . .

TIME BLOCKING

6

7

8

9

10

11

12

1

2

3

4

5

6

7

8

9

Thursday
/

TOP 3 PRIORITIES
. . . .
. . . .
. . . .

DAILY GRATITUDE
. . . .
. . . .
. . . .
. . . .
. . . .

TO-DO
- ☐ . . . .
- ☐ . . . .
- ☐ . . . .
- ☐ . . . .
- ☐ . . . .

TIME BLOCKING
6
7
8
9
10
11
12
1
2
3
4
5
6
7
8
9

Friday
/

TOP 3 PRIORITIES
. . . .
. . . .
. . . .

DAILY GRATITUDE
. . . .
. . . .
. . . .
. . . .
. . . .

TO-DO
- ☐ . . . .
- ☐ . . . .
- ☐ . . . .
- ☐ . . . .
- ☐ . . . .

TIME BLOCKING
6
7
8
9
10
11
12
1
2
3
4
5
6
7
8
9

Weekend
/

TOP 3 PRIORITIES
. . . .
. . . .
. . . .

DAILY GRATITUDE
. . . .
. . . .
. . . .
. . . .

TO-DO
- ☐ . . . .
- ☐ . . . .
- ☐ . . . .
- ☐ . . . .
- ☐ . . . .

NOTES
. . . .
. . . .
. . . .
. . . .
. . . .
. . . .
. . . .
. . . .
. . . .
. . . .
. . . .
. . . .

DATES / / - / /

MON

TUE

WED

THU

FRI

SAT

SUN

WORD OF THE WEEK

....

THIS WEEKS TOP PRIORITIES

☐ ....
☐ ....
☐ ....
☐ ....
☐ ....

TO - DO

☐ ....
☐ ....
☐ ....
☐ ....
☐ ....
☐ ....
☐ ....
☐ ....
☐ ....
☐ ....

HABIT / RITUAL TRACKER

	M	T	W	T	F	S	S
....							
....							
....							
....							
....							
....							
....							

STAYING FOCUSED ON YOUR GOALS

- [ ] REVIEW WEEKLY GOALS
- [ ] REVIEW MONTHLY GOALS
- [ ] REVIEW 6-MONTH GOALS

NOTES

THIS WEEKS NUMBERS

NEW LISTINGS	. . . .
CLOSINGS	. . . .
COMMISSIONS	. . . .
CONTRACTS ACCEPTED	. . . .
SHOWINGS	. . . .
CALLS MADE	. . . .
NEW LEADS	. . . .
APPOINTMENTS SET	. . . .
SOCIAL MEDIA POSTS	. . . .
OTHER:	. . . .
OTHER:	. . . .

WHAT ACTIONS DO I NEED TO TAKE THIS WEEK IN ORDER TO MOVE THE NEEDLE FORWARD?

WHAT ARE MY MAIN GOALS THIS WEEK?

HOW WILL I CELEBRATE MY WINS THIS WEEK?

IS THERE ANYTHING I'VE BEEN AVOIDING THAT NEEDS TO BE COMPLETED OR STARTED THIS WEEK?

WHAT MIGHT TRIP ME UP THIS WEEK AND MOVE ME OFF COURSE? HOW CAN I AVOID THESE PITFALLS?

Monday
/

Tuesday
/

Wednesday
/

TOP 3 PRIORITIES	TOP 3 PRIORITIES	TOP 3 PRIORITIES
. . . .	. . . .	. . . .
. . . .	. . . .	. . . .
. . . .	. . . .	. . . .

DAILY GRATITUDE

DAILY GRATITUDE

DAILY GRATITUDE

TO-DO

☐ . . . .
☐ . . . .
☐ . . . .
☐ . . . .
☐ . . . .

TO-DO

☐
☐
☐
☐
☐

TO-DO

☐
☐
☐
☐
☐

TIME BLOCKING

Monday	Tuesday	Wednesday
6	6	6
7	7	7
8	8	8
9	9	9
10	10	10
11	11	11
12	12	12
1	1	1
2	2	2
3	3	3
4	4	4
5	5	5
6	6	6
7	7	7
8	8	8
9	9	9

Thursday	**Friday**	**Weekend**
/	/	/
TOP 3 PRIORITIES	TOP 3 PRIORITIES	TOP 3 PRIORITIES
. . . .	. . . .	. . . .
. . . .	. . . .	. . . .
. . . .	. . . .	. . . .
DAILY GRATITUDE	DAILY GRATITUDE	DAILY GRATITUDE
. . . .	. . . .	. . . .
. . . .	. . . .	. . . .
. . . .	. . . .	. . . .
. . . .	. . . .	. . . .
. . . .	. . . .	. . . .
TO-DO	TO-DO	TO-DO
☐	☐	☐ . . . .
☐	☐	☐ . . . .
☐	☐	☐ . . . .
☐	☐	☐ . . . .
☐	☐	☐ . . . .
TIME BLOCKING	TIME BLOCKING	NOTES
6	6	. . . .
7	7	. . . .
8	8	. . . .
9	9	. . . .
10	10	. . . .
11	11	. . . .
12	12	. . . .
1	1	. . . .
2	2	. . . .
3	3	. . . .
4	4	. . . .
5	5	. . . .
6	6	. . . .
7	7	. . . .
8	8	. . . .
9	9	. . . .

Reminder:
if you
play small
you stay small.

So play BIG!

MONTH

MONTH:

This Months Goals

COMMISSION TOTAL

GOAL:	ACTUAL:

CLOSINGS

GOAL:	ACTUAL:

NEW LISTINGS

GOAL:	ACTUAL:

#NEW CONTACTS

GOAL:	ACTUAL:

APPOINTMENTS SET

GOAL:	ACTUAL:

NEW SELLER PROSPECTS

GOAL:	ACTUAL:

NEW BUYER PROSPECTS

GOAL:	ACTUAL:

. . . .

GOAL:	ACTUAL:

. . . .

GOAL:	ACTUAL:

. . . .

GOAL:	ACTUAL:

Monday	Tuesday	Wednesday	Thursday
☐	☐	☐	☐
☐	☐	☐	☐
☐	☐	☐	☐
☐	☐	☐	☐
☐	☐	☐	☐

THIS MONTHS MAIN GOALS

☐ . . . .

☐ . . . .

☐ . . . .

☐ . . . .

☐ . . . .

Friday	Saturday	Sunday
☐	☐	☐
☐	☐	☐
☐	☐	☐
☐	☐	☐
☐	☐	☐

ACTIONS TO TAKE

☐ ....
☐ ....
☐ ....
☐ ....
☐ ....
☐ ....

BUSINESS EXPENSES

MLS FEES	....	CLIENT GIFTS	....
OFFICE FEES	....	LUNCHES	....
DUES / FEES	....	COFFEE	....
OFFICE SUPPLIES	....	SIGNAGE	....
TRAVEL MILEAGE	....	MAILERS	....
SUBSCRIPTIONS	....	FUEL	....
PARKING FEES	....	MISC.	....
ONLINE MARKETING	....	MISC.	....

NOTES

....
....
....
....
....
....

WHAT POSITIVE HABITS DO I WANT TO NURTURE THIS MONTH?

☐ ....
☐ ....
☐ ....
☐ ....
☐ ....

DATES / / - / /

MON

TUE

WED

THU

FRI

SAT

SUN

WORD OF THE WEEK

....

THIS WEEKS TOP PRIORITIES

☐ ....
☐ ....
☐ ....
☐ ....
☐ ....

TO - DO

☐ ....
☐ ....
☐ ....
☐ ....
☐ ....
☐ ....
☐ ....
☐ ....
☐ ....
☐ ....

HABIT / RITUAL TRACKER

M T W T F S S

STAYING FOCUSED ON YOUR GOALS

- [ ] REVIEW WEEKLY GOALS
- [ ] REVIEW MONTHLY GOALS
- [ ] REVIEW 6-MONTH GOALS

NOTES

THIS WEEKS NUMBERS

NEW LISTINGS	. . . .
CLOSINGS	. . . .
COMMISSIONS	. . . .
CONTRACTS ACCEPTED	. . . .
SHOWINGS	. . . .
CALLS MADE	. . . .
NEW LEADS	. . . .
APPOINTMENTS SET	. . . .
SOCIAL MEDIA POSTS	. . . .
OTHER:	. . . .
OTHER:	. . . .

WHAT ACTIONS DO I NEED TO TAKE THIS WEEK IN ORDER TO MOVE THE NEEDLE FORWARD?

WHAT ARE MY MAIN GOALS THIS WEEK?

HOW WILL I CELEBRATE MY WINS THIS WEEK?

IS THERE ANYTHING I'VE BEEN AVOIDING THAT NEEDS TO BE COMPLETED OR STARTED THIS WEEK?

WHAT MIGHT TRIP ME UP THIS WEEK AND MOVE ME OFF COURSE? HOW CAN I AVOID THESE PITFALLS?

Monday
/

Tuesday
/

Wednesday
/

TOP 3 PRIORITIES	TOP 3 PRIORITIES	TOP 3 PRIORITIES
. . . .	. . . .	. . . .
. . . .	. . . .	. . . .
. . . .	. . . .	. . . .

DAILY GRATITUDE	DAILY GRATITUDE	DAILY GRATITUDE
. . . .	. . . .	. . . .
. . . .	. . . .	. . . .
. . . .	. . . .	. . . .
. . . .	. . . .	. . . .
. . . .		

TO-DO

Monday	Tuesday	Wednesday
☐	☐	☐ . . . .
☐	☐	☐ . . . .
☐	☐	☐ . . . .
☐	☐	☐ . . . .
☐	☐	☐ . . . .

TIME BLOCKING

	Monday	Tuesday	Wednesday
6			
7			
8			
9			
10			
11			
12			
1			
2			
3			
4			
5			
6			
7			
8			
9			

Thursday
/

TOP 3 PRIORITIES
. . . .
. . . .
. . . .

DAILY GRATITUDE
. . . .
. . . .
. . . .
. . . .
. . . .

TO-DO
- ☐ . . . .
- ☐ . . . .
- ☐ . . . .
- ☐ . . . .
- ☐ . . . .

TIME BLOCKING
6
7
8
9
10
11
12
1
2
3
4
5
6
7
8
9

Friday
/

TOP 3 PRIORITIES
. . . .
. . . .
. . . .

DAILY GRATITUDE
. . . .
. . . .
. . . .
. . . .
. . . .

TO-DO
- ☐ . . . .
- ☐ . . . .
- ☐ . . . .
- ☐ . . . .
- ☐ . . . .

TIME BLOCKING
6
7
8
9
10
11
12
1
2
3
4
5
6
7
8
9

Weekend
/

TOP 3 PRIORITIES
. . . .
. . . .
. . . .

DAILY GRATITUDE
. . . .
. . . .
. . . .
. . . .
. . . .

TO-DO
- ☐ . . . .
- ☐ . . . .
- ☐ . . . .
- ☐ . . . .
- ☐ . . . .

NOTES
. . . .
. . . .
. . . .
. . . .
. . . .
. . . .
. . . .
. . . .
. . . .
. . . .
. . . .
. . . .
. . . .
. . . .

DATES / / - / /

MON

TUE

WED

THU

FRI

SAT

SUN

WORD OF THE WEEK

....

THIS WEEKS TOP PRIORITIES

☐ ....
☐ ....
☐ ....
☐ ....
☐ ....

TO - DO

☐ ....
☐ ....
☐ ....
☐ ....
☐ ....
☐ ....
☐ ....
☐ ....
☐ ....
☐ ....

HABIT / RITUAL TRACKER

M T W T F S S

....
....
....
....
....
....
....

STAYING FOCUSED ON YOUR GOALS

- [ ] REVIEW WEEKLY GOALS
- [ ] REVIEW MONTHLY GOALS
- [ ] REVIEW 6-MONTH GOALS

NOTES

THIS WEEKS NUMBERS

NEW LISTINGS	. . . .
CLOSINGS	. . . .
COMMISSIONS	. . . .
CONTRACTS ACCEPTED	. . . .
SHOWINGS	. . . .
CALLS MADE	. . . .
NEW LEADS	. . . .
APPOINTMENTS SET	. . . .
SOCIAL MEDIA POSTS	. . . .
OTHER:	. . . .
OTHER:	. . . .

WHAT ACTIONS DO I NEED TO TAKE THIS WEEK IN ORDER TO MOVE THE NEEDLE FORWARD?

WHAT ARE MY MAIN GOALS THIS WEEK?

HOW WILL I CELEBRATE MY WINS THIS WEEK?

IS THERE ANYTHING I'VE BEEN AVOIDING THAT NEEDS TO BE COMPLETED OR STARTED THIS WEEK?

WHAT MIGHT TRIP ME UP THIS WEEK AND MOVE ME OFF COURSE? HOW CAN I AVOID THESE PITFALLS?

Monday

/

TOP 3 PRIORITIES

. . . .
. . . .
. . . .

DAILY GRATITUDE

. . . .
. . . .
. . . .
. . . .

TO-DO

☐ . . . .
☐ . . . .
☐ . . . .
☐ . . . .
☐ . . . .

TIME BLOCKING

6
7
8
9
10
11
12
1
2
3
4
5
6
7
8
9

Tuesday

/

TOP 3 PRIORITIES

. . . .
. . . .
. . . .

DAILY GRATITUDE

. . . .
. . . .
. . . .
. . . .

TO-DO

☐ . . . .
☐ . . . .
☐ . . . .
☐ . . . .
☐ . . . .

TIME BLOCKING

6
7
8
9
10
11
12
1
2
3
4
5
6
7
8
9

Wednesday

/

TOP 3 PRIORITIES

. . . .
. . . .
. . . .

DAILY GRATITUDE

. . . .
. . . .
. . . .
. . . .

TO-DO

☐ . . . .
☐ . . . .
☐ . . . .
☐ . . . .
☐ . . . .

TIME BLOCKING

6
7
8
9
10
11
12
1
2
3
4
5
6
7
8
9

QUOTE OF THE WEEK:

Thursday
/

TOP 3 PRIORITIES

....
....
....

DAILY GRATITUDE

....
....
....
....
....

TO-DO

☐ ....
☐ ....
☐ ....
☐ ....
☐ ....

TIME BLOCKING

6 _____
7 _____
8 _____
9 _____
10 _____
11 _____
12 _____
1 _____
2 _____
3 _____
4 _____
5 _____
6 _____
7 _____
8 _____
9 _____

Friday
/

TOP 3 PRIORITIES

....
....
....

DAILY GRATITUDE

....
....
....
....
....

TO-DO

☐ ....
☐ ....
☐ ....
☐ ....
☐ ....

TIME BLOCKING

6 _____
7 _____
8 _____
9 _____
10 _____
11 _____
12 _____
1 _____
2 _____
3 _____
4 _____
5 _____
6 _____
7 _____
8 _____
9 _____

Weekend
/

TOP 3 PRIORITIES

....
....
....

DAILY GRATITUDE

....
....
....
....
....

TO-DO

☐ ....
☐ ....
☐ ....
☐ ....
☐ ....

NOTES

....
....
....
....
....
....
....
....
....
....
....
....
....
....
....

DATES / / - / /

MON

TUE

WED

THU

FRI

SAT

SUN

WORD OF THE WEEK

....

THIS WEEKS TOP PRIORITIES

☐ ....
☐ ....
☐ ....
☐ ....
☐ ....

TO - DO

☐ ....
☐ ....
☐ ....
☐ ....
☐ ....
☐ ....
☐ ....
☐ ....
☐ ....
☐ ....

HABIT / RITUAL TRACKER

M T W T F S S

....
....
....
....
....
....
....

STAYING FOCUSED ON YOUR GOALS

- ☐ REVIEW WEEKLY GOALS
- ☐ REVIEW MONTHLY GOALS
- ☐ REVIEW 6-MONTH GOALS

THIS WEEKS NUMBERS

NEW LISTINGS	. . . .
CLOSINGS	. . . .
COMMISSIONS	. . . .
CONTRACTS ACCEPTED	. . . .
SHOWINGS	. . . .
CALLS MADE	. . . .
NEW LEADS	. . . .
APPOINTMENTS SET	. . . .
SOCIAL MEDIA POSTS	. . . .
OTHER:	. . . .
OTHER:	. . . .

NOTES

WHAT ACTIONS DO I NEED TO TAKE THIS WEEK IN ORDER TO MOVE THE NEEDLE FORWARD?

WHAT ARE MY MAIN GOALS THIS WEEK?

HOW WILL I CELEBRATE MY WINS THIS WEEK?

IS THERE ANYTHING I'VE BEEN AVOIDING THAT NEEDS TO BE COMPLETED OR STARTED THIS WEEK?

WHAT MIGHT TRIP ME UP THIS WEEK AND MOVE ME OFF COURSE? HOW CAN I AVOID THESE PITFALLS?

Monday
/

TOP 3 PRIORITIES
. . . .
. . . .
. . . .

DAILY GRATITUDE
. . . .
. . . .
. . . .
. . . .

TO-DO
☐ . . . .
☐ . . . .
☐ . . . .
☐ . . . .
☐ . . . .

TIME BLOCKING
6
7
8
9
10
11
12
1
2
3
4
5
6
7
8
9

Tuesday
/

TOP 3 PRIORITIES
. . . .
. . . .
. . . .

DAILY GRATITUDE
. . . .
. . . .
. . . .
. . . .

TO-DO
☐ . . . .
☐ . . . .
☐ . . . .
☐ . . . .
☐ . . . .

TIME BLOCKING
6
7
8
9
10
11
12
1
2
3
4
5
6
7
8
9

Wednesday
/

TOP 3 PRIORITIES
. . . .
. . . .
. . . .

DAILY GRATITUDE
. . . .
. . . .
. . . .
. . . .

TO-DO
☐ . . . .
☐ . . . .
☐ . . . .
☐ . . . .
☐ . . . .

TIME BLOCKING
6
7
8
9
10
11
12
1
2
3
4
5
6
7
8
9

Thursday

/

TOP 3 PRIORITIES

. . . .

. . . .

. . . .

DAILY GRATITUDE

. . . .

. . . .

. . . .

. . . .

. . . .

TO-DO

- ☐
- ☐
- ☐
- ☐
- ☐

TIME BLOCKING

6

7

8

9

10

11

12

1

2

3

4

5

6

7

8

9

Friday

/

TOP 3 PRIORITIES

. . . .

. . . .

. . . .

DAILY GRATITUDE

. . . .

. . . .

. . . .

. . . .

. . . .

TO-DO

- ☐
- ☐
- ☐
- ☐
- ☐

TIME BLOCKING

6

7

8

9

10

11

12

1

2

3

4

5

6

7

8

9

Weekend

/

TOP 3 PRIORITIES

. . . .

. . . .

. . . .

DAILY GRATITUDE

. . . .

. . . .

. . . .

. . . .

TO-DO

- ☐
- ☐
- ☐
- ☐
- ☐

NOTES

. . . .

. . . .

. . . .

. . . .

. . . .

. . . .

. . . .

. . . .

. . . .

. . . .

. . . .

. . . .

. . . .

DATES / / - / /

MON

TUE

WED

THU

FRI

SAT

SUN

WORD OF THE WEEK

....

THIS WEEKS TOP PRIORITIES

☐ ....
☐ ....
☐ ....
☐ ....
☐ ....

TO - DO

☐ ....
☐ ....
☐ ....
☐ ....
☐ ....
☐ ....
☐ ....
☐ ....
☐ ....
☐ ....

HABIT / RITUAL TRACKER

	M	T	W	T	F	S	S
....							
....							
....							
....							
....							
....							
....							

STAYING FOCUSED ON YOUR GOALS

- ☐ REVIEW WEEKLY GOALS
- ☐ REVIEW MONTHLY GOALS
- ☐ REVIEW 6-MONTH GOALS

THIS WEEKS NUMBERS

NEW LISTINGS	. . . .
CLOSINGS	. . . .
COMMISSIONS	. . . .
CONTRACTS ACCEPTED	. . . .
SHOWINGS	. . . .
CALLS MADE	. . . .
NEW LEADS	. . . .
APPOINTMENTS SET	. . . .
SOCIAL MEDIA POSTS	. . . .
OTHER:	. . . .
OTHER:	. . . .

NOTES

WHAT ACTIONS DO I NEED TO TAKE THIS WEEK IN ORDER TO MOVE THE NEEDLE FORWARD?

WHAT ARE MY MAIN GOALS THIS WEEK?

HOW WILL I CELEBRATE MY WINS THIS WEEK?

IS THERE ANYTHING I'VE BEEN AVOIDING THAT NEEDS TO BE COMPLETED OR STARTED THIS WEEK?

WHAT MIGHT TRIP ME UP THIS WEEK AND MOVE ME OFF COURSE? HOW CAN I AVOID THESE PITFALLS?

Monday
/

TOP 3 PRIORITIES
. . . .
. . . .
. . . .

DAILY GRATITUDE
. . . .
. . . .
. . . .
. . . .

TO-DO
☐ . . . .
☐ . . . .
☐ . . . .
☐ . . . .
☐ . . . .

TIME BLOCKING
6
7
8
9
10
11
12
1
2
3
4
5
6
7
8
9

Tuesday
/

TOP 3 PRIORITIES
. . . .
. . . .
. . . .

DAILY GRATITUDE
. . . .
. . . .
. . . .
. . . .

TO-DO
☐ . . . .
☐ . . . .
☐ . . . .
☐ . . . .
☐ . . . .

TIME BLOCKING
6
7
8
9
10
11
12
1
2
3
4
5
6
7
8
9

Wednesday
/

TOP 3 PRIORITIES
. . . .
. . . .
. . . .

DAILY GRATITUDE
. . . .
. . . .
. . . .
. . . .

TO-DO
☐ . . . .
☐ . . . .
☐ . . . .
☐ . . . .
☐ . . . .

TIME BLOCKING
6
7
8
9
10
11
12
1
2
3
4
5
6
7
8
9

Thursday

/

TOP 3 PRIORITIES

. . . .

. . . .

. . . .

DAILY GRATITUDE

. . . .

. . . .

. . . .

. . . .

. . . .

TO-DO

☐

☐

☐

☐

☐

TIME BLOCKING

6

7

8

9

10

11

12

1

2

3

4

5

6

7

8

9

Friday

/

TOP 3 PRIORITIES

. . . .

. . . .

. . . .

DAILY GRATITUDE

. . . .

. . . .

. . . .

. . . .

. . . .

TO-DO

☐

☐

☐

☐

☐

TIME BLOCKING

6

7

8

9

10

11

12

1

2

3

4

5

6

7

8

9

Weekend

/

TOP 3 PRIORITIES

. . . .

. . . .

. . . .

DAILY GRATITUDE

. . . .

. . . .

. . . .

. . . .

. . . .

TO-DO

☐

☐

☐

☐

☐

NOTES

. . . .

. . . .

. . . .

. . . .

. . . .

. . . .

. . . .

. . . .

. . . .

. . . .

. . . .

. . . .

DATES / / - / /

MON

TUE

WED

THU

FRI

SAT

SUN

WORD OF THE WEEK

. . . .

THIS WEEKS TOP PRIORITIES

☐ . . . .
☐ . . . .
☐ . . . .
☐ . . . .
☐ . . . .

TO - DO

☐ . . . .
☐ . . . .
☐ . . . .
☐ . . . .
☐ . . . .
☐ . . . .
☐ . . . .
☐ . . . .
☐ . . . .
☐ . . . .

HABIT / RITUAL TRACKER

	M	T	W	T	F	S	S
. . . .							
. . . .							
. . . .							
. . . .							
. . . .							
. . . .							
. . . .							

STAYING FOCUSED ON YOUR GOALS

- ☐ REVIEW WEEKLY GOALS
- ☐ REVIEW MONTHLY GOALS
- ☐ REVIEW 6-MONTH GOALS

NOTES

THIS WEEKS NUMBERS

NEW LISTINGS	. . . .
CLOSINGS	. . . .
COMMISSIONS	. . . .
CONTRACTS ACCEPTED	. . . .
SHOWINGS	. . . .
CALLS MADE	. . . .
NEW LEADS	. . . .
APPOINTMENTS SET	. . . .
SOCIAL MEDIA POSTS	. . . .
OTHER:	. . . .
OTHER:	. . . .

WHAT ACTIONS DO I NEED TO TAKE THIS WEEK IN ORDER TO MOVE THE NEEDLE FORWARD?

WHAT ARE MY MAIN GOALS THIS WEEK?

HOW WILL I CELEBRATE MY WINS THIS WEEK?

IS THERE ANYTHING I'VE BEEN AVOIDING THAT NEEDS TO BE COMPLETED OR STARTED THIS WEEK?

WHAT MIGHT TRIP ME UP THIS WEEK AND MOVE ME OFF COURSE? HOW CAN I AVOID THESE PITFALLS?

Monday

/

Tuesday

/

Wednesday

/

TOP 3 PRIORITIES

. . . .

. . . .

. . . .

TOP 3 PRIORITIES

. . . .

. . . .

. . . .

TOP 3 PRIORITIES

. . . .

. . . .

. . . .

DAILY GRATITUDE

. . . .

. . . .

. . . .

. . . .

DAILY GRATITUDE

. . . .

. . . .

. . . .

. . . .

DAILY GRATITUDE

. . . .

. . . .

. . . .

. . . .

TO-DO

☐ . . . .
☐ . . . .
☐ . . . .
☐ . . . .
☐ . . . .

TO-DO

☐
☐
☐
☐
☐

TO-DO

☐
☐
☐
☐
☐

TIME BLOCKING

6
7
8
9
10
11
12
1
2
3
4
5
6
7
8
9

TIME BLOCKING

6
7
8
9
10
11
12
1
2
3
4
5
6
7
8
9

TIME BLOCKING

6
7
8
9
10
11
12
1
2
3
4
5
6
7
8
9

QUOTE OF THE WEEK:

Thursday
/

Friday
/

Weekend
/

TOP 3 PRIORITIES

· ·

· ·

· ·

DAILY GRATITUDE

· ·

· ·

· ·

· ·

TO-DO

☐ ·

☐ ·

☐ ·

☐ ·

☐ ·

TIME BLOCKING

6
7
8
9
10
11
12
1
2
3
4
5
6
7
8
9

TOP 3 PRIORITIES

· ·

· ·

· ·

DAILY GRATITUDE

· ·

· ·

· ·

· ·

TO-DO

☐ ·

☐ ·

☐ ·

☐ ·

☐ ·

TIME BLOCKING

6
7
8
9
10
11
12
1
2
3
4
5
6
7
8
9

TOP 3 PRIORITIES

· ·

· ·

· ·

DAILY GRATITUDE

· ·

· ·

· ·

· ·

TO-DO

☐ ·

☐ ·

☐ ·

☐ ·

☐ ·

NOTES

Great things never came from staying in your comfort zone.

MONTH

MONTH:

This Months Goals

COMMISSION TOTAL

GOAL:	ACTUAL:

CLOSINGS

GOAL:	ACTUAL:

NEW LISTINGS

GOAL:	ACTUAL:

#NEW CONTACTS

GOAL:	ACTUAL:

APPOINTMENTS SET

GOAL:	ACTUAL:

NEW SELLER PROSPECTS

GOAL:	ACTUAL:

NEW BUYER PROSPECTS

GOAL:	ACTUAL:

. . . .

GOAL:	ACTUAL:

. . . .

GOAL:	ACTUAL:

. . . .

GOAL:	ACTUAL:

Monday	Tuesday	Wednesday	Thursday
☐	☐	☐	☐
☐	☐	☐	☐
☐	☐	☐	☐
☐	☐	☐	☐
☐	☐	☐	☐

THIS MONTHS MAIN GOALS

☐ . . . .

☐ . . . .

☐ . . . .

☐ . . . .

☐ . . . .

Friday	Saturday	Sunday
☐	☐	☐
☐	☐	☐
☐	☐	☐
☐	☐	☐
☐	☐	☐

ACTIONS TO TAKE

☐ ....

☐ ....

☐ ....

☐ ....

☐ ....

☐ ....

BUSINESS EXPENSES

MLS FEES	....	CLIENT GIFTS	....
OFFICE FEES	....	LUNCHES	....
DUES / FEES	....	COFFEE	....
OFFICE SUPPLIES	....	SIGNAGE	....
TRAVEL MILEAGE	....	MAILERS	....
SUBSCRIPTIONS	....	FUEL	....
PARKING FEES	....	MISC.	....
ONLINE MARKETING	....	MISC.	....

NOTES

....

....

....

....

....

....

WHAT POSITIVE HABITS DO I WANT TO NURTURE THIS MONTH?

☐ ....

☐ ....

☐ ....

☐ ....

☐ ....

DATES / / - / /

MON

TUE

WED

THU

FRI

SAT

SUN

WORD OF THE WEEK

....

THIS WEEKS TOP PRIORITIES

☐ ....
☐ ....
☐ ....
☐ ....
☐ ....

TO - DO

☐ ....
☐ ....
☐ ....
☐ ....
☐ ....
☐ ....
☐ ....
☐ ....
☐ ....
☐ ....

HABIT / RITUAL TRACKER

	M	T	W	T	F	S	S
....							
....							
....							
....							
....							
....							
....							

STAYING FOCUSED ON YOUR GOALS

- ☐ REVIEW WEEKLY GOALS
- ☐ REVIEW MONTHLY GOALS
- ☐ REVIEW 6-MONTH GOALS

THIS WEEKS NUMBERS

NEW LISTINGS	. . . .
CLOSINGS	. . . .
COMMISSIONS	. . . .
CONTRACTS ACCEPTED	. . . .
SHOWINGS	. . . .
CALLS MADE	. . . .
NEW LEADS	. . . .
APPOINTMENTS SET	. . . .
SOCIAL MEDIA POSTS	. . . .
OTHER:	. . . .
OTHER:	. . . .

NOTES

WHAT ACTIONS DO I NEED TO TAKE THIS WEEK IN ORDER TO MOVE THE NEEDLE FORWARD?

WHAT ARE MY MAIN GOALS THIS WEEK?

HOW WILL I CELEBRATE MY WINS THIS WEEK?

IS THERE ANYTHING I'VE BEEN AVOIDING THAT NEEDS TO BE COMPLETED OR STARTED THIS WEEK?

WHAT MIGHT TRIP ME UP THIS WEEK AND MOVE ME OFF COURSE? HOW CAN I AVOID THESE PITFALLS?

Monday	Tuesday	Wednesday
/	/	/

TOP 3 PRIORITIES

. . . .

. . . .

. . . .

DAILY GRATITUDE

. . . .

. . . .

. . . .

. . . .

TO-DO

☐ ....

☐ ....

☐ ....

☐ ....

☐ ....

TIME BLOCKING

6

7

8

9

10

11

12

1

2

3

4

5

6

7

8

9

TOP 3 PRIORITIES

. . . .

. . . .

. . . .

DAILY GRATITUDE

. . . .

. . . .

. . . .

. . . .

TO-DO

☐ ....

☐ ....

☐ ....

☐ ....

☐ ....

TIME BLOCKING

6

7

8

9

10

11

12

1

2

3

4

5

6

7

8

9

TOP 3 PRIORITIES

. . . .

. . . .

. . . .

DAILY GRATITUDE

. . . .

. . . .

. . . .

. . . .

TO-DO

☐ ....

☐ ....

☐ ....

☐ ....

☐ ....

TIME BLOCKING

6

7

8

9

10

11

12

1

2

3

4

5

6

7

8

9

Thursday

/

TOP 3 PRIORITIES

. . . .

. . . .

. . . .

DAILY GRATITUDE

. . . .

. . . .

. . . .

. . . .

. . . .

TO-DO

☐
☐
☐
☐
☐

TIME BLOCKING

6

7

8

9

10

11

12

1

2

3

4

5

6

7

8

9

Friday

/

TOP 3 PRIORITIES

. . . .

. . . .

. . . .

DAILY GRATITUDE

. . . .

. . . .

. . . .

. . . .

. . . .

TO-DO

☐
☐
☐
☐
☐

TIME BLOCKING

6

7

8

9

10

11

12

1

2

3

4

5

6

7

8

9

Weekend

/

TOP 3 PRIORITIES

. . . .

. . . .

. . . .

DAILY GRATITUDE

. . . .

. . . .

. . . .

. . . .

. . . .

TO-DO

☐
☐
☐
☐
☐

NOTES

. . . .

. . . .

. . . .

. . . .

. . . .

. . . .

. . . .

. . . .

. . . .

. . . .

. . . .

. . . .

DATES / / - / /

MON

TUE

WED

THU

FRI

SAT

SUN

WORD OF THE WEEK

....

THIS WEEKS TOP PRIORITIES

☐ ....
☐ ....
☐ ....
☐ ....
☐ ....

TO - DO

☐ ....
☐ ....
☐ ....
☐ ....
☐ ....
☐ ....
☐ ....
☐ ....
☐ ....
☐ ....

HABIT / RITUAL TRACKER

M T W T F S S

....
....
....
....
....
....
....

STAYING FOCUSED ON YOUR GOALS

☐ REVIEW WEEKLY GOALS

☐ REVIEW MONTHLY GOALS

☐ REVIEW 6-MONTH GOALS

THIS WEEKS NUMBERS

NEW LISTINGS	. . . .
CLOSINGS	. . . .
COMMISSIONS	. . . .
CONTRACTS ACCEPTED	. . . .
SHOWINGS	. . . .
CALLS MADE	. . . .
NEW LEADS	. . . .
APPOINTMENTS SET	. . . .
SOCIAL MEDIA POSTS	. . . .
OTHER:	. . . .
OTHER:	. . . .

NOTES

WHAT ACTIONS DO I NEED TO TAKE THIS WEEK IN ORDER TO MOVE THE NEEDLE FORWARD?

WHAT ARE MY MAIN GOALS THIS WEEK?

HOW WILL I CELEBRATE MY WINS THIS WEEK?

IS THERE ANYTHING I'VE BEEN AVOIDING THAT NEEDS TO BE COMPLETED OR STARTED THIS WEEK?

WHAT MIGHT TRIP ME UP THIS WEEK AND MOVE ME OFF COURSE? HOW CAN I AVOID THESE PITFALLS?

WEEK#   THIS WEEKS FOCUS:

Monday
/

Tuesday
/

Wednesday
/

TOP 3 PRIORITIES

. . . .
. . . .
. . . .

TOP 3 PRIORITIES

. . . .
. . . .
. . . .

TOP 3 PRIORITIES

. . . .
. . . .
. . . .

DAILY GRATITUDE

. . . .
. . . .
. . . .
. . . .
. . . .

DAILY GRATITUDE

. . . .
. . . .
. . . .
. . . .
. . . .

DAILY GRATITUDE

. . . .
. . . .
. . . .
. . . .
. . . .

TO-DO

☐
☐
☐
☐
☐

TO-DO

☐
☐
☐
☐
☐

TO-DO

☐
☐
☐
☐
☐

TIME BLOCKING

6
7
8
9
10
11
12
1
2
3
4
5
6
7
8
9

TIME BLOCKING

6
7
8
9
10
11
12
1
2
3
4
5
6
7
8
9

TIME BLOCKING

6
7
8
9
10
11
12
1
2
3
4
5
6
7
8
9

Thursday
/

TOP 3 PRIORITIES

. . . .
. . . .
. . . .

DAILY GRATITUDE

. . . .
. . . .
. . . .
. . . .
. . . .

TO-DO

- [ ]
- [ ]
- [ ]
- [ ]
- [ ]

TIME BLOCKING

6
7
8
9
10
11
12
1
2
3
4
5
6
7
8
9

Friday
/

TOP 3 PRIORITIES

. . . .
. . . .
. . . .

DAILY GRATITUDE

. . . .
. . . .
. . . .
. . . .
. . . .

TO-DO

- [ ]
- [ ]
- [ ]
- [ ]
- [ ]

TIME BLOCKING

6
7
8
9
10
11
12
1
2
3
4
5
6
7
8
9

Weekend
/

TOP 3 PRIORITIES

. . . .
. . . .
. . . .

DAILY GRATITUDE

. . . .
. . . .
. . . .
. . . .
. . . .

TO-DO

- [ ]
- [ ]
- [ ]
- [ ]
- [ ]

NOTES

. . . .
. . . .
. . . .
. . . .
. . . .
. . . .
. . . .
. . . .
. . . .
. . . .
. . . .
. . . .
. . . .
. . . .

DATES / / - / /

MON

TUE

WED

THU

FRI

SAT

SUN

WORD OF THE WEEK

....

THIS WEEKS TOP PRIORITIES

☐ ....
☐ ....
☐ ....
☐ ....
☐ ....

TO - DO

☐ ....
☐ ....
☐ ....
☐ ....
☐ ....
☐ ....
☐ ....
☐ ....
☐ ....
☐ ....

HABIT / RITUAL TRACKER

          M T W T F S S

....
....
....
....
....
....
....

STAYING FOCUSED ON YOUR GOALS

- [ ] REVIEW WEEKLY GOALS
- [ ] REVIEW MONTHLY GOALS
- [ ] REVIEW 6-MONTH GOALS

NOTES

THIS WEEKS NUMBERS

NEW LISTINGS	. . . .
CLOSINGS	. . . .
COMMISSIONS	. . . .
CONTRACTS ACCEPTED	. . . .
SHOWINGS	. . . .
CALLS MADE	. . . .
NEW LEADS	. . . .
APPOINTMENTS SET	. . . .
SOCIAL MEDIA POSTS	. . . .
OTHER:	. . . .
OTHER:	. . . .

WHAT ACTIONS DO I NEED TO TAKE THIS WEEK IN ORDER TO MOVE THE NEEDLE FORWARD?

WHAT ARE MY MAIN GOALS THIS WEEK?

HOW WILL I CELEBRATE MY WINS THIS WEEK?

IS THERE ANYTHING I'VE BEEN AVOIDING THAT NEEDS TO BE COMPLETED OR STARTED THIS WEEK?

WHAT MIGHT TRIP ME UP THIS WEEK AND MOVE ME OFF COURSE? HOW CAN I AVOID THESE PITFALLS?

Monday

/

Tuesday

/

Wednesday

/

TOP 3 PRIORITIES

. . . .

. . . .

. . . .

DAILY GRATITUDE

. . . .

. . . .

. . . .

. . . .

. . . .

TO-DO

☐ . . . .

☐ . . . .

☐ . . . .

☐ . . . .

☐

TIME BLOCKING

6

7

8

9

10

11

12

1

2

3

4

5

6

7

8

9

TOP 3 PRIORITIES

. . . .

. . . .

. . . .

DAILY GRATITUDE

. . . .

. . . .

. . . .

. . . .

. . . .

TO-DO

☐

☐

☐

☐

☐

TIME BLOCKING

6

7

8

9

10

11

12

1

2

3

4

5

6

7

8

9

TOP 3 PRIORITIES

. . . .

. . . .

. . . .

DAILY GRATITUDE

. . . .

. . . .

. . . .

. . . .

. . . .

TO-DO

☐

☐

☐

☐

☐

TIME BLOCKING

6

7

8

9

10

11

12

1

2

3

4

5

6

7

8

9

Thursday
/

Friday
/

Weekend
/

TOP 3 PRIORITIES	TOP 3 PRIORITIES	TOP 3 PRIORITIES
. . . .	. . . .	. . . .
. . . .	. . . .	. . . .
. . . .	. . . .	. . . .

DAILY GRATITUDE	DAILY GRATITUDE	DAILY GRATITUDE
. . . .	. . . .	. . . .
. . . .	. . . .	. . . .
. . . .	. . . .	. . . .
. . . .	. . . .	. . . .
. . . .		

TO-DO (Thursday)
- ☐ . . . .
- ☐ . . . .
- ☐ . . . .
- ☐ . . . .
- ☐ . . . .

TO-DO (Friday)
- ☐ . . . .
- ☐ . . . .
- ☐ . . . .
- ☐ . . . .
- ☐ . . . .

TO-DO (Weekend)
- ☐ . . . .
- ☐ . . . .
- ☐ . . . .
- ☐ . . . .
- ☐ . . . .

TIME BLOCKING	TIME BLOCKING	NOTES
6	6	. . . .
7	7	. . . .
8	8	. . . .
9	9	. . . .
10	10	. . . .
11	11	. . . .
12	12	. . . .
1	1	. . . .
2	2	. . . .
3	3	. . . .
4	4	. . . .
5	5	. . . .
6	6	. . . .
7	7	. . . .
8	8	. . . .
9	9	. . . .
		. . . .

DATES / / - / /

WED

THU

FRI

SAT

SUN

WORD OF THE WEEK

. . . .

THIS WEEKS TOP PRIORITIES

☐ . . . .
☐ . . . .
☐ . . . .
☐ . . . .
☐ . . . .

TO - DO

☐ . . . .
☐ . . . .
☐ . . . .
☐ . . . .
☐ . . . .
☐ . . . .
☐ . . . .
☐ . . . .
☐ . . . .
☐ . . . .

HABIT / RITUAL TRACKER

M T W T F S S

. . . .
. . . .
. . . .
. . . .
. . . .
. . . .
. . . .
. . . .

STAYING FOCUSED ON YOUR GOALS

☐ REVIEW WEEKLY GOALS

☐ REVIEW MONTHLY GOALS

☐ REVIEW 6-MONTH GOALS

THIS WEEKS NUMBERS

NEW LISTINGS	. . . .
CLOSINGS	. . . .
COMMISSIONS	. . . .
CONTRACTS ACCEPTED	. . . .
SHOWINGS	. . . .
CALLS MADE	. . . .
NEW LEADS	. . . .
APPOINTMENTS SET	. . . .
SOCIAL MEDIA POSTS	. . . .
OTHER:	. . . .
OTHER:	. . . .

NOTES

WHAT ACTIONS DO I NEED TO TAKE THIS WEEK IN ORDER TO MOVE THE NEEDLE FORWARD?

WHAT ARE MY MAIN GOALS THIS WEEK?

HOW WILL I CELEBRATE MY WINS THIS WEEK?

IS THERE ANYTHING I'VE BEEN AVOIDING THAT NEEDS TO BE COMPLETED OR STARTED THIS WEEK?

WHAT MIGHT TRIP ME UP THIS WEEK AND MOVE ME OFF COURSE? HOW CAN I AVOID THESE PITFALLS?

Monday
/

Tuesday
/

Wednesday
/

Monday	Tuesday	Wednesday
TOP 3 PRIORITIES	TOP 3 PRIORITIES	TOP 3 PRIORITIES
. . . .	. . . .	. . . .
. . . .	. . . .	. . . .
. . . .	. . . .	. . . .
DAILY GRATITUDE	DAILY GRATITUDE	DAILY GRATITUDE
. . . .	. . . .	. . . .
. . . .	. . . .	. . . .
. . . .	. . . .	. . . .
. . . .	. . . .	. . . .
TO-DO	TO-DO	TO-DO
☐	☐	☐
☐	☐	☐
☐	☐	☐
☐	☐	☐
☐	☐	☐
TIME BLOCKING	TIME BLOCKING	TIME BLOCKING
6	6	6
7	7	7
8	8	8
9	9	9
10	10	10
11	11	11
12	12	12
1	1	1
2	2	2
3	3	3
4	4	4
5	5	5
6	6	6
7	7	7
8	8	8
9	9	9

Thursday
/

TOP 3 PRIORITIES
. . . .
. . . .
. . . .

DAILY GRATITUDE
. . . .
. . . .
. . . .
. . . .
. . . .

TO-DO
☐
☐
☐
☐
☐

TIME BLOCKING
6
7
8
9
10
11
12
1
2
3
4
5
6
7
8
9

Friday
/

TOP 3 PRIORITIES
. . . .
. . . .
. . . .

DAILY GRATITUDE
. . . .
. . . .
. . . .
. . . .
. . . .

TO-DO
☐
☐
☐
☐
☐

TIME BLOCKING
6
7
8
9
10
11
12
1
2
3
4
5
6
7
8
9

Weekend
/

TOP 3 PRIORITIES
. . . .
. . . .
. . . .

DAILY GRATITUDE
. . . .
. . . .
. . . .
. . . .
. . . .

TO-DO
☐
☐
☐
☐
☐

NOTES
. . . .
. . . .
. . . .
. . . .
. . . .
. . . .
. . . .
. . . .
. . . .
. . . .
. . . .
. . . .
. . . .

DATES / / - / /

MON

TUE

WED

THU

FRI

SAT

SUN

WORD OF THE WEEK

....

THIS WEEKS TOP PRIORITIES

☐ ....
☐ ....
☐ ....
☐ ....
☐ ....

TO - DO

☐ ....
☐ ....
☐ ....
☐ ....
☐ ....
☐ ....
☐ ....
☐ ....
☐ ....
☐ ....

HABIT / RITUAL TRACKER

	M	T	W	T	F	S	S
....							
....							
....							
....							
....							
....							
....							

STAYING FOCUSED ON YOUR GOALS

- ☐ REVIEW WEEKLY GOALS
- ☐ REVIEW MONTHLY GOALS
- ☐ REVIEW 6-MONTH GOALS

THIS WEEKS NUMBERS

NEW LISTINGS	. . . .
CLOSINGS	. . . .
COMMISSIONS	. . . .
CONTRACTS ACCEPTED	. . . .
SHOWINGS	. . . .
CALLS MADE	. . . .
NEW LEADS	. . . .
APPOINTMENTS SET	. . . .
SOCIAL MEDIA POSTS	. . . .
OTHER:	. . . .
OTHER:	. . . .

NOTES

WHAT ACTIONS DO I NEED TO TAKE THIS WEEK IN ORDER TO MOVE THE NEEDLE FORWARD?

WHAT ARE MY MAIN GOALS THIS WEEK?

HOW WILL I CELEBRATE MY WINS THIS WEEK?

IS THERE ANYTHING I'VE BEEN AVOIDING THAT NEEDS TO BE COMPLETED OR STARTED THIS WEEK?

WHAT MIGHT TRIP ME UP THIS WEEK AND MOVE ME OFF COURSE? HOW CAN I AVOID THESE PITFALLS?

Monday
/

Tuesday
/

Wednesday
/

TOP 3 PRIORITIES

. . . .

. . . .

. . . .

DAILY GRATITUDE

. . . .

. . . .

. . . .

. . . .

. . . .

TO-DO

☐ . . . .
☐ . . . .
☐ . . . .
☐ . . . .
☐ . . . .

TIME BLOCKING

6
7
8
9
10
11
12
1
2
3
4
5
6
7
8
9

TOP 3 PRIORITIES

. . . .

. . . .

. . . .

DAILY GRATITUDE

. . . .

. . . .

. . . .

. . . .

. . . .

TO-DO

☐ . . . .
☐ . . . .
☐ . . . .
☐ . . . .
☐ . . . .

TIME BLOCKING

6
7
8
9
10
11
12
1
2
3
4
5
6
7
8
9

TOP 3 PRIORITIES

. . . .

. . . .

. . . .

DAILY GRATITUDE

. . . .

. . . .

. . . .

. . . .

. . . .

TO-DO

☐ . . . .
☐ . . . .
☐ . . . .
☐ . . . .
☐ . . . .

TIME BLOCKING

6
7
8
9
10
11
12
1
2
3
4
5
6
7
8
9

Thursday
/

TOP 3 PRIORITIES
....
....
....

DAILY GRATITUDE
....
....
....
....
....

TO-DO
☐ ....
☐ ....
☐ ....
☐ ....
☐ ....

TIME BLOCKING
6
7
8
9
10
11
12
1
2
3
4
5
6
7
8
9

Friday
/

TOP 3 PRIORITIES
....
....
....

DAILY GRATITUDE
....
....
....
....
....

TO-DO
☐ ....
☐ ....
☐ ....
☐ ....
☐ ....

TIME BLOCKING
6
7
8
9
10
11
12
1
2
3
4
5
6
7
8
9

Weekend
/

TOP 3 PRIORITIES
....
....
....

DAILY GRATITUDE
....
....
....
....
....

TO-DO
☐ ....
☐ ....
☐ ....
☐ ....
☐ ....

NOTES
....
....
....
....
....
....
....
....
....
....
....
....
....
....

Mindset is what separates the best from the rest.

MONTH

MONTH:

This Months Goals

COMMISSION TOTAL

| GOAL: | ACTUAL: |

CLOSINGS

| GOAL: | ACTUAL: |

NEW LISTINGS

| GOAL: | ACTUAL: |

#NEW CONTACTS

| GOAL: | ACTUAL: |

APPOINTMENTS SET

| GOAL: | ACTUAL: |

NEW SELLER PROSPECTS

| GOAL: | ACTUAL: |

NEW BUYER PROSPECTS

| GOAL: | ACTUAL: |

. . . .

| GOAL: | ACTUAL: |

. . . .

| GOAL: | ACTUAL: |

. . . .

| GOAL: | ACTUAL: |

Monday	Tuesday	Wednesday	Thursday
☐	☐	☐	☐
☐	☐	☐	☐
☐	☐	☐	☐
☐	☐	☐	☐
☐	☐	☐	☐

THIS MONTHS MAIN GOALS

☐ . . . .
☐ . . . .
☐ . . . .
☐ . . . .
☐ . . . .

Friday	Saturday	Sunday
☐	☐	☐
☐	☐	☐
☐	☐	☐
☐	☐	☐
☐	☐	☐

ACTIONS TO TAKE

☐ ....
☐ ....
☐ ....
☐ ....
☐ ....
☐ ....

BUSINESS EXPENSES

MLS FEES	....	CLIENT GIFTS	....
OFFICE FEES	....	LUNCHES	....
DUES / FEES	....	COFFEE	....
OFFICE SUPPLIES	....	SIGNAGE	....
TRAVEL MILEAGE	....	MAILERS	....
SUBSCRIPTIONS	....	FUEL	....
PARKING FEES	....	MISC.	....
ONLINE MARKETING	....	MISC.	....

NOTES

....
....
....
....
....
....

WHAT POSITIVE HABITS DO I WANT TO NURTURE THIS MONTH?

☐ ....
☐ ....
☐ ....
☐ ....
☐ ....

DATES / / - / /

MON

TUE

WED

THU

FRI

SAT

SUN

WORD OF THE WEEK

....

THIS WEEKS TOP PRIORITIES

☐ ....
☐ ....
☐ ....
☐ ....
☐ ....

TO - DO

☐ ....
☐ ....
☐ ....
☐ ....
☐ ....
☐ ....
☐ ....
☐ ....
☐ ....
☐ ....

HABIT / RITUAL TRACKER

	M	T	W	T	F	S	S
....							
....							
....							
....							
....							
....							
....							

STAYING FOCUSED ON YOUR GOALS

- ☐ REVIEW WEEKLY GOALS
- ☐ REVIEW MONTHLY GOALS
- ☐ REVIEW 6-MONTH GOALS

THIS WEEKS NUMBERS

NEW LISTINGS	. . . .
CLOSINGS	. . . .
COMMISSIONS	. . . .
CONTRACTS ACCEPTED	. . . .
SHOWINGS	. . . .
CALLS MADE	. . . .
NEW LEADS	. . . .
APPOINTMENTS SET	. . . .
SOCIAL MEDIA POSTS	. . . .
OTHER:	. . . .
OTHER:	. . . .

NOTES

WHAT ACTIONS DO I NEED TO TAKE THIS WEEK IN ORDER TO MOVE THE NEEDLE FORWARD?

WHAT ARE MY MAIN GOALS THIS WEEK?

HOW WILL I CELEBRATE MY WINS THIS WEEK?

IS THERE ANYTHING I'VE BEEN AVOIDING THAT NEEDS TO BE COMPLETED OR STARTED THIS WEEK?

WHAT MIGHT TRIP ME UP THIS WEEK AND MOVE ME OFF COURSE? HOW CAN I AVOID THESE PITFALLS?

Monday
/

TOP 3 PRIORITIES

....

....

....

DAILY GRATITUDE

....

....

....

....

....

TO-DO

☐ ....

☐ ....

☐ ....

☐ ....

☐ ....

TIME BLOCKING

6

7

8

9

10

11

12

1

2

3

4

5

6

7

8

9

Tuesday
/

TOP 3 PRIORITIES

....

....

....

DAILY GRATITUDE

....

....

....

....

....

TO-DO

☐ ....

☐ ....

☐ ....

☐ ....

☐ ....

TIME BLOCKING

6

7

8

9

10

11

12

1

2

3

4

5

6

7

8

9

Wednesday
/

TOP 3 PRIORITIES

....

....

....

DAILY GRATITUDE

....

....

....

....

....

TO-DO

☐ ....

☐ ....

☐ ....

☐ ....

☐ ....

TIME BLOCKING

6

7

8

9

10

11

12

1

2

3

4

5

6

7

8

9

Thursday
/

TOP 3 PRIORITIES

....
....
....

DAILY GRATITUDE

....
....
....
....
....

TO-DO

☐ ....
☐ ....
☐ ....
☐ ....
☐ ....

TIME BLOCKING

6
7
8
9
10
11
12
1
2
3
4
5
6
7
8
9

Friday
/

TOP 3 PRIORITIES

....
....
....

DAILY GRATITUDE

....
....
....
....
....

TO-DO

☐ ....
☐ ....
☐ ....
☐ ....
☐ ....

TIME BLOCKING

6
7
8
9
10
11
12
1
2
3
4
5
6
7
8
9

Weekend
/

TOP 3 PRIORITIES

....
....
....

DAILY GRATITUDE

....
....
....
....
....

TO-DO

☐ ....
☐ ....
☐ ....
☐ ....
☐ ....

NOTES

....
....
....
....
....
....
....
....
....
....
....
....
....
....
....
....

DATES / / - / /

MON

TUE

WED

THU

FRI

SAT

SUN

WORD OF THE WEEK

....

THIS WEEKS TOP PRIORITIES

☐ ....
☐ ....
☐ ....
☐ ....
☐ ....

TO - DO

☐ ....
☐ ....
☐ ....
☐ ....
☐ ....
☐ ....
☐ ....
☐ ....
☐ ....
☐ ....

HABIT / RITUAL TRACKER

	M	T	W	T	F	S	S
....							
....							
....							
....							
....							
....							
....							

STAYING FOCUSED ON YOUR GOALS

- ☐ REVIEW WEEKLY GOALS
- ☐ REVIEW MONTHLY GOALS
- ☐ REVIEW 6-MONTH GOALS

THIS WEEKS NUMBERS

NEW LISTINGS	. . . .
CLOSINGS	. . . .
COMMISSIONS	. . . .
CONTRACTS ACCEPTED	. . . .
SHOWINGS	. . . .
CALLS MADE	. . . .
NEW LEADS	. . . .
APPOINTMENTS SET	. . . .
SOCIAL MEDIA POSTS	. . . .
OTHER:	. . . .
OTHER:	. . . .

NOTES

WHAT ACTIONS DO I NEED TO TAKE THIS WEEK IN ORDER TO MOVE THE NEEDLE FORWARD?

WHAT ARE MY MAIN GOALS THIS WEEK?

HOW WILL I CELEBRATE MY WINS THIS WEEK?

IS THERE ANYTHING I'VE BEEN AVOIDING THAT NEEDS TO BE COMPLETED OR STARTED THIS WEEK?

WHAT MIGHT TRIP ME UP THIS WEEK AND MOVE ME OFF COURSE? HOW CAN I AVOID THESE PITFALLS?

Monday	**Tuesday**	**Wednesday**
/	/	/

TOP 3 PRIORITIES	TOP 3 PRIORITIES	TOP 3 PRIORITIES
. . . .	. . . .	. . . .
. . . .	. . . .	. . . .
. . . .	. . . .	. . . .

DAILY GRATITUDE	DAILY GRATITUDE	DAILY GRATITUDE
. . . .	. . . .	. . . .
. . . .	. . . .	. . . .
. . . .	. . . .	. . . .
. . . .	. . . .	. . . .
. . . .	. . . .	. . . .

TO-DO

☐
☐
☐
☐
☐

TO-DO

☐
☐
☐
☐
☐

TO-DO

☐
☐
☐
☐
☐

TIME BLOCKING	TIME BLOCKING	TIME BLOCKING
6	6	6
7	7	7
8	8	8
9	9	9
10	10	10
11	11	11
12	12	12
1	1	1
2	2	2
3	3	3
4	4	4
5	5	5
6	6	6
7	7	7
8	8	8
9	9	9

Thursday
/

TOP 3 PRIORITIES
....
....
....

DAILY GRATITUDE
....
....
....
....
....

TO-DO
☐ ....
☐ ....
☐ ....
☐ ....
☐ ....

TIME BLOCKING
6
7
8
9
10
11
12
1
2
3
4
5
6
7
8
9

Friday
/

TOP 3 PRIORITIES
....
....
....

DAILY GRATITUDE
....
....
....
....
....

TO-DO
☐ ....
☐ ....
☐ ....
☐ ....
☐ ....

TIME BLOCKING
6
7
8
9
10
11
12
1
2
3
4
5
6
7
8
9

Weekend
/

TOP 3 PRIORITIES
....
....
....

DAILY GRATITUDE
....
....
....
....
....

TO-DO
☐ ....
☐ ....
☐ ....
☐ ....
☐ ....

NOTES
....
....
....
....
....
....
....
....
....
....
....
....
....
....

DATES /   /   -   /   /

WORD OF THE WEEK

MON

TUE

WED

THU

FRI

SAT

SUN

....

THIS WEEKS TOP PRIORITIES

☐ ....
☐ ....
☐ ....
☐ ....
☐ ....

TO - DO

☐ ....
☐ ....
☐ ....
☐ ....
☐ ....
☐ ....
☐ ....
☐ ....
☐ ....
☐ ....

HABIT / RITUAL TRACKER

	M	T	W	T	F	S	S
....							
....							
....							
....							
....							
....							
....							

STAYING FOCUSED ON YOUR GOALS

- ☐ REVIEW WEEKLY GOALS
- ☐ REVIEW MONTHLY GOALS
- ☐ REVIEW 6-MONTH GOALS

THIS WEEKS NUMBERS

NEW LISTINGS	. . . .
CLOSINGS	. . . .
COMMISSIONS	. . . .
CONTRACTS ACCEPTED	. . . .
SHOWINGS	. . . .
CALLS MADE	. . . .
NEW LEADS	. . . .
APPOINTMENTS SET	. . . .
SOCIAL MEDIA POSTS	. . . .
OTHER:	. . . .
OTHER:	. . . .

NOTES

WHAT ACTIONS DO I NEED TO TAKE THIS WEEK IN ORDER TO MOVE THE NEEDLE FORWARD?

WHAT ARE MY MAIN GOALS THIS WEEK?

HOW WILL I CELEBRATE MY WINS THIS WEEK?

IS THERE ANYTHING I'VE BEEN AVOIDING THAT NEEDS TO BE COMPLETED OR STARTED THIS WEEK?

WHAT MIGHT TRIP ME UP THIS WEEK AND MOVE ME OFF COURSE? HOW CAN I AVOID THESE PITFALLS?

Monday

/

TOP 3 PRIORITIES

. . . .

. . . .

. . . .

DAILY GRATITUDE

. . . .

. . . .

. . . .

. . . .

TO-DO

☐ . . . .

☐ . . . .

☐ . . . .

☐ . . . .

☐

TIME BLOCKING

6

7

8

9

10

11

12

1

2

3

4

5

6

7

8

9

Tuesday

/

TOP 3 PRIORITIES

. . . .

. . . .

. . . .

DAILY GRATITUDE

. . . .

. . . .

. . . .

. . . .

TO-DO

☐

☐

☐

☐

☐

TIME BLOCKING

6

7

8

9

10

11

12

1

2

3

4

5

6

7

8

9

Wednesday

/

TOP 3 PRIORITIES

. . . .

. . . .

. . . .

DAILY GRATITUDE

. . . .

. . . .

. . . .

. . . .

TO-DO

☐

☐

☐

☐

☐

TIME BLOCKING

6

7

8

9

10

11

12

1

2

3

4

5

6

7

8

9

Thursday
/

TOP 3 PRIORITIES
....
....
....

DAILY GRATITUDE
....
....
....
....
....

TO-DO
☐ ....
☐ ....
☐ ....
☐ ....
☐ ....

TIME BLOCKING
6
7
8
9
10
11
12
1
2
3
4
5
6
7
8
9

Friday
/

TOP 3 PRIORITIES
....
....
....

DAILY GRATITUDE
....
....
....
....
....

TO-DO
☐ ....
☐ ....
☐ ....
☐ ....
☐ ....

TIME BLOCKING
6
7
8
9
10
11
12
1
2
3
4
5
6
7
8
9

Weekend
/

TOP 3 PRIORITIES
....
....
....

DAILY GRATITUDE
....
....
....
....
....

TO-DO
☐
☐
☐
☐
☐

NOTES
....
....
....
....
....
....
....
....
....
....
....
....
....
....

DATES / / - / /

MON

TUE

WED

THU

FRI

SAT

SUN

WORD OF THE WEEK

. . . .

THIS WEEKS TOP PRIORITIES

☐ . . . .
☐ . . . .
☐ . . . .
☐ . . . .
☐ . . . .

TO - DO

☐ . . . .
☐ . . . .
☐ . . . .
☐ . . . .
☐ . . . .
☐ . . . .
☐ . . . .
☐ . . . .
☐ . . . .
☐ . . . .

HABIT / RITUAL TRACKER

M T W T F S S

. . . .
. . . .
. . . .
. . . .
. . . .
. . . .
. . . .

STAYING FOCUSED ON YOUR GOALS

- ☐ REVIEW WEEKLY GOALS
- ☐ REVIEW MONTHLY GOALS
- ☐ REVIEW 6-MONTH GOALS

THIS WEEKS NUMBERS

NEW LISTINGS	. . . .
CLOSINGS	. . . .
COMMISSIONS	. . . .
CONTRACTS ACCEPTED	. . . .
SHOWINGS	. . . .
CALLS MADE	. . . .
NEW LEADS	. . . .
APPOINTMENTS SET	. . . .
SOCIAL MEDIA POSTS	. . . .
OTHER:	. . . .
OTHER:	. . . .

NOTES

WHAT ACTIONS DO I NEED TO TAKE THIS WEEK IN ORDER TO MOVE THE NEEDLE FORWARD?

WHAT ARE MY MAIN GOALS THIS WEEK?

HOW WILL I CELEBRATE MY WINS THIS WEEK?

IS THERE ANYTHING I'VE BEEN AVOIDING THAT NEEDS TO BE COMPLETED OR STARTED THIS WEEK?

WHAT MIGHT TRIP ME UP THIS WEEK AND MOVE ME OFF COURSE? HOW CAN I AVOID THESE PITFALLS?

Monday   # Tuesday   # Wednesday

/   /   /

TOP 3 PRIORITIES   TOP 3 PRIORITIES   TOP 3 PRIORITIES

. . . .

. . . .

. . . .

DAILY GRATITUDE   DAILY GRATITUDE   DAILY GRATITUDE

. . . .

. . . .

. . . .

. . . .

. . . .

TO-DO   TO-DO   TO-DO

☐   ☐   ☐

☐   ☐   ☐

☐   ☐   ☐

☐   ☐   ☐

☐   ☐   ☐

TIME BLOCKING   TIME BLOCKING   TIME BLOCKING

Monday	Tuesday	Wednesday
6	6	6
7	7	7
8	8	8
9	9	9
10	10	10
11	11	11
12	12	12
1	1	1
2	2	2
3	3	3
4	4	4
5	5	5
6	6	6
7	7	7
8	8	8
9	9	9

Thursday
/

TOP 3 PRIORITIES

....

....

....

DAILY GRATITUDE

....

....

....

....

....

TO-DO

☐ ....

☐ ....

☐ ....

☐ ....

☐

TIME BLOCKING

6

7

8

9

10

11

12

1

2

3

4

5

6

7

8

9

Friday
/

TOP 3 PRIORITIES

....

....

....

DAILY GRATITUDE

....

....

....

....

....

TO-DO

☐ ....

☐ ....

☐ ....

☐ ....

☐

TIME BLOCKING

6

7

8

9

10

11

12

1

2

3

4

5

6

7

8

9

Weekend
/

TOP 3 PRIORITIES

....

....

....

DAILY GRATITUDE

....

....

....

....

....

TO-DO

☐

☐

☐

☐

☐

NOTES

....

....

....

....

....

....

....

....

....

....

....

....

....

....

....

D A T E S / / - / /

MON

TUE

WED

THU

FRI

SAT

SUN

WORD OF THE WEEK

....

THIS WEEKS TOP PRIORITIES

☐ ....
☐ ....
☐ ....
☐ ....
☐ ....

TO - DO

☐ ....
☐ ....
☐ ....
☐ ....
☐ ....
☐ ....
☐ ....
☐ ....
☐ ....

HABIT / RITUAL TRACKER

M T W T F S S

....
....
....
....
....
....
....

STAYING FOCUSED ON YOUR GOALS

- ☐ REVIEW WEEKLY GOALS
- ☐ REVIEW MONTHLY GOALS
- ☐ REVIEW 6-MONTH GOALS

THIS WEEKS NUMBERS

NEW LISTINGS	. . . .
CLOSINGS	. . . .
COMMISSIONS	. . . .
CONTRACTS ACCEPTED	. . . .
SHOWINGS	. . . .
CALLS MADE	. . . .
NEW LEADS	. . . .
APPOINTMENTS SET	. . . .
SOCIAL MEDIA POSTS	. . . .
OTHER:	. . . .
OTHER:	. . . .

NOTES

WHAT ACTIONS DO I NEED TO TAKE THIS WEEK IN ORDER TO MOVE THE NEEDLE FORWARD?

WHAT ARE MY MAIN GOALS THIS WEEK?

HOW WILL I CELEBRATE MY WINS THIS WEEK?

IS THERE ANYTHING I'VE BEEN AVOIDING THAT NEEDS TO BE COMPLETED OR STARTED THIS WEEK?

WHAT MIGHT TRIP ME UP THIS WEEK AND MOVE ME OFF COURSE? HOW CAN I AVOID THESE PITFALLS?

Monday
/

TOP 3 PRIORITIES
. . . .
. . . .
. . . .

DAILY GRATITUDE
. . . .
. . . .
. . . .
. . . .

TO-DO
☐ . . . .
☐ . . . .
☐ . . . .
☐ . . . .
☐ . . . .

TIME BLOCKING
6
7
8
9
10
11
12
1
2
3
4
5
6
7
8
9

Tuesday
/

TOP 3 PRIORITIES
. . . .
. . . .
. . . .

DAILY GRATITUDE
. . . .
. . . .
. . . .
. . . .

TO-DO
☐ . . . .
☐ . . . .
☐ . . . .
☐ . . . .
☐ . . . .

TIME BLOCKING
6
7
8
9
10
11
12
1
2
3
4
5
6
7
8
9

Wednesday
/

TOP 3 PRIORITIES
. . . .
. . . .
. . . .

DAILY GRATITUDE
. . . .
. . . .
. . . .
. . . .

TO-DO
☐ . . . .
☐ . . . .
☐ . . . .
☐ . . . .
☐ . . . .

TIME BLOCKING
6
7
8
9
10
11
12
1
2
3
4
5
6
7
8
9

Thursday
/

Friday
/

Weekend
/

TOP 3 PRIORITIES

. . . .

. . . .

. . . .

DAILY GRATITUDE

. . . .

. . . .

. . . .

. . . .

. . . .

TO-DO

☐ . . . .

☐ . . . .

☐ . . . .

☐ . . . .

☐ . . . .

TIME BLOCKING

6

7

8

9

10

11

12

1

2

3

4

5

6

7

8

9

TOP 3 PRIORITIES

. . . .

. . . .

. . . .

DAILY GRATITUDE

. . . .

. . . .

. . . .

. . . .

. . . .

TO-DO

☐ . . . .

☐ . . . .

☐ . . . .

☐ . . . .

☐ . . . .

TIME BLOCKING

6

7

8

9

10

11

12

1

2

3

4

5

6

7

8

9

TOP 3 PRIORITIES

. . . .

. . . .

. . . .

DAILY GRATITUDE

. . . .

. . . .

. . . .

. . . .

. . . .

TO-DO

☐ . . . .

☐ . . . .

☐ . . . .

☐ . . . .

☐ . . . .

NOTES

. . . .

. . . .

. . . .

. . . .

. . . .

. . . .

. . . .

. . . .

. . . .

. . . .

. . . .

. . . .

. . . .

. . . .

. . . .

I can.
I will.
End of
story.

MONTH

MONTH:

This Months Goals

COMMISSION TOTAL

| GOAL: | ACTUAL: |

CLOSINGS

| GOAL: | ACTUAL: |

NEW LISTINGS

| GOAL: | ACTUAL: |

#NEW CONTACTS

| GOAL: | ACTUAL: |

APPOINTMENTS SET

| GOAL: | ACTUAL: |

NEW SELLER PROSPECTS

| GOAL: | ACTUAL: |

NEW BUYER PROSPECTS

| GOAL: | ACTUAL: |

. . . .

| GOAL: | ACTUAL: |

. . . .

| GOAL: | ACTUAL: |

. . . .

| GOAL: | ACTUAL: |

Monday	Tuesday	Wednesday	Thursday
☐	☐	☐	☐
☐	☐	☐	☐
☐	☐	☐	☐
☐	☐	☐	☐
☐	☐	☐	☐

THIS MONTHS MAIN GOALS

☐ . . . .

☐ . . . .

☐ . . . .

☐ . . . .

☐ . . . .

Friday	Saturday	Sunday
☐	☐	☐
☐	☐	☐
☐	☐	☐
☐	☐	☐
☐	☐	☐

ACTIONS TO TAKE

☐ ....
☐ ....
☐ ....
☐ ....
☐ ....
☐ ....

BUSINESS EXPENSES

MLS FEES	....	CLIENT GIFTS	....
OFFICE FEES	....	LUNCHES	....
DUES / FEES	....	COFFEE	....
OFFICE SUPPLIES	....	SIGNAGE	....
TRAVEL MILEAGE	....	MAILERS	....
SUBSCRIPTIONS	....	FUEL	....
PARKING FEES	....	MISC.	....
ONLINE MARKETING	....	MISC.	....

NOTES

....
....
....
....
....
....

WHAT POSITIVE HABITS DO I WANT TO NURTURE THIS MONTH?

☐ ....
☐ ....
☐ ....
☐ ....
☐ ....

DATES / / - / /

MON

TUE

WED

THU

FRI

SAT

SUN

WORD OF THE WEEK

....

THIS WEEKS TOP PRIORITIES

☐ ....
☐ ....
☐ ....
☐ ....
☐ ....

TO - DO

☐ ....
☐ ....
☐ ....
☐ ....
☐ ....
☐ ....
☐ ....
☐ ....
☐ ....
☐ ....

HABIT / RITUAL TRACKER

	M	T	W	T	F	S	S
....	☐	☐	☐	☐	☐	☐	☐
....	☐	☐	☐	☐	☐	☐	☐
....	☐	☐	☐	☐	☐	☐	☐
....	☐	☐	☐	☐	☐	☐	☐
....	☐	☐	☐	☐	☐	☐	☐
....	☐	☐	☐	☐	☐	☐	☐
....	☐	☐	☐	☐	☐	☐	☐

STAYING FOCUSED ON YOUR GOALS

- [ ] REVIEW WEEKLY GOALS
- [ ] REVIEW MONTHLY GOALS
- [ ] REVIEW 6-MONTH GOALS

NOTES

THIS WEEKS NUMBERS

NEW LISTINGS	. . . .
CLOSINGS	. . . .
COMMISSIONS	. . . .
CONTRACTS ACCEPTED	. . . .
SHOWINGS	. . . .
CALLS MADE	. . . .
NEW LEADS	. . . .
APPOINTMENTS SET	. . . .
SOCIAL MEDIA POSTS	. . . .
OTHER:	. . . .
OTHER:	. . . .

WHAT ACTIONS DO I NEED TO TAKE THIS WEEK IN ORDER TO MOVE THE NEEDLE FORWARD?

WHAT ARE MY MAIN GOALS THIS WEEK?

HOW WILL I CELEBRATE MY WINS THIS WEEK?

IS THERE ANYTHING I'VE BEEN AVOIDING THAT NEEDS TO BE COMPLETED OR STARTED THIS WEEK?

WHAT MIGHT TRIP ME UP THIS WEEK AND MOVE ME OFF COURSE? HOW CAN I AVOID THESE PITFALLS?

Monday	Tuesday	Wednesday
/	/	/

TOP 3 PRIORITIES

. . . .

. . . .

. . . .

DAILY GRATITUDE

. . . .

. . . .

. . . .

. . . .

. . . .

TO-DO

☐ . . . .

☐ . . . .

☐ . . . .

☐ . . . .

☐ . . . .

TIME BLOCKING

6

7

8

9

10

11

12

1

2

3

4

5

6

7

8

9

TOP 3 PRIORITIES

. . . .

. . . .

. . . .

DAILY GRATITUDE

. . . .

. . . .

. . . .

. . . .

. . . .

TO-DO

☐ . . . .

☐ . . . .

☐ . . . .

☐ . . . .

☐ . . . .

TIME BLOCKING

6

7

8

9

10

11

12

1

2

3

4

5

6

7

8

9

TOP 3 PRIORITIES

. . . .

. . . .

. . . .

DAILY GRATITUDE

. . . .

. . . .

. . . .

. . . .

. . . .

TO-DO

☐ . . . .

☐ . . . .

☐ . . . .

☐ . . . .

☐ . . . .

TIME BLOCKING

6

7

8

9

10

11

12

1

2

3

4

5

6

7

8

9

Thursday
/

Friday
/

Weekend
/

TOP 3 PRIORITIES	TOP 3 PRIORITIES	TOP 3 PRIORITIES
. . . .	. . . .	. . . .
. . . .	. . . .	. . . .
. . . .	. . . .	. . . .

DAILY GRATITUDE	DAILY GRATITUDE	DAILY GRATITUDE
. . . .	. . . .	. . . .
. . . .	. . . .	. . . .
. . . .	. . . .	. . . .
. . . .	. . . .	. . . .
. . . .	. . . .	. . . .

TO-DO
- ☐
- ☐
- ☐
- ☐
- ☐

TO-DO
- ☐
- ☐
- ☐
- ☐
- ☐

TO-DO
- ☐
- ☐
- ☐
- ☐
- ☐

TIME BLOCKING	TIME BLOCKING	NOTES
6	6	. . . .
7	7	. . . .
8	8	. . . .
9	9	. . . .
10	10	. . . .
11	11	. . . .
12	12	. . . .
1	1	. . . .
2	2	. . . .
3	3	. . . .
4	4	. . . .
5	5	. . . .
6	6	. . . .
7	7	. . . .
8	8	. . . .
9	9	. . . .

DATES / / - / /

MON

TUE

WED

THU

FRI

SAT

SUN

WORD OF THE WEEK

. . . .

THIS WEEKS TOP PRIORITIES

☐ . . . .
☐ . . . .
☐ . . . .
☐ . . . .
☐ . . . .

TO - DO

☐ . . . .
☐ . . . .
☐ . . . .
☐ . . . .
☐ . . . .
☐ . . . .
☐ . . . .
☐ . . . .
☐ . . . .
☐ . . . .

HABIT / RITUAL TRACKER

	M	T	W	T	F	S	S
. . . .	☐	☐	☐	☐	☐	☐	☐
. . . .	☐	☐	☐	☐	☐	☐	☐
. . . .	☐	☐	☐	☐	☐	☐	☐
. . . .	☐	☐	☐	☐	☐	☐	☐
. . . .	☐	☐	☐	☐	☐	☐	☐
. . . .	☐	☐	☐	☐	☐	☐	☐
. . . .	☐	☐	☐	☐	☐	☐	☐

STAYING FOCUSED ON YOUR GOALS

- [ ] REVIEW WEEKLY GOALS
- [ ] REVIEW MONTHLY GOALS
- [ ] REVIEW 6-MONTH GOALS

THIS WEEKS NUMBERS

NEW LISTINGS . . . .

CLOSINGS . . . .

COMMISSIONS . . . .

CONTRACTS ACCEPTED . . . .

SHOWINGS . . . .

CALLS MADE . . . .

NEW LEADS . . . .

APPOINTMENTS SET . . . .

SOCIAL MEDIA POSTS . . . .

OTHER: . . . .

OTHER: . . . .

NOTES

WHAT ACTIONS DO I NEED TO TAKE THIS WEEK IN ORDER TO MOVE THE NEEDLE FORWARD?

WHAT ARE MY MAIN GOALS THIS WEEK?

HOW WILL I CELEBRATE MY WINS THIS WEEK?

IS THERE ANYTHING I'VE BEEN AVOIDING THAT NEEDS TO BE COMPLETED OR STARTED THIS WEEK?

WHAT MIGHT TRIP ME UP THIS WEEK AND MOVE ME OFF COURSE? HOW CAN I AVOID THESE PITFALLS?

Monday
/

TOP 3 PRIORITIES

. . . .

. . . .

. . . .

DAILY GRATITUDE

. . . .

. . . .

. . . .

. . . .

TO-DO

☐ . . . .

☐ . . . .

☐ . . . .

☐ . . . .

☐ . . . .

TIME BLOCKING

6

7

8

9

10

11

12

1

2

3

4

5

6

7

8

9

Tuesday
/

TOP 3 PRIORITIES

. . . .

. . . .

. . . .

DAILY GRATITUDE

. . . .

. . . .

. . . .

. . . .

TO-DO

☐ . . . .

☐ . . . .

☐ . . . .

☐ . . . .

☐ . . . .

TIME BLOCKING

6

7

8

9

10

11

12

1

2

3

4

5

6

7

8

9

Wednesday
/

TOP 3 PRIORITIES

. . . .

. . . .

. . . .

DAILY GRATITUDE

. . . .

. . . .

. . . .

. . . .

TO-DO

☐ . . . .

☐ . . . .

☐ . . . .

☐ . . . .

☐ . . . .

TIME BLOCKING

6

7

8

9

10

11

12

1

2

3

4

5

6

7

8

9

Thursday

/

TOP 3 PRIORITIES

. . . .
. . . .
. . . .

DAILY GRATITUDE

. . . .
. . . .
. . . .
. . . .
. . . .

TO-DO

- ☐ . . . .
- ☐ . . . .
- ☐ . . . .
- ☐ . . . .
- ☐ . . . .

TIME BLOCKING

6
7
8
9
10
11
12
1
2
3
4
5
6
7
8
9

Friday

/

TOP 3 PRIORITIES

. . . .
. . . .
. . . .

DAILY GRATITUDE

. . . .
. . . .
. . . .
. . . .
. . . .

TO-DO

- ☐ . . . .
- ☐ . . . .
- ☐ . . . .
- ☐ . . . .
- ☐ . . . .

TIME BLOCKING

6
7
8
9
10
11
12
1
2
3
4
5
6
7
8
9

Weekend

/

TOP 3 PRIORITIES

. . . .
. . . .

DAILY GRATITUDE

. . . .
. . . .
. . . .
. . . .

TO-DO

- ☐ . . . .
- ☐ . . . .
- ☐ . . . .
- ☐ . . . .
- ☐

NOTES

. . . .
. . . .
. . . .
. . . .
. . . .
. . . .
. . . .
. . . .
. . . .
. . . .
. . . .
. . . .
. . . .
. . . .
. . . .
. . . .
. . . .

D A T E S / / - / /

MON

TUE

WED

THU

FRI

SAT

SUN

WORD OF THE WEEK

....

THIS WEEKS TOP PRIORITIES

☐ ....

☐ ....

☐ ....

☐ ....

☐ ....

TO - DO

☐ ....

☐ ....

☐ ....

☐ ....

☐ ....

☐ ....

☐ ....

☐ ....

☐ ....

☐ ....

HABIT / RITUAL TRACKER

M T W T F S S

....

....

....

....

....

....

....

STAYING FOCUSED ON YOUR GOALS

- ☐ REVIEW WEEKLY GOALS
- ☐ REVIEW MONTHLY GOALS
- ☐ REVIEW 6-MONTH GOALS

THIS WEEKS NUMBERS

NEW LISTINGS	. . . .
CLOSINGS	. . . .
COMMISSIONS	. . . .
CONTRACTS ACCEPTED	. . . .
SHOWINGS	. . . .
CALLS MADE	. . . .
NEW LEADS	. . . .
APPOINTMENTS SET	. . . .
SOCIAL MEDIA POSTS	. . . .
OTHER:	. . . .
OTHER:	. . . .

NOTES

WHAT ACTIONS DO I NEED TO TAKE THIS WEEK IN ORDER TO MOVE THE NEEDLE FORWARD?

WHAT ARE MY MAIN GOALS THIS WEEK?

HOW WILL I CELEBRATE MY WINS THIS WEEK?

IS THERE ANYTHING I'VE BEEN AVOIDING THAT NEEDS TO BE COMPLETED OR STARTED THIS WEEK?

WHAT MIGHT TRIP ME UP THIS WEEK AND MOVE ME OFF COURSE? HOW CAN I AVOID THESE PITFALLS?

Monday
/

Tuesday
/

Wednesday
/

TOP 3 PRIORITIES

....
....
....

TOP 3 PRIORITIES

....
....
....

TOP 3 PRIORITIES

....
....
....

DAILY GRATITUDE

....
....
....
....
....

DAILY GRATITUDE

....
....
....
....
....

DAILY GRATITUDE

....
....
....
....
....

TO-DO

- ☐ ....
- ☐ ....
- ☐ ....
- ☐ ....
- ☐ ....

TO-DO

- ☐ ....
- ☐ ....
- ☐ ....
- ☐ ....
- ☐ ....

TO-DO

- ☐ ....
- ☐ ....
- ☐ ....
- ☐ ....
- ☐ ....

TIME BLOCKING

6
7
8
9
10
11
12
1
2
3
4
5
6
7
8
9

TIME BLOCKING

6
7
8
9
10
11
12
1
2
3
4
5
6
7
8
9

TIME BLOCKING

6
7
8
9
10
11
12
1
2
3
4
5
6
7
8
9

QUOTE OF THE WEEK:

Thursday
/

TOP 3 PRIORITIES

. . . .

. . . .

. . . .

DAILY GRATITUDE

. . . .

. . . .

. . . .

. . . .

. . . .

TO-DO

- ☐ . . . .
- ☐ . . . .
- ☐ . . . .
- ☐ . . . .
- ☐ . . . .

TIME BLOCKING

6
7
8
9
10
11
12
1
2
3
4
5
6
7
8
9

Friday
/

TOP 3 PRIORITIES

. . . .

. . . .

. . . .

DAILY GRATITUDE

. . . .

. . . .

. . . .

. . . .

. . . .

TO-DO

- ☐ . . . .
- ☐ . . . .
- ☐ . . . .
- ☐ . . . .
- ☐ . . . .

TIME BLOCKING

6
7
8
9
10
11
12
1
2
3
4
5
6
7
8
9

Weekend
/

TOP 3 PRIORITIES

. . . .

. . . .

. . . .

DAILY GRATITUDE

. . . .

. . . .

. . . .

. . . .

. . . .

TO-DO

- ☐ . . . .
- ☐ . . . .
- ☐ . . . .
- ☐ . . . .
- ☐ . . . .

NOTES

. . . .

. . . .

. . . .

. . . .

. . . .

. . . .

. . . .

. . . .

. . . .

. . . .

. . . .

. . . .

. . . .

. . . .

DATES / / - / /

MON

TUE

WED

THU

FRI

SAT

SUN

WORD OF THE WEEK

....

THIS WEEKS TOP PRIORITIES

☐ ....
☐ ....
☐ ....
☐ ....
☐ ....

TO - DO

☐ ....
☐ ....
☐ ....
☐ ....
☐ ....
☐ ....
☐ ....
☐ ....
☐ ....
☐ ....

HABIT / RITUAL TRACKER

	M	T	W	T	F	S	S
....							
....							
....							
....							
....							
....							
....							

STAYING FOCUSED ON YOUR GOALS

- ☐ REVIEW WEEKLY GOALS
- ☐ REVIEW MONTHLY GOALS
- ☐ REVIEW 6-MONTH GOALS

NOTES

THIS WEEKS NUMBERS

NEW LISTINGS	. . . .
CLOSINGS	. . . .
COMMISSIONS	. . . .
CONTRACTS ACCEPTED	. . . .
SHOWINGS	. . . .
CALLS MADE	. . . .
NEW LEADS	. . . .
APPOINTMENTS SET	. . . .
SOCIAL MEDIA POSTS	. . . .
OTHER:	. . . .
OTHER:	. . . .

WHAT ACTIONS DO I NEED TO TAKE THIS WEEK IN ORDER TO MOVE THE NEEDLE FORWARD?

WHAT ARE MY MAIN GOALS THIS WEEK?

HOW WILL I CELEBRATE MY WINS THIS WEEK?

IS THERE ANYTHING I'VE BEEN AVOIDING THAT NEEDS TO BE COMPLETED OR STARTED THIS WEEK?

WHAT MIGHT TRIP ME UP THIS WEEK AND MOVE ME OFF COURSE? HOW CAN I AVOID THESE PITFALLS?

Monday
/

Tuesday
/

Wednesday
/

Monday	Tuesday	Wednesday

TOP 3 PRIORITIES

. . . .
. . . .
. . . .

TOP 3 PRIORITIES

. . . .
. . . .
. . . .

TOP 3 PRIORITIES

. . . .
. . . .
. . . .

DAILY GRATITUDE

. . . .
. . . .
. . . .
. . . .

DAILY GRATITUDE

. . . .
. . . .
. . . .
. . . .

DAILY GRATITUDE

. . . .
. . . .
. . . .
. . . .

TO-DO

☐
☐
☐
☐
☐

TO-DO

☐
☐
☐
☐
☐

TO-DO

☐
☐
☐
☐
☐

TIME BLOCKING

6
7
8
9
10
11
12
1
2
3
4
5
6
7
8
9

TIME BLOCKING

6
7
8
9
10
11
12
1
2
3
4
5
6
7
8
9

TIME BLOCKING

6
7
8
9
10
11
12
1
2
3
4
5
6
7
8
9

Thursday
/

Friday
/

Weekend
/

Thursday	Friday	Weekend
TOP 3 PRIORITIES	**TOP 3 PRIORITIES**	**TOP 3 PRIORITIES**
. . . .	. . . .	. . . .
. . . .	. . . .	. . . .
. . . .	. . . .	. . . .
DAILY GRATITUDE	**DAILY GRATITUDE**	**DAILY GRATITUDE**

Thursday

TOP 3 PRIORITIES
- . . . .
- . . . .
- . . . .

DAILY GRATITUDE
. . . .
. . . .
. . . .
. . . .
. . . .

TO-DO
- ☐ . . . .
- ☐ . . . .
- ☐ . . . .
- ☐ . . . .
- ☐ . . . .

TIME BLOCKING
6
7
8
9
10
11
12
1
2
3
4
5
6
7
8
9

Friday

TOP 3 PRIORITIES
- . . . .
- . . . .
- . . . .

DAILY GRATITUDE
. . . .
. . . .
. . . .
. . . .
. . . .

TO-DO
- ☐ . . . .
- ☐ . . . .
- ☐ . . . .
- ☐ . . . .
- ☐ . . . .

TIME BLOCKING
6
7
8
9
10
11
12
1
2
3
4
5
6
7
8
9

Weekend

TOP 3 PRIORITIES
- . . . .
- . . . .
- . . . .

DAILY GRATITUDE
. . . .
. . . .
. . . .
. . . .
. . . .

TO-DO
- ☐ . . . .
- ☐ . . . .
- ☐ . . . .
- ☐ . . . .
- ☐ . . . .

NOTES
. . . .
. . . .
. . . .
. . . .
. . . .
. . . .
. . . .
. . . .
. . . .
. . . .
. . . .
. . . .
. . . .
. . . .

DATES / / - / /

MON

TUE

WED

THU

FRI

SAT

SUN

WORD OF THE WEEK

....

THIS WEEKS TOP PRIORITIES

☐ ....
☐ ....
☐ ....
☐ ....
☐ ....

TO - DO

☐ ....
☐ ....
☐ ....
☐ ....
☐ ....
☐ ....
☐ ....
☐ ....
☐ ....
☐ ....

HABIT / RITUAL TRACKER

	M	T	W	T	F	S	S
....							
....							
....							
....							
....							
....							
....							

STAYING FOCUSED ON YOUR GOALS

- ☐ REVIEW WEEKLY GOALS
- ☐ REVIEW MONTHLY GOALS
- ☐ REVIEW 6-MONTH GOALS

THIS WEEKS NUMBERS

NEW LISTINGS	. . . .
CLOSINGS	. . . .
COMMISSIONS	. . . .
CONTRACTS ACCEPTED	. . . .
SHOWINGS	. . . .
CALLS MADE	. . . .
NEW LEADS	. . . .
APPOINTMENTS SET	. . . .
SOCIAL MEDIA POSTS	. . . .
OTHER:	. . . .
OTHER:	. . . .

NOTES

WHAT ACTIONS DO I NEED TO TAKE THIS WEEK IN ORDER TO MOVE THE NEEDLE FORWARD?

WHAT ARE MY MAIN GOALS THIS WEEK?

HOW WILL I CELEBRATE MY WINS THIS WEEK?

IS THERE ANYTHING I'VE BEEN AVOIDING THAT NEEDS TO BE COMPLETED OR STARTED THIS WEEK?

WHAT MIGHT TRIP ME UP THIS WEEK AND MOVE ME OFF COURSE? HOW CAN I AVOID THESE PITFALLS?

Monday	Tuesday	Wednesday
/	/	/

TOP 3 PRIORITIES | **TOP 3 PRIORITIES** | **TOP 3 PRIORITIES**

....

....

....

DAILY GRATITUDE

....

....

....

....

....

TO-DO

☐ ....
☐ ....
☐ ....
☐ ....
☐ ....

TIME BLOCKING

6 _____
7 _____
8 _____
9 _____
10 _____
11 _____
12 _____
1 _____
2 _____
3 _____
4 _____
5 _____
6 _____
7 _____
8 _____
9 _____

Thursday
/

TOP 3 PRIORITIES

. . . .

. . . .

. . . .

DAILY GRATITUDE

. . . .

. . . .

. . . .

. . . .

. . . .

TO-DO

☐ . . . .

☐ . . . .

☐ . . . .

☐ . . . .

☐

TIME BLOCKING

6

7

8

9

10

11

12

1

2

3

4

5

6

7

8

9

Friday
/

TOP 3 PRIORITIES

. . . .

. . . .

. . . .

DAILY GRATITUDE

. . . .

. . . .

. . . .

. . . .

. . . .

TO-DO

☐ . . . .

☐ . . . .

☐ . . . .

☐ . . . .

☐

TIME BLOCKING

6

7

8

9

10

11

12

1

2

3

4

5

6

7

8

9

Weekend
/

TOP 3 PRIORITIES

. . . .

. . . .

. . . .

DAILY GRATITUDE

. . . .

. . . .

. . . .

. . . .

TO-DO

☐ . . . .

☐ . . . .

☐ . . . .

☐ . . . .

☐

NOTES

. . . .

. . . .

. . . .

. . . .

. . . .

. . . .

. . . .

. . . .

. . . .

. . . .

. . . .

. . . .

Enjoy the journey.

MONTH

MONTH:

This Months Goals

COMMISSION TOTAL

GOAL: ACTUAL:

CLOSINGS

GOAL: ACTUAL:

NEW LISTINGS

GOAL: ACTUAL:

#NEW CONTACTS

GOAL: ACTUAL:

APPOINTMENTS SET

GOAL: ACTUAL:

NEW SELLER PROSPECTS

GOAL: ACTUAL:

NEW BUYER PROSPECTS

GOAL: ACTUAL:

. . . .

GOAL: ACTUAL:

. . . .

GOAL: ACTUAL:

. . . .

GOAL: ACTUAL:

Monday	Tuesday	Wednesday	Thursday

THIS MONTHS MAIN GOALS

☐ . . . .

☐ . . . .

☐ . . . .

☐ . . . .

☐ . . . .

Friday	Saturday	Sunday
☐	☐	☐
☐	☐	☐
☐	☐	☐
☐	☐	☐
☐	☐	☐

ACTIONS TO TAKE

☐ ....
☐ ....
☐ ....
☐ ....
☐ ....
☐ ....

BUSINESS EXPENSES

MLS FEES	CLIENT GIFTS ....
OFFICE FEES	LUNCHES ....
DUES / FEES	COFFEE ....
OFFICE SUPPLIES	SIGNAGE ....
TRAVEL MILEAGE	MAILERS ....
SUBSCRIPTIONS	FUEL ....
PARKING FEES	MISC. ....
ONLINE MARKETING	MISC. ....

NOTES

....
....
....
....
....
....

WHAT POSITIVE HABITS DO I WANT TO NURTURE THIS MONTH?

☐ ....
☐ ....
☐ ....
☐ ....
☐ ....

DATES / / - / /

MON

TUE

WED

THU

FRI

SAT

SUN

WORD OF THE WEEK

....

THIS WEEKS TOP PRIORITIES

☐ ....
☐ ....
☐ ....
☐ ....
☐ ....

TO - DO

☐ ....
☐ ....
☐ ....
☐ ....
☐ ....
☐ ....
☐ ....
☐ ....
☐ ....
☐ ....

HABIT / RITUAL TRACKER

M T W T F S S
....
....
....
....
....
....
....

STAYING FOCUSED ON YOUR GOALS

- [ ] REVIEW WEEKLY GOALS
- [ ] REVIEW MONTHLY GOALS
- [ ] REVIEW 6-MONTH GOALS

NOTES

THIS WEEKS NUMBERS

NEW LISTINGS	. . . .
CLOSINGS	. . . .
COMMISSIONS	. . . .
CONTRACTS ACCEPTED	. . . .
SHOWINGS	. . . .
CALLS MADE	. . . .
NEW LEADS	. . . .
APPOINTMENTS SET	. . . .
SOCIAL MEDIA POSTS	. . . .
OTHER:	. . . .
OTHER:	. . . .

WHAT ACTIONS DO I NEED TO TAKE THIS WEEK IN ORDER TO MOVE THE NEEDLE FORWARD?

WHAT ARE MY MAIN GOALS THIS WEEK?

HOW WILL I CELEBRATE MY WINS THIS WEEK?

IS THERE ANYTHING I'VE BEEN AVOIDING THAT NEEDS TO BE COMPLETED OR STARTED THIS WEEK?

WHAT MIGHT TRIP ME UP THIS WEEK AND MOVE ME OFF COURSE? HOW CAN I AVOID THESE PITFALLS?

Monday
/

TOP 3 PRIORITIES

. . . .

. . . .

. . . .

DAILY GRATITUDE

. . . .

. . . .

. . . .

. . . .

TO-DO

☐ . . . .
☐ . . . .
☐ . . . .
☐ . . . .
☐ . . . .

TIME BLOCKING

6
7
8
9
10
11
12
1
2
3
4
5
6
7
8
9

Tuesday
/

TOP 3 PRIORITIES

. . . .

. . . .

. . . .

DAILY GRATITUDE

. . . .

. . . .

. . . .

. . . .

TO-DO

☐ . . . .
☐ . . . .
☐ . . . .
☐ . . . .
☐ . . . .

TIME BLOCKING

6
7
8
9
10
11
12
1
2
3
4
5
6
7
8
9

Wednesday
/

TOP 3 PRIORITIES

. . . .

. . . .

. . . .

DAILY GRATITUDE

. . . .

. . . .

. . . .

. . . .

TO-DO

☐ . . . .
☐ . . . .
☐ . . . .
☐ . . . .
☐ . . . .

TIME BLOCKING

6
7
8
9
10
11
12
1
2
3
4
5
6
7
8
9

Thursday
/

TOP 3 PRIORITIES

．．．．．．．．．．．．．．．．．．．．．．．．．．．．

．．．．．．．．．．．．．．．．．．．．．．．．．．．．

．．．．．．．．．．．．．．．．．．．．．．．．．．．．

DAILY GRATITUDE

．．．．．．．．．．．．．．．．．．．．．．．．．．．．

．．．．．．．．．．．．．．．．．．．．．．．．．．．．

．．．．．．．．．．．．．．．．．．．．．．．．．．．．

．．．．．．．．．．．．．．．．．．．．．．．．．．．．

TO-DO

☐ ．．．．．．．．．．．．．．．．．．．．．．．．．．

☐ ．．．．．．．．．．．．．．．．．．．．．．．．．．

☐ ．．．．．．．．．．．．．．．．．．．．．．．．．．

☐ ．．．．．．．．．．．．．．．．．．．．．．．．．．

☐

TIME BLOCKING

6

7

8

9

10

11

12

1

2

3

4

5

6

7

8

9

Friday
/

TOP 3 PRIORITIES

．．．．．．．．．．．．．．．．．．．．．．．．．．．．

．．．．．．．．．．．．．．．．．．．．．．．．．．．．

．．．．．．．．．．．．．．．．．．．．．．．．．．．．

DAILY GRATITUDE

．．．．．．．．．．．．．．．．．．．．．．．．．．．．

．．．．．．．．．．．．．．．．．．．．．．．．．．．．

．．．．．．．．．．．．．．．．．．．．．．．．．．．．

．．．．．．．．．．．．．．．．．．．．．．．．．．．．

TO-DO

☐ ．．．．．．．．．．．．．．．．．．．．．．．．．．

☐ ．．．．．．．．．．．．．．．．．．．．．．．．．．

☐ ．．．．．．．．．．．．．．．．．．．．．．．．．．

☐ ．．．．．．．．．．．．．．．．．．．．．．．．．．

☐

TIME BLOCKING

6

7

8

9

10

11

12

1

2

3

4

5

6

7

8

9

Weekend
/

TOP 3 PRIORITIES

．．．．．．．．．．．．．．．．．．．．．．．．．．．．

．．．．．．．．．．．．．．．．．．．．．．．．．．．．

．．．．．．．．．．．．．．．．．．．．．．．．．．．．

DAILY GRATITUDE

．．．．．．．．．．．．．．．．．．．．．．．．．．．．

．．．．．．．．．．．．．．．．．．．．．．．．．．．．

．．．．．．．．．．．．．．．．．．．．．．．．．．．．

．．．．．．．．．．．．．．．．．．．．．．．．．．．．

TO-DO

☐ ．．．．．．．．．．．．．．．．．．．．．．．．．．

☐ ．．．．．．．．．．．．．．．．．．．．．．．．．．

☐ ．．．．．．．．．．．．．．．．．．．．．．．．．．

☐ ．．．．．．．．．．．．．．．．．．．．．．．．．．

☐

NOTES

．．．．．．．．．．．．．．．．．．．．．．．．．．．．

．．．．．．．．．．．．．．．．．．．．．．．．．．．．

．．．．．．．．．．．．．．．．．．．．．．．．．．．．

．．．．．．．．．．．．．．．．．．．．．．．．．．．．

．．．．．．．．．．．．．．．．．．．．．．．．．．．．

．．．．．．．．．．．．．．．．．．．．．．．．．．．．

．．．．．．．．．．．．．．．．．．．．．．．．．．．．

．．．．．．．．．．．．．．．．．．．．．．．．．．．．

．．．．．．．．．．．．．．．．．．．．．．．．．．．．

．．．．．．．．．．．．．．．．．．．．．．．．．．．．

．．．．．．．．．．．．．．．．．．．．．．．．．．．．

．．．．．．．．．．．．．．．．．．．．．．．．．．．．

．．．．．．．．．．．．．．．．．．．．．．．．．．．．

DATES ___ / ___ / ___ - ___ / ___ /

MON

TUE

WED

THU

FRI

SAT

SUN

WORD OF THE WEEK

. . . .

THIS WEEKS TOP PRIORITIES

☐ . . . .
☐ . . . .
☐ . . . .
☐ . . . .
☐ . . . .

TO - DO

☐ . . . .
☐ . . . .
☐ . . . .
☐ . . . .
☐ . . . .
☐ . . . .
☐ . . . .
☐ . . . .
☐ . . . .
☐ . . . .

HABIT / RITUAL TRACKER

M T W T F S S

STAYING FOCUSED ON YOUR GOALS

- ☐ REVIEW WEEKLY GOALS
- ☐ REVIEW MONTHLY GOALS
- ☐ REVIEW 6-MONTH GOALS

THIS WEEKS NUMBERS

NEW LISTINGS	. . . .
CLOSINGS	. . . .
COMMISSIONS	. . . .
CONTRACTS ACCEPTED	. . . .
SHOWINGS	. . . .
CALLS MADE	. . . .
NEW LEADS	. . . .
APPOINTMENTS SET	. . . .
SOCIAL MEDIA POSTS	. . . .
OTHER:	. . . .
OTHER:	. . . .

NOTES

WHAT ACTIONS DO I NEED TO TAKE THIS WEEK IN ORDER TO MOVE THE NEEDLE FORWARD?

WHAT ARE MY MAIN GOALS THIS WEEK?

HOW WILL I CELEBRATE MY WINS THIS WEEK?

IS THERE ANYTHING I'VE BEEN AVOIDING THAT NEEDS TO BE COMPLETED OR STARTED THIS WEEK?

WHAT MIGHT TRIP ME UP THIS WEEK AND MOVE ME OFF COURSE? HOW CAN I AVOID THESE PITFALLS?

Monday
/

Tuesday
/

Wednesday
/

TOP 3 PRIORITIES
. . . .
. . . .
. . . .

DAILY GRATITUDE
. . . .
. . . .
. . . .
. . . .

TO-DO
☐ . . . .
☐ . . . .
☐ . . . .
☐ . . . .
☐ . . . .

TIME BLOCKING
6
7
8
9
10
11
12
1
2
3
4
5
6
7
8
9

TOP 3 PRIORITIES
. . . .
. . . .
. . . .

DAILY GRATITUDE
. . . .
. . . .
. . . .
. . . .

TO-DO
☐ . . . .
☐ . . . .
☐ . . . .
☐ . . . .
☐ . . . .

TIME BLOCKING
6
7
8
9
10
11
12
1
2
3
4
5
6
7
8
9

TOP 3 PRIORITIES
. . . .
. . . .
. . . .

DAILY GRATITUDE
. . . .
. . . .
. . . .
. . . .

TO-DO
☐ . . . .
☐ . . . .
☐ . . . .
☐ . . . .
☐ . . . .

TIME BLOCKING
6
7
8
9
10
11
12
1
2
3
4
5
6
7
8
9

Thursday
/

TOP 3 PRIORITIES
. . . .
. . . .
. . . .

DAILY GRATITUDE
. . . .
. . . .
. . . .
. . . .
. . . .

TO-DO
- ☐ . . . .
- ☐ . . . .
- ☐ . . . .
- ☐ . . . .
- ☐

TIME BLOCKING
6
7
8
9
10
11
12
1
2
3
4
5
6
7
8
9

Friday
/

TOP 3 PRIORITIES
. . . .
. . . .
. . . .

DAILY GRATITUDE
. . . .
. . . .
. . . .
. . . .
. . . .

TO-DO
- ☐ . . . .
- ☐ . . . .
- ☐ . . . .
- ☐ . . . .
- ☐

TIME BLOCKING
6
7
8
9
10
11
12
1
2
3
4
5
6
7
8
9

Weekend
/

TOP 3 PRIORITIES
. . . .
. . . .
. . . .

DAILY GRATITUDE
. . . .
. . . .
. . . .
. . . .
. . . .

TO-DO
- ☐ . . . .
- ☐ . . . .
- ☐ . . . .
- ☐ . . . .
- ☐

NOTES
. . . .
. . . .
. . . .
. . . .
. . . .
. . . .
. . . .
. . . .
. . . .
. . . .
. . . .
. . . .
. . . .
. . . .
. . . .
. . . .

DATES / / - / /

MON

TUE

WED

THU

FRI

SAT

SUN

WORD OF THE WEEK

. . . .

THIS WEEKS TOP PRIORITIES

☐ . . . .
☐ . . . .
☐ . . . .
☐ . . . .
☐ . . . .

TO - DO

☐ . . . .
☐ . . . .
☐ . . . .
☐ . . . .
☐ . . . .
☐ . . . .
☐ . . . .
☐ . . . .
☐ . . . .
☐ . . . .

HABIT / RITUAL TRACKER

M T W T F S S

. . . .
. . . .
. . . .
. . . .
. . . .
. . . .
. . . .

STAYING FOCUSED ON YOUR GOALS

- ☐ REVIEW WEEKLY GOALS
- ☐ REVIEW MONTHLY GOALS
- ☐ REVIEW 6-MONTH GOALS

THIS WEEKS NUMBERS

NEW LISTINGS	. . . .
CLOSINGS	. . . .
COMMISSIONS	. . . .
CONTRACTS ACCEPTED	. . . .
SHOWINGS	. . . .
CALLS MADE	. . . .
NEW LEADS	. . . .
APPOINTMENTS SET	. . . .
SOCIAL MEDIA POSTS	. . . .
OTHER:	. . . .
OTHER:	. . . .

NOTES

WHAT ACTIONS DO I NEED TO TAKE THIS WEEK IN ORDER TO MOVE THE NEEDLE FORWARD?

WHAT ARE MY MAIN GOALS THIS WEEK?

HOW WILL I CELEBRATE MY WINS THIS WEEK?

IS THERE ANYTHING I'VE BEEN AVOIDING THAT NEEDS TO BE COMPLETED OR STARTED THIS WEEK?

WHAT MIGHT TRIP ME UP THIS WEEK AND MOVE ME OFF COURSE? HOW CAN I AVOID THESE PITFALLS?

Monday
/

Tuesday
/

Wednesday
/

TOP 3 PRIORITIES

. . . .

. . . .

. . . .

DAILY GRATITUDE

. . . .

. . . .

. . . .

. . . .

TO-DO

☐ . . . .

☐ . . . .

☐ . . . .

☐ . . . .

☐ . . . .

TIME BLOCKING

6

7

8

9

10

11

12

1

2

3

4

5

6

7

8

9

TOP 3 PRIORITIES

. . . .

. . . .

. . . .

DAILY GRATITUDE

. . . .

. . . .

. . . .

. . . .

TO-DO

☐ . . . .

☐ . . . .

☐ . . . .

☐ . . . .

☐ . . . .

TIME BLOCKING

6

7

8

9

10

11

12

1

2

3

4

5

6

7

8

9

TOP 3 PRIORITIES

. . . .

. . . .

. . . .

DAILY GRATITUDE

. . . .

. . . .

. . . .

. . . .

TO-DO

☐ . . . .

☐ . . . .

☐ . . . .

☐ . . . .

☐ . . . .

TIME BLOCKING

6

7

8

9

10

11

12

1

2

3

4

5

6

7

8

9

Thursday
/

TOP 3 PRIORITIES
. . . .
. . . .
. . . .

DAILY GRATITUDE
. . . .
. . . .
. . . .
. . . .
. . . .

TO-DO
☐ . . . .
☐ . . . .
☐ . . . .
☐ . . . .
☐ . . . .

TIME BLOCKING
6
7
8
9
10
11
12
1
2
3
4
5
6
7
8
9

Friday
/

TOP 3 PRIORITIES
. . . .
. . . .
. . . .

DAILY GRATITUDE
. . . .
. . . .
. . . .
. . . .
. . . .

TO-DO
☐ . . . .
☐ . . . .
☐ . . . .
☐ . . . .
☐ . . . .

TIME BLOCKING
6
7
8
9
10
11
12
1
2
3
4
5
6
7
8
9

Weekend
/

TOP 3 PRIORITIES
. . . .
. . . .
. . . .

DAILY GRATITUDE
. . . .
. . . .
. . . .
. . . .
. . . .

TO-DO
☐
☐
☐
☐
☐

NOTES
. . . .
. . . .
. . . .
. . . .
. . . .
. . . .
. . . .
. . . .
. . . .
. . . .
. . . .
. . . .
. . . .
. . . .
. . . .
. . . .

DATES / / - / /

MON

TUE

WED

THU

FRI

SAT

SUN

WORD OF THE WEEK

....

THIS WEEKS TOP PRIORITIES

☐ ....
☐ ....
☐ ....
☐ ....
☐ ....

TO - DO

☐ ....
☐ ....
☐ ....
☐ ....
☐ ....
☐ ....
☐ ....
☐ ....
☐ ....
☐ ....

HABIT / RITUAL TRACKER

	M	T	W	T	F	S	S
....							
....							
....							
....							
....							
....							
....							

STAYING FOCUSED ON YOUR GOALS

☐ REVIEW WEEKLY GOALS

☐ REVIEW MONTHLY GOALS

☐ REVIEW 6-MONTH GOALS

THIS WEEKS NUMBERS

NEW LISTINGS	. . . .
CLOSINGS	. . . .
COMMISSIONS	. . . .
CONTRACTS ACCEPTED	. . . .
SHOWINGS	. . . .
CALLS MADE	. . . .
NEW LEADS	. . . .
APPOINTMENTS SET	. . . .
SOCIAL MEDIA POSTS	. . . .
OTHER:	. . . .
OTHER:	. . . .

NOTES

WHAT ACTIONS DO I NEED TO TAKE THIS WEEK IN ORDER TO MOVE THE NEEDLE FORWARD?

WHAT ARE MY MAIN GOALS THIS WEEK?

HOW WILL I CELEBRATE MY WINS THIS WEEK?

IS THERE ANYTHING I'VE BEEN AVOIDING THAT NEEDS TO BE COMPLETED OR STARTED THIS WEEK?

WHAT MIGHT TRIP ME UP THIS WEEK AND MOVE ME OFF COURSE? HOW CAN I AVOID THESE PITFALLS?

Monday

/

TOP 3 PRIORITIES

. . . .

. . . .

. . . .

DAILY GRATITUDE

. . . .

. . . .

. . . .

. . . .

TO-DO

☐ . . . .
☐ . . . .
☐ . . . .
☐ . . . .
☐ . . . .

TIME BLOCKING

6
7
8
9
10
11
12
1
2
3
4
5
6
7
8
9

Tuesday

/

TOP 3 PRIORITIES

. . . .

. . . .

. . . .

DAILY GRATITUDE

. . . .

. . . .

. . . .

. . . .

TO-DO

☐ . . . .
☐ . . . .
☐ . . . .
☐ . . . .
☐ . . . .

TIME BLOCKING

6
7
8
9
10
11
12
1
2
3
4
5
6
7
8
9

Wednesday

/

TOP 3 PRIORITIES

. . . .

. . . .

. . . .

DAILY GRATITUDE

. . . .

. . . .

. . . .

. . . .

TO-DO

☐ . . . .
☐ . . . .
☐ . . . .
☐ . . . .
☐ . . . .

TIME BLOCKING

6
7
8
9
10
11
12
1
2
3
4
5
6
7
8
9

Thursday
/

TOP 3 PRIORITIES
. . . .
. . . .
. . . .

DAILY GRATITUDE
. . . .
. . . .
. . . .
. . . .
. . . .

TO-DO
☐
☐
☐
☐
☐

TIME BLOCKING
6
7
8
9
10
11
12
1
2
3
4
5
6
7
8
9

Friday
/

TOP 3 PRIORITIES
. . . .
. . . .
. . . .

DAILY GRATITUDE
. . . .
. . . .
. . . .
. . . .
. . . .

TO-DO
☐
☐
☐
☐
☐

TIME BLOCKING
6
7
8
9
10
11
12
1
2
3
4
5
6
7
8
9

Weekend
/

TOP 3 PRIORITIES
. . . .
. . . .
. . . .

DAILY GRATITUDE
. . . .
. . . .
. . . .
. . . .
. . . .

TO-DO
☐
☐
☐
☐
☐

NOTES
. . . .
. . . .
. . . .
. . . .
. . . .
. . . .
. . . .
. . . .
. . . .
. . . .
. . . .
. . . .
. . . .
. . . .
. . . .
. . . .
. . . .

DATES /   /   -   /   /

MON

TUE

WED

THU

FRI

SAT

SUN

WORD OF THE WEEK

....

THIS WEEKS TOP PRIORITIES

☐ ....
☐ ....
☐ ....
☐ ....
☐ ....

TO - DO

☐ ....
☐ ....
☐ ....
☐ ....
☐ ....
☐ ....
☐ ....
☐ ....
☐ ....
☐ ....

HABIT / RITUAL TRACKER

M T W T F S S

....
....
....
....
....
....
....

STAYING FOCUSED ON YOUR GOALS

☐ REVIEW WEEKLY GOALS

☐ REVIEW MONTHLY GOALS

☐ REVIEW 6-MONTH GOALS

THIS WEEKS NUMBERS

NEW LISTINGS	. . . .
CLOSINGS	. . . .
COMMISSIONS	. . . .
CONTRACTS ACCEPTED	. . . .
SHOWINGS	. . . .
CALLS MADE	. . . .
NEW LEADS	. . . .
APPOINTMENTS SET	. . . .
SOCIAL MEDIA POSTS	. . . .
OTHER:	. . . .
OTHER:	. . . .

NOTES

WHAT ACTIONS DO I NEED TO TAKE THIS WEEK IN ORDER TO MOVE THE NEEDLE FORWARD?

WHAT ARE MY MAIN GOALS THIS WEEK?

HOW WILL I CELEBRATE MY WINS THIS WEEK?

IS THERE ANYTHING I'VE BEEN AVOIDING THAT NEEDS TO BE COMPLETED OR STARTED THIS WEEK?

WHAT MIGHT TRIP ME UP THIS WEEK AND MOVE ME OFF COURSE? HOW CAN I AVOID THESE PITFALLS?

Monday
/

Tuesday
/

Wednesday
/

TOP 3 PRIORITIES   TOP 3 PRIORITIES   TOP 3 PRIORITIES

. . . .

. . . .

. . . .

DAILY GRATITUDE   DAILY GRATITUDE   DAILY GRATITUDE

. . . .

. . . .

. . . .

. . . .

TO-DO   TO-DO   TO-DO

☐   ☐   ☐

☐   ☐   ☐

☐   ☐   ☐

☐   ☐   ☐

☐   ☐   ☐

TIME BLOCKING   TIME BLOCKING   TIME BLOCKING

Monday	Tuesday	Wednesday
6	6	6
7	7	7
8	8	8
9	9	9
10	10	10
11	11	11
12	12	12
1	1	1
2	2	2
3	3	3
4	4	4
5	5	5
6	6	6
7	7	7
8	8	8
9	9	9

Thursday
/

Friday
/

Weekend
/

TOP 3 PRIORITIES	TOP 3 PRIORITIES	TOP 3 PRIORITIES
. . . .	. . . .	. . . .
. . . .	. . . .	. . . .
. . . .	. . . .	. . . .

DAILY GRATITUDE	DAILY GRATITUDE	DAILY GRATITUDE
. . . .	. . . .	. . . .
. . . .	. . . .	. . . .
. . . .	. . . .	. . . .
. . . .	. . . .	. . . .
. . . .	. . . .	. . . .

TO-DO ☐ ☐ ☐ ☐ ☐

TO-DO ☐ ☐ ☐ ☐ ☐

TO-DO ☐ ☐ ☐ ☐ ☐

TIME BLOCKING	TIME BLOCKING	NOTES
6	6	. . . .
7	7	. . . .
8	8	. . . .
9	9	. . . .
10	10	. . . .
11	11	. . . .
12	12	. . . .
1	1	. . . .
2	2	. . . .
3	3	. . . .
4	4	. . . .
5	5	. . . .
6	6	. . . .
7	7	. . . .
8	8	. . . .
9	9	. . . .

Remember your goal & why you started.

6-Month Goals

6-Month Goals

	LAST YEAR	GOAL	ACTUAL	CHANGE
TOTAL COMMISSIONS	_____	_____	_____	_____
TOTAL VOLUME	_____	_____	_____	_____
TOTAL CLOSINGS	_____	_____	_____	_____
TOTAL BUYERS	_____	_____	_____	_____
TOTAL LISTINGS	_____	_____	_____	_____

LISTINGS

CLOSINGS

BUDGET	BUDGETED	ACTUAL		BUDGETED	ACTUAL
REAL ESTATE DUES	_____	_____	FUEL	_____	_____
OFFICE FEES	_____	_____	MAILERS	_____	_____
MLS FEES	_____	_____	SIGNAGE	_____	_____
SUBSCRIPTIONS	_____	_____	GIFTS	_____	_____
OFFICE SUPPLIES	_____	_____	OTHER	_____	_____
PHOTOGRAPHER	_____	_____	OTHER	_____	_____
ONLINE MARKETING	_____	_____	OTHER	_____	_____

Six Month Goals

BEING A TOP AGENT ISN'T JUST ABOUT BUSINESS, IT'S ALSO IMPORTANT TO HAVE SOME BALANCE IN ALL AREAS OF LIFE. IN THE FOLLOWING SPACES CREATE GOALS YOU WANT TO ACCOMPLISH WITHIN THE NEXT SIX MONTHS IN EACH OF THE TEN LIFE AREAS.

Family & Friends

Personal Development

Spirituality

Finances

Business

Relationship

Fun & Recreation

Giving & Contribution

Environment

Health & Fitness

Focus on your goals.

Look nowhere but ahead.

Cashflow Tracking

Month:

Income   ## Amount

....
....
....
....
....
....
....
....
....

Expenses

....
....
....
....
....
....
....
....
....
....
....
....
....
....
....
....
....

Monthly Cash Flow

TOTAL INCOME $ ....
TOTAL EXPENSES $ ....
TOTAL $ ....

Month:

INCOME GOAL:
SAVINGS GOAL:

Income   ## Amount

....
....
....
....
....
....
....
....
....

Expenses

....
....
....
....
....
....
....
....
....
....
....
....
....
....
....
....
....

Monthly Cash Flow

TOTAL INCOME $ ....
TOTAL EXPENSES $ ....
TOTAL $ ....

Month:

Income	Amount
....	....
....	....
....	....
....	....
....	....
....	....
....	....
....	....
....	....
....	....

Expenses

....	....
....	....
....	....
....	....
....	....
....	....
....	....
....	....
....	....
....	....
....	....
....	....
....	....
....	....
....	....
....	....
....	....
....	....

Monthly Cash Flow

TOTAL INCOME	$ ....
TOTAL EXPENSES	$ ....
TOTAL	$ ....

Month:

Income	Amount
....	....
....	....
....	....
....	....
....	....
....	....
....	....
....	....
....	....

Expenses

....	....
....	....
....	....
....	....
....	....
....	....
....	....
....	....
....	....
....	....
....	....
....	....
....	....
....	....
....	....
....	....
....	....

Monthly Cash Flow

TOTAL INCOME	$ ....
TOTAL EXPENSES	$ ....
TOTAL	$ ....

Month:

Income	Amount
. . . .	. . . .
. . . .	. . . .
. . . .	. . . .
. . . .	. . . .
. . . .	. . . .
. . . .	. . . .
. . . .	. . . .
. . . .	. . . .
. . . .	. . . .

Expenses

. . . .	. . . .
. . . .	. . . .
. . . .	. . . .
. . . .	. . . .
. . . .	. . . .
. . . .	. . . .
. . . .	. . . .
. . . .	. . . .
. . . .	. . . .
. . . .	. . . .
. . . .	. . . .
. . . .	. . . .
. . . .	. . . .
. . . .	. . . .
. . . .	. . . .
. . . .	. . . .

Monthly Cash Flow

TOTAL INCOME $ . . . .

TOTAL EXPENSES $ . . . .

TOTAL $ . . . .

Month:

INCOME GOAL:
SAVINGS GOAL:

Income	Amount
. . . .	. . . .
. . . .	. . . .
. . . .	. . . .
. . . .	. . . .
. . . .	. . . .
. . . .	. . . .
. . . .	. . . .
. . . .	. . . .
. . . .	. . . .

Expenses

. . . .	. . . .
. . . .	. . . .
. . . .	. . . .
. . . .	. . . .
. . . .	. . . .
. . . .	. . . .
. . . .	. . . .
. . . .	. . . .
. . . .	. . . .
. . . .	. . . .
. . . .	. . . .
. . . .	. . . .
. . . .	. . . .
. . . .	. . . .
. . . .	. . . .
. . . .	. . . .

Monthly Cash Flow

TOTAL INCOME $ . . . .

TOTAL EXPENSES $ . . . .

TOTAL $ . . . .

Success is going from failure to failure

without losing enthusiasm.

Pending
Sale Trackers

Pending Sale Tracker

- [ ] LISTING SIDE   PURCHASE PRICE $ . . . .
- [ ] BUYERS SIDE   COMMISSION RATE   . . . . %
- [ ] REFERRAL   COMMISSION $ . . . .

PROPERTY INFORMATION

MLS ID # . . . .

ADDRESS . . . .

CITY . . . .

STATE . . . . ZIP . . . .

CLIENT INFORMATION

NAME . . . .

PHONE . . . .

EMAIL . . . .

CO BUYER/SELLER . . . .

LENDER

NAME . . . .

COMPANY . . . .

PHONE . . . .

EMAIL . . . .

TITLE / ATTORNEY

NAME . . . .

COMPANY . . . .

PHONE . . . .

EMAIL . . . .

COOPERATING AGENT

NAME . . . .

BROKERAGE . . . .

PHONE . . . .

EMAIL . . . .

INSPECTOR

NAME . . . .

COMPANY . . . .

PHONE . . . .

EMAIL . . . .

TIMELINE

CONTRACT DATE . . . .

ACCEPTANCE DATE . . . .

INSPECTION DATE . . . .

INSPECTION END DATE . . . .

APPRAISAL DATE . . . .

FINAL WALK DATE . . . .

SIGNING FINAL DOCS . . . .

CLOSING DATE . . . .

- [ ] GIVE GIFT TO CLIENT
- [ ] TAKE DOWN SIGN / LOCKBOX
- [ ] CLOSE LISTING ON MLS

DOCUMENT CHECKLIST

- [ ] PURCHASE CONTRACT
- [ ] COUNTERS
- [ ] ADDENDUMS
- [ ] AGENCY DISCLOSURE
- [ ] SPDS
- [ ] BINSR
- [ ] INSURANCE CLAIMS HISTORY
- [ ] EARNEST MONEY RECEIPT
- [ ] PRELIM. TITLE PAPERWORK
- [ ] SCHEDULE B DOCS
- [ ] PRE-QUAL FROM LENDER
- [ ] SELLER FINANCING ADDENDUM
- [ ] FINAL WALKTHROUGH
- [ ] COMMISSION INSTRUCTIONS

- [ ] COMMISSION DISBURSMENT
- [ ] REFERRAL AGREEMENT
- [ ] REFERRING BROKERAGE W9
- [ ] CLOSING PACKAGE
- [ ] LIMITED REPRESENTATION DISC.
- [ ] ON-SITE WASTE WATER ADD.
- [ ] SWIMMING POOL ADD.
- [ ] LEAD BASED PAINT ADDENDUM
- [ ] HOA ADDENDUM
- [ ] WELL SPDS
- [ ] LOAN STATUS UPDATE
- [ ] BUYER CONTINGENCY ADD.
- [ ] BUYER BROKER AGREEMENT
- [ ] MISC.

Pending Sale Tracker

☐ LISTING SIDE   PURCHASE PRICE $ . . . .

☐ BUYERS SIDE   COMMISSION RATE   . . . . %

☐ REFERRAL   COMMISSION $ . . . .

PROPERTY INFORMATION

MLS ID # . . . .

ADDRESS . . . .

CITY . . . .

STATE . . . . ZIP . . . .

CLIENT INFORMATION

NAME . . . .

PHONE . . . .

EMAIL . . . .

CO BUYER/SELLER . . . .

LENDER

NAME . . . .

COMPANY . . . .

PHONE . . . .

EMAIL . . . .

TITLE / ATTORNEY

NAME . . . .

COMPANY . . . .

PHONE . . . .

EMAIL . . . .

COOPERATING AGENT

NAME . . . .

BROKERAGE . . . .

PHONE . . . .

EMAIL . . . .

INSPECTOR

NAME . . . .

COMPANY . . . .

PHONE . . . .

EMAIL . . . .

TIMELINE

CONTRACT DATE . . . .

ACCEPTANCE DATE . . . .

INSPECTION DATE . . . .

INSPECTION END DATE . . . .

APPRAISAL DATE . . . .

FINAL WALK DATE . . . .

SIGNING FINAL DOCS . . . .

CLOSING DATE . . . .

☐ GIVE GIFT TO CLIENT

☐ TAKE DOWN SIGN / LOCKBOX

☐ CLOSE LISTING ON MLS

DOCUMENT CHECKLIST

☐ PURCHASE CONTRACT

☐ COUNTERS

☐ ADDENDUMS

☐ AGENCY DISCLOSURE

☐ SPDS

☐ BINSR

☐ INSURANCE CLAIMS HISTORY

☐ EARNEST MONEY RECEIPT

☐ PRELIM. TITLE PAPERWORK

☐ SCHEDULE B DOCS

☐ PRE-QUAL FROM LENDER

☐ SELLER FINANCING ADDENDUM

☐ FINAL WALKTHROUGH

☐ COMMISSION INSTRUCTIONS

☐ COMMISSION DISBURSMENT

☐ REFERRAL AGREEMENT

☐ REFERRING BROKERAGE W9

☐ CLOSING PACKAGE

☐ LIMITED REPRESENTATION DISC.

☐ ON-SITE WASTE WATER ADD.

☐ SWIMMING POOL ADD.

☐ LEAD BASED PAINT ADDENDUM

☐ HOA ADDENDUM

☐ WELL SPDS

☐ LOAN STATUS UPDATE

☐ BUYER CONTINGENCY ADD.

☐ BUYER BROKER AGREEMENT

☐ MISC.

Pending Sale Tracker

- ☐ LISTING SIDE   PURCHASE PRICE $ . . . .
- ☐ BUYERS SIDE   COMMISSION RATE   . . . . %
- ☐ REFERRAL   COMMISSION $ . . . .

PROPERTY INFORMATION

MLS ID # . . . .
ADDRESS . . . .
CITY . . . .
STATE . . . . ZIP . . . .

CLIENT INFORMATION

NAME . . . .
PHONE . . . .
EMAIL . . . .
CO BUYER/SELLER . . . .

LENDER

NAME . . . .
COMPANY . . . .
PHONE . . . .
EMAIL . . . .

TITLE / ATTORNEY

NAME . . . .
COMPANY . . . .
PHONE . . . .
EMAIL . . . .

COOPERATING AGENT

NAME . . . .
BROKERAGE . . . .
PHONE . . . .
EMAIL . . . .

INSPECTOR

NAME . . . .
COMPANY . . . .
PHONE . . . .
EMAIL . . . .

TIMELINE

CONTRACT DATE . . . .
ACCEPTANCE DATE . . . .
INSPECTION DATE . . . .
INSPECTION END DATE . . . .
APPRAISAL DATE . . . .
FINAL WALK DATE . . . .
SIGNING FINAL DOCS . . . .
CLOSING DATE . . . .

- ☐ GIVE GIFT TO CLIENT
- ☐ TAKE DOWN SIGN / LOCKBOX
- ☐ CLOSE LISTING ON MLS

DOCUMENT CHECKLIST

- ☐ PURCHASE CONTRACT
- ☐ COUNTERS
- ☐ ADDENDUMS
- ☐ AGENCY DISCLOSURE
- ☐ SPDS
- ☐ BINSR
- ☐ INSURANCE CLAIMS HISTORY
- ☐ EARNEST MONEY RECEIPT
- ☐ PRELIM. TITLE PAPERWORK
- ☐ SCHEDULE B DOCS
- ☐ PRE-QUAL FROM LENDER
- ☐ SELLER FINANCING ADDENDUM
- ☐ FINAL WALKTHROUGH
- ☐ COMMISSION INSTRUCTIONS

- ☐ COMMISSION DISBURSMENT
- ☐ REFERRAL AGREEMENT
- ☐ REFERRING BROKERAGE W9
- ☐ CLOSING PACKAGE
- ☐ LIMITED REPRESENTATION DISC.
- ☐ ON-SITE WASTE WATER ADD.
- ☐ SWIMMING POOL ADD.
- ☐ LEAD BASED PAINT ADDENDUM
- ☐ HOA ADDENDUM
- ☐ WELL SPDS
- ☐ LOAN STATUS UPDATE
- ☐ BUYER CONTINGENCY ADD.
- ☐ BUYER BROKER AGREEMENT
- ☐ MISC.

Pending Sale Tracker

☐ LISTING SIDE   PURCHASE PRICE $ . . . .
☐ BUYERS SIDE   COMMISSION RATE   . . . . %
☐ REFERRAL   COMMISSION $ . . . .

PROPERTY INFORMATION

MLS ID # . . . .
ADDRESS . . . .
CITY . . . .
STATE . . . . ZIP . . . .

CLIENT INFORMATION

NAME . . . .
PHONE . . . .
EMAIL . . . .
CO BUYER/SELLER . . . .

LENDER

NAME . . . .
COMPANY . . . .
PHONE . . . .
EMAIL . . . .

TITLE / ATTORNEY

NAME . . . .
COMPANY . . . .
PHONE . . . .
EMAIL . . . .

COOPERATING AGENT

NAME . . . .
BROKERAGE . . . .
PHONE . . . .
EMAIL . . . .

INSPECTOR

NAME . . . .
COMPANY . . . .
PHONE . . . .
EMAIL . . . .

TIMELINE

CONTRACT DATE . . . .
ACCEPTANCE DATE . . . .
INSPECTION DATE . . . .
INSPECTION END DATE . . . .
APPRAISAL DATE . . . .
FINAL WALK DATE . . . .
SIGNING FINAL DOCS . . . .
CLOSING DATE . . . .
☐ GIVE GIFT TO CLIENT
☐ TAKE DOWN SIGN / LOCKBOX
☐ CLOSE LISTING ON MLS

DOCUMENT CHECKLIST

☐ PURCHASE CONTRACT
☐ COUNTERS
☐ ADDENDUMS
☐ AGENCY DISCLOSURE
☐ SPDS
☐ BINSR
☐ INSURANCE CLAIMS HISTORY
☐ EARNEST MONEY RECEIPT
☐ PRELIM. TITLE PAPERWORK
☐ SCHEDULE B DOCS
☐ PRE-QUAL FROM LENDER
☐ SELLER FINANCING ADDENDUM
☐ FINAL WALKTHROUGH
☐ COMMISSION INSTRUCTIONS

☐ COMMISSION DISBURSMENT
☐ REFERRAL AGREEMENT
☐ REFERRING BROKERAGE W9
☐ CLOSING PACKAGE
☐ LIMITED REPRESENTATION DISC.
☐ ON-SITE WASTE WATER ADD.
☐ SWIMMING POOL ADD.
☐ LEAD BASED PAINT ADDENDUM
☐ HOA ADDENDUM
☐ WELL SPDS
☐ LOAN STATUS UPDATE
☐ BUYER CONTINGENCY ADD.
☐ BUYER BROKER AGREEMENT
☐ MISC.

Pending Sale Tracker

- [ ] LISTING SIDE
- [ ] BUYERS SIDE
- [ ] REFERRAL

PURCHASE PRICE $ . . . .
COMMISSION RATE . . . . %
COMMISSION $ . . . .

PROPERTY INFORMATION

MLS ID # . . . .
ADDRESS . . . .
CITY . . . .
STATE . . . . ZIP . . . .

CLIENT INFORMATION

NAME . . . .
PHONE . . . .
EMAIL . . . .
CO BUYER/SELLER . . . .

LENDER

NAME . . . .
COMPANY . . . .
PHONE . . . .
EMAIL . . . .

TITLE / ATTORNEY

NAME . . . .
COMPANY . . . .
PHONE . . . .
EMAIL . . . .

COOPERATING AGENT

NAME . . . .
BROKERAGE . . . .
PHONE . . . .
EMAIL . . . .

INSPECTOR

NAME . . . .
COMPANY . . . .
PHONE . . . .
EMAIL . . . .

TIMELINE

CONTRACT DATE . . . .
ACCEPTANCE DATE . . . .
INSPECTION DATE . . . .
INSPECTION END DATE . . . .
APPRAISAL DATE . . . .
FINAL WALK DATE . . . .
SIGNING FINAL DOCS . . . .
CLOSING DATE . . . .

- [ ] GIVE GIFT TO CLIENT
- [ ] TAKE DOWN SIGN / LOCKBOX
- [ ] CLOSE LISTING ON MLS

DOCUMENT CHECKLIST

- [ ] PURCHASE CONTRACT
- [ ] COUNTERS
- [ ] ADDENDUMS
- [ ] AGENCY DISCLOSURE
- [ ] SPDS
- [ ] BINSR
- [ ] INSURANCE CLAIMS HISTORY
- [ ] EARNEST MONEY RECEIPT
- [ ] PRELIM. TITLE PAPERWORK
- [ ] SCHEDULE B DOCS
- [ ] PRE-QUAL FROM LENDER
- [ ] SELLER FINANCING ADDENDUM
- [ ] FINAL WALKTHROUGH
- [ ] COMMISSION INSTRUCTIONS

- [ ] COMMISSION DISBURSMENT
- [ ] REFERRAL AGREEMENT
- [ ] REFERRING BROKERAGE W9
- [ ] CLOSING PACKAGE
- [ ] LIMITED REPRESENTATION DISC.
- [ ] ON-SITE WASTE WATER ADD.
- [ ] SWIMMING POOL ADD.
- [ ] LEAD BASED PAINT ADDENDUM
- [ ] HOA ADDENDUM
- [ ] WELL SPDS
- [ ] LOAN STATUS UPDATE
- [ ] BUYER CONTINGENCY ADD.
- [ ] BUYER BROKER AGREEMENT
- [ ] MISC.

Pending Sale Tracker

☐ LISTING SIDE   PURCHASE PRICE $ . . . .

☐ BUYERS SIDE   COMMISSION RATE   . . . . %

☐ REFERRAL   COMMISSION $ . . . .

PROPERTY INFORMATION

MLS ID # . . . .

ADDRESS . . . .

CITY . . . .

STATE . . . . ZIP . . . .

CLIENT INFORMATION

NAME . . . .

PHONE . . . .

EMAIL . . . .

CO BUYER/SELLER . . . .

LENDER

NAME . . . .

COMPANY . . . .

PHONE . . . .

EMAIL . . . .

TITLE / ATTORNEY

NAME . . . .

COMPANY . . . .

PHONE . . . .

EMAIL . . . .

COOPERATING AGENT

NAME . . . .

BROKERAGE . . . .

PHONE . . . .

EMAIL . . . .

INSPECTOR

NAME . . . .

COMPANY . . . .

PHONE . . . .

EMAIL . . . .

TIMELINE

CONTRACT DATE . . . .

ACCEPTANCE DATE . . . .

INSPECTION DATE . . . .

INSPECTION END DATE . . . .

APPRAISAL DATE . . . .

FINAL WALK DATE . . . .

SIGNING FINAL DOCS . . . .

CLOSING DATE . . . .

☐ GIVE GIFT TO CLIENT

☐ TAKE DOWN SIGN / LOCKBOX

☐ CLOSE LISTING ON MLS

DOCUMENT CHECKLIST

☐ PURCHASE CONTRACT

☐ COUNTERS

☐ ADDENDUMS

☐ AGENCY DISCLOSURE

☐ SPDS

☐ BINSR

☐ INSURANCE CLAIMS HISTORY

☐ EARNEST MONEY RECEIPT

☐ PRELIM. TITLE PAPERWORK

☐ SCHEDULE B DOCS

☐ PRE-QUAL FROM LENDER

☐ SELLER FINANCING ADDENDUM

☐ FINAL WALKTHROUGH

☐ COMMISSION INSTRUCTIONS

☐ COMMISSION DISBURSMENT

☐ REFERRAL AGREEMENT

☐ REFERRING BROKERAGE W9

☐ CLOSING PACKAGE

☐ LIMITED REPRESENTATION DISC.

☐ ON-SITE WASTE WATER ADD.

☐ SWIMMING POOL ADD.

☐ LEAD BASED PAINT ADDENDUM

☐ HOA ADDENDUM

☐ WELL SPDS

☐ LOAN STATUS UPDATE

☐ BUYER CONTINGENCY ADD.

☐ BUYER BROKER AGREEMENT

☐ MISC.

Pending Sale Tracker

☐ LISTING SIDE   PURCHASE PRICE $ . . . .

☐ BUYERS SIDE   COMMISSION RATE   . . . . %

☐ REFERRAL   COMMISSION $ . . . .

PROPERTY INFORMATION

MLS ID # . . . .

ADDRESS . . . .

CITY . . . .

STATE . . . . ZIP . . . .

CLIENT INFORMATION

NAME . . . .

PHONE . . . .

EMAIL . . . .

CO BUYER/SELLER . . . .

LENDER

NAME . . . .

COMPANY . . . .

PHONE . . . .

EMAIL . . . .

TITLE / ATTORNEY

NAME . . . .

COMPANY . . . .

PHONE . . . .

EMAIL . . . .

COOPERATING AGENT

NAME . . . .

BROKERAGE . . . .

PHONE . . . .

EMAIL . . . .

INSPECTOR

NAME . . . .

COMPANY . . . .

PHONE . . . .

EMAIL . . . .

TIMELINE

CONTRACT DATE . . . .

ACCEPTANCE DATE . . . .

INSPECTION DATE . . . .

INSPECTION END DATE . . . .

APPRAISAL DATE . . . .

FINAL WALK DATE . . . .

SIGNING FINAL DOCS . . . .

CLOSING DATE . . . .

☐ GIVE GIFT TO CLIENT

☐ TAKE DOWN SIGN / LOCKBOX

☐ CLOSE LISTING ON MLS

DOCUMENT CHECKLIST

☐ PURCHASE CONTRACT

☐ COUNTERS

☐ ADDENDUMS

☐ AGENCY DISCLOSURE

☐ SPDS

☐ BINSR

☐ INSURANCE CLAIMS HISTORY

☐ EARNEST MONEY RECEIPT

☐ PRELIM. TITLE PAPERWORK

☐ SCHEDULE B DOCS

☐ PRE-QUAL FROM LENDER

☐ SELLER FINANCING ADDENDUM

☐ FINAL WALKTHROUGH

☐ COMMISSION INSTRUCTIONS

☐ COMMISSION DISBURSMENT

☐ REFERRAL AGREEMENT

☐ REFERRING BROKERAGE W9

☐ CLOSING PACKAGE

☐ LIMITED REPRESENTATION DISC.

☐ ON-SITE WASTE WATER ADD.

☐ SWIMMING POOL ADD.

☐ LEAD BASED PAINT ADDENDUM

☐ HOA ADDENDUM

☐ WELL SPDS

☐ LOAN STATUS UPDATE

☐ BUYER CONTINGENCY ADD.

☐ BUYER BROKER AGREEMENT

☐ MISC.

Pending Sale Tracker

- [ ] LISTING SIDE
- [ ] BUYERS SIDE
- [ ] REFERRAL

PURCHASE PRICE $ . . . .
COMMISSION RATE . . . . %
COMMISSION $ . . . .

PROPERTY INFORMATION

MLS ID # . . . .
ADDRESS . . . .
CITY . . . .
STATE . . . . ZIP . . . .

CLIENT INFORMATION

NAME . . . .
PHONE . . . .
EMAIL . . . .
CO BUYER/SELLER . . . .

LENDER

NAME . . . .
COMPANY . . . .
PHONE . . . .
EMAIL . . . .

TITLE / ATTORNEY

NAME . . . .
COMPANY . . . .
PHONE . . . .
EMAIL . . . .

COOPERATING AGENT

NAME . . . .
BROKERAGE . . . .
PHONE . . . .
EMAIL . . . .

INSPECTOR

NAME . . . .
COMPANY . . . .
PHONE . . . .
EMAIL . . . .

TIMELINE

CONTRACT DATE . . . .
ACCEPTANCE DATE . . . .
INSPECTION DATE . . . .
INSPECTION END DATE . . . .
APPRAISAL DATE . . . .
FINAL WALK DATE . . . .
SIGNING FINAL DOCS . . . .
CLOSING DATE . . . .
- [ ] GIVE GIFT TO CLIENT
- [ ] TAKE DOWN SIGN / LOCKBOX
- [ ] CLOSE LISTING ON MLS

DOCUMENT CHECKLIST

- [ ] PURCHASE CONTRACT
- [ ] COUNTERS
- [ ] ADDENDUMS
- [ ] AGENCY DISCLOSURE
- [ ] SPDS
- [ ] BINSR
- [ ] INSURANCE CLAIMS HISTORY
- [ ] EARNEST MONEY RECEIPT
- [ ] PRELIM. TITLE PAPERWORK
- [ ] SCHEDULE B DOCS
- [ ] PRE-QUAL FROM LENDER
- [ ] SELLER FINANCING ADDENDUM
- [ ] FINAL WALKTHROUGH
- [ ] COMMISSION INSTRUCTIONS

- [ ] COMMISSION DISBURSMENT
- [ ] REFERRAL AGREEMENT
- [ ] REFERRING BROKERAGE W9
- [ ] CLOSING PACKAGE
- [ ] LIMITED REPRESENTATION DISC.
- [ ] ON-SITE WASTE WATER ADD.
- [ ] SWIMMING POOL ADD.
- [ ] LEAD BASED PAINT ADDENDUM
- [ ] HOA ADDENDUM
- [ ] WELL SPDS
- [ ] LOAN STATUS UPDATE
- [ ] BUYER CONTINGENCY ADD.
- [ ] BUYER BROKER AGREEMENT
- [ ] MISC.

Pending Sale Tracker

☐ LISTING SIDE PURCHASE PRICE $ . . . .
☐ BUYERS SIDE   COMMISSION RATE   . . . . %
☐ REFERRAL   COMMISSION $ . . . .

PROPERTY INFORMATION

MLS ID # . . . .
ADDRESS . . . .
CITY . . . .
STATE . . . . ZIP . . . .

CLIENT INFORMATION

NAME . . . .
PHONE . . . .
EMAIL . . . .
CO BUYER/SELLER . . . .

LENDER

NAME . . . .
COMPANY . . . .
PHONE . . . .
EMAIL . . . .

TITLE / ATTORNEY

NAME . . . .
COMPANY . . . .
PHONE . . . .
EMAIL . . . .

COOPERATING AGENT

NAME . . . .
BROKERAGE . . . .
PHONE . . . .
EMAIL . . . .

INSPECTOR

NAME . . . .
COMPANY . . . .
PHONE . . . .
EMAIL . . . .

TIMELINE

CONTRACT DATE . . . .
ACCEPTANCE DATE . . . .
INSPECTION DATE . . . .
INSPECTION END DATE . . . .
APPRAISAL DATE . . . .
FINAL WALK DATE . . . .
SIGNING FINAL DOCS . . . .
CLOSING DATE . . . .
☐ GIVE GIFT TO CLIENT
☐ TAKE DOWN SIGN / LOCKBOX
☐ CLOSE LISTING ON MLS

DOCUMENT CHECKLIST

☐ PURCHASE CONTRACT
☐ COUNTERS
☐ ADDENDUMS
☐ AGENCY DISCLOSURE
☐ SPDS
☐ BINSR
☐ INSURANCE CLAIMS HISTORY
☐ EARNEST MONEY RECEIPT
☐ PRELIM. TITLE PAPERWORK
☐ SCHEDULE B DOCS
☐ PRE-QUAL FROM LENDER
☐ SELLER FINANCING ADDENDUM
☐ FINAL WALKTHROUGH
☐ COMMISSION INSTRUCTIONS

☐ COMMISSION DISBURSMENT
☐ REFERRAL AGREEMENT
☐ REFERRING BROKERAGE W9
☐ CLOSING PACKAGE
☐ LIMITED REPRESENTATION DISC.
☐ ON-SITE WASTE WATER ADD.
☐ SWIMMING POOL ADD.
☐ LEAD BASED PAINT ADDENDUM
☐ HOA ADDENDUM
☐ WELL SPDS
☐ LOAN STATUS UPDATE
☐ BUYER CONTINGENCY ADD.
☐ BUYER BROKER AGREEMENT
☐ MISC.

Pending Sale Tracker

- [ ] LISTING SIDE
- [ ] BUYERS SIDE
- [ ] REFERRAL

PURCHASE PRICE $ . . . .

COMMISSION RATE   . . . . %

COMMISSION $ . . . .

PROPERTY INFORMATION

MLS ID # . . . .

ADDRESS . . . .

CITY . . . .

STATE . . . . ZIP . . . .

CLIENT INFORMATION

NAME . . . .

PHONE . . . .

EMAIL . . . .

CO BUYER/SELLER . . . .

LENDER

NAME . . . .

COMPANY . . . .

PHONE . . . .

EMAIL . . . .

TITLE / ATTORNEY

NAME . . . .

COMPANY . . . .

PHONE . . . .

EMAIL . . . .

COOPERATING AGENT

NAME . . . .

BROKERAGE . . . .

PHONE . . . .

EMAIL . . . .

INSPECTOR

NAME . . . .

COMPANY . . . .

PHONE . . . .

EMAIL . . . .

TIMELINE

CONTRACT DATE . . . .

ACCEPTANCE DATE . . . .

INSPECTION DATE . . . .

INSPECTION END DATE . . . .

APPRAISAL DATE . . . .

FINAL WALK DATE . . . .

SIGNING FINAL DOCS . . . .

CLOSING DATE . . . .

- [ ] GIVE GIFT TO CLIENT
- [ ] TAKE DOWN SIGN / LOCKBOX
- [ ] CLOSE LISTING ON MLS

DOCUMENT CHECKLIST

- [ ] PURCHASE CONTRACT
- [ ] COUNTERS
- [ ] ADDENDUMS
- [ ] AGENCY DISCLOSURE
- [ ] SPDS
- [ ] BINSR
- [ ] INSURANCE CLAIMS HISTORY
- [ ] EARNEST MONEY RECEIPT
- [ ] PRELIM. TITLE PAPERWORK
- [ ] SCHEDULE B DOCS
- [ ] PRE-QUAL FROM LENDER
- [ ] SELLER FINANCING ADDENDUM
- [ ] FINAL WALKTHROUGH
- [ ] COMMISSION INSTRUCTIONS

- [ ] COMMISSION DISBURSMENT
- [ ] REFERRAL AGREEMENT
- [ ] REFERRING BROKERAGE W9
- [ ] CLOSING PACKAGE
- [ ] LIMITED REPRESENTATION DISC.
- [ ] ON-SITE WASTE WATER ADD.
- [ ] SWIMMING POOL ADD.
- [ ] LEAD BASED PAINT ADDENDUM
- [ ] HOA ADDENDUM
- [ ] WELL SPDS
- [ ] LOAN STATUS UPDATE
- [ ] BUYER CONTINGENCY ADD.
- [ ] BUYER BROKER AGREEMENT
- [ ] MISC.

Pending Sale Tracker

- ☐ LISTING SIDE PURCHASE PRICE $ . . . .
- ☐ BUYERS SIDE COMMISSION RATE . . . . %
- ☐ REFERRAL COMMISSION $ . . . .

PROPERTY INFORMATION

MLS ID # . . . .
ADDRESS . . . .
CITY . . . .
STATE . . . . ZIP . . . .

CLIENT INFORMATION

NAME . . . .
PHONE . . . .
EMAIL . . . .
CO BUYER/SELLER . . . .

LENDER

NAME . . . .
COMPANY . . . .
PHONE . . . .
EMAIL . . . .

TITLE / ATTORNEY

NAME . . . .
COMPANY . . . .
PHONE . . . .
EMAIL . . . .

COOPERATING AGENT

NAME . . . .
BROKERAGE . . . .
PHONE . . . .
EMAIL . . . .

INSPECTOR

NAME . . . .
COMPANY . . . .
PHONE . . . .
EMAIL . . . .

TIMELINE

CONTRACT DATE . . . .
ACCEPTANCE DATE . . . .
INSPECTION DATE . . . .
INSPECTION END DATE . . . .
APPRAISAL DATE . . . .
FINAL WALK DATE . . . .
SIGNING FINAL DOCS . . . .
CLOSING DATE . . . .
- ☐ GIVE GIFT TO CLIENT
- ☐ TAKE DOWN SIGN / LOCKBOX
- ☐ CLOSE LISTING ON MLS

DOCUMENT CHECKLIST

- ☐ PURCHASE CONTRACT
- ☐ COUNTERS
- ☐ ADDENDUMS
- ☐ AGENCY DISCLOSURE
- ☐ SPDS
- ☐ BINSR
- ☐ INSURANCE CLAIMS HISTORY
- ☐ EARNEST MONEY RECEIPT
- ☐ PRELIM. TITLE PAPERWORK
- ☐ SCHEDULE B DOCS
- ☐ PRE-QUAL FROM LENDER
- ☐ SELLER FINANCING ADDENDUM
- ☐ FINAL WALKTHROUGH
- ☐ COMMISSION INSTRUCTIONS

- ☐ COMMISSION DISBURSMENT
- ☐ REFERRAL AGREEMENT
- ☐ REFERRING BROKERAGE W9
- ☐ CLOSING PACKAGE
- ☐ LIMITED REPRESENTATION DISC.
- ☐ ON-SITE WASTE WATER ADD.
- ☐ SWIMMING POOL ADD.
- ☐ LEAD BASED PAINT ADDENDUM
- ☐ HOA ADDENDUM
- ☐ WELL SPDS
- ☐ LOAN STATUS UPDATE
- ☐ BUYER CONTINGENCY ADD.
- ☐ BUYER BROKER AGREEMENT
- ☐ MISC.

Pending Sale Tracker

☐ LISTING SIDE   PURCHASE PRICE $ . . . .

☐ BUYERS SIDE   COMMISSION RATE   . . . . %

☐ REFERRAL   COMMISSION $ . . . .

PROPERTY INFORMATION

MLS ID # . . . .

ADDRESS . . . .

CITY . . . .

STATE . . . . ZIP . . . .

CLIENT INFORMATION

NAME . . . .

PHONE . . . .

EMAIL . . . .

CO BUYER/SELLER . . . .

LENDER

NAME . . . .

COMPANY . . . .

PHONE . . . .

EMAIL . . . .

TITLE / ATTORNEY

NAME . . . .

COMPANY . . . .

PHONE . . . .

EMAIL . . . .

COOPERATING AGENT

NAME . . . .

BROKERAGE . . . .

PHONE . . . .

EMAIL . . . .

INSPECTOR

NAME . . . .

COMPANY . . . .

PHONE . . . .

EMAIL . . . .

TIMELINE

CONTRACT DATE . . . .

ACCEPTANCE DATE . . . .

INSPECTION DATE . . . .

INSPECTION END DATE . . . .

APPRAISAL DATE . . . .

FINAL WALK DATE . . . .

SIGNING FINAL DOCS . . . .

CLOSING DATE . . . .

☐ GIVE GIFT TO CLIENT

☐ TAKE DOWN SIGN / LOCKBOX

☐ CLOSE LISTING ON MLS

DOCUMENT CHECKLIST

☐ PURCHASE CONTRACT
☐ COUNTERS
☐ ADDENDUMS
☐ AGENCY DISCLOSURE
☐ SPDS
☐ BINSR
☐ INSURANCE CLAIMS HISTORY
☐ EARNEST MONEY RECEIPT
☐ PRELIM. TITLE PAPERWORK
☐ SCHEDULE B DOCS
☐ PRE-QUAL FROM LENDER
☐ SELLER FINANCING ADDENDUM
☐ FINAL WALKTHROUGH
☐ COMMISSION INSTRUCTIONS

☐ COMMISSION DISBURSMENT
☐ REFERRAL AGREEMENT
☐ REFERRING BROKERAGE W9
☐ CLOSING PACKAGE
☐ LIMITED REPRESENTATION DISC.
☐ ON-SITE WASTE WATER ADD.
☐ SWIMMING POOL ADD.
☐ LEAD BASED PAINT ADDENDUM
☐ HOA ADDENDUM
☐ WELL SPDS
☐ LOAN STATUS UPDATE
☐ BUYER CONTINGENCY ADD.
☐ BUYER BROKER AGREEMENT
☐ MISC.

Pending Sale Tracker

[ ] LISTING SIDE   PURCHASE PRICE $ . . . .

[ ] BUYERS SIDE   COMMISSION RATE   . . . .%

[ ] REFERRAL   COMMISSION $ . . . .

PROPERTY INFORMATION

MLS ID # . . . .

ADDRESS . . . .

CITY . . . .

STATE . . . . ZIP . . . .

CLIENT INFORMATION

NAME . . . .

PHONE . . . .

EMAIL . . . .

CO BUYER/SELLER . . . .

LENDER

NAME . . . .

COMPANY . . . .

PHONE . . . .

EMAIL . . . .

TITLE / ATTORNEY

NAME . . . .

COMPANY . . . .

PHONE . . . .

EMAIL . . . .

COOPERATING AGENT

NAME . . . .

BROKERAGE . . . .

PHONE . . . .

EMAIL . . . .

INSPECTOR

NAME . . . .

COMPANY . . . .

PHONE . . . .

EMAIL . . . .

TIMELINE

CONTRACT DATE . . . .

ACCEPTANCE DATE . . . .

INSPECTION DATE . . . .

INSPECTION END DATE . . . .

APPRAISAL DATE . . . .

FINAL WALK DATE . . . .

SIGNING FINAL DOCS . . . .

CLOSING DATE . . . .

[ ] GIVE GIFT TO CLIENT

[ ] TAKE DOWN SIGN / LOCKBOX

[ ] CLOSE LISTING ON MLS

DOCUMENT CHECKLIST

[ ] PURCHASE CONTRACT

[ ] COUNTERS

[ ] ADDENDUMS

[ ] AGENCY DISCLOSURE

[ ] SPDS

[ ] BINSR

[ ] INSURANCE CLAIMS HISTORY

[ ] EARNEST MONEY RECEIPT

[ ] PRELIM. TITLE PAPERWORK

[ ] SCHEDULE B DOCS

[ ] PRE-QUAL FROM LENDER

[ ] SELLER FINANCING ADDENDUM

[ ] FINAL WALKTHROUGH

[ ] COMMISSION INSTRUCTIONS

[ ] COMMISSION DISBURSMENT

[ ] REFERRAL AGREEMENT

[ ] REFERRING BROKERAGE W9

[ ] CLOSING PACKAGE

[ ] LIMITED REPRESENTATION DISC.

[ ] ON-SITE WASTE WATER ADD.

[ ] SWIMMING POOL ADD.

[ ] LEAD BASED PAINT ADDENDUM

[ ] HOA ADDENDUM

[ ] WELL SPDS

[ ] LOAN STATUS UPDATE

[ ] BUYER CONTINGENCY ADD.

[ ] BUYER BROKER AGREEMENT

[ ] MISC.

Pending Sale Tracker

☐ LISTING SIDE PURCHASE PRICE $ . . . .
☐ BUYERS SIDE COMMISSION RATE . . . .%
☐ REFERRAL COMMISSION $ . . . .

PROPERTY INFORMATION

MLS ID # . . . .
ADDRESS . . . .
CITY . . . .
STATE . . . . ZIP . . . .

CLIENT INFORMATION

NAME . . . .
PHONE . . . .
EMAIL . . . .
CO BUYER/SELLER . . . .

LENDER

NAME . . . .
COMPANY . . . .
PHONE . . . .
EMAIL . . . .

TITLE / ATTORNEY

NAME . . . .
COMPANY . . . .
PHONE . . . .
EMAIL . . . .

COOPERATING AGENT

NAME . . . .
BROKERAGE . . . .
PHONE . . . .
EMAIL . . . .

INSPECTOR

NAME . . . .
COMPANY . . . .
PHONE . . . .
EMAIL . . . .

TIMELINE

CONTRACT DATE . . . .
ACCEPTANCE DATE . . . .
INSPECTION DATE . . . .
INSPECTION END DATE . . . .
APPRAISAL DATE . . . .
FINAL WALK DATE . . . .
SIGNING FINAL DOCS . . . .
CLOSING DATE . . . .
☐ GIVE GIFT TO CLIENT
☐ TAKE DOWN SIGN / LOCKBOX
☐ CLOSE LISTING ON MLS

DOCUMENT CHECKLIST

☐ PURCHASE CONTRACT
☐ COUNTERS
☐ ADDENDUMS
☐ AGENCY DISCLOSURE
☐ SPDS
☐ BINSR
☐ INSURANCE CLAIMS HISTORY
☐ EARNEST MONEY RECEIPT
☐ PRELIM. TITLE PAPERWORK
☐ SCHEDULE B DOCS
☐ PRE-QUAL FROM LENDER
☐ SELLER FINANCING ADDENDUM
☐ FINAL WALKTHROUGH
☐ COMMISSION INSTRUCTIONS

☐ COMMISSION DISBURSMENT
☐ REFERRAL AGREEMENT
☐ REFERRING BROKERAGE W9
☐ CLOSING PACKAGE
☐ LIMITED REPRESENTATION DISC.
☐ ON-SITE WASTE WATER ADD.
☐ SWIMMING POOL ADD.
☐ LEAD BASED PAINT ADDENDUM
☐ HOA ADDENDUM
☐ WELL SPDS
☐ LOAN STATUS UPDATE
☐ BUYER CONTINGENCY ADD.
☐ BUYER BROKER AGREEMENT
☐ MISC.

Pending Sale Tracker

- [ ] LISTING SIDE
- [ ] BUYERS SIDE
- [ ] REFERRAL

PURCHASE PRICE $ . . . .

COMMISSION RATE . . . . %

COMMISSION $ . . . .

PROPERTY INFORMATION

MLS ID # . . . .
ADDRESS . . . .
CITY . . . .
STATE . . . . ZIP . . . .

CLIENT INFORMATION

NAME . . . .
PHONE . . . .
EMAIL . . . .
CO BUYER/SELLER . . . .

LENDER

NAME . . . .
COMPANY . . . .
PHONE . . . .
EMAIL . . . .

TITLE / ATTORNEY

NAME . . . .
COMPANY . . . .
PHONE . . . .
EMAIL . . . .

COOPERATING AGENT

NAME . . . .
BROKERAGE . . . .
PHONE . . . .
EMAIL . . . .

INSPECTOR

NAME . . . .
COMPANY . . . .
PHONE . . . .
EMAIL . . . .

TIMELINE

CONTRACT DATE . . . .
ACCEPTANCE DATE . . . .
INSPECTION DATE . . . .
INSPECTION END DATE . . . .
APPRAISAL DATE . . . .
FINAL WALK DATE . . . .
SIGNING FINAL DOCS . . . .
CLOSING DATE . . . .

- [ ] GIVE GIFT TO CLIENT
- [ ] TAKE DOWN SIGN / LOCKBOX
- [ ] CLOSE LISTING ON MLS

DOCUMENT CHECKLIST

- [ ] PURCHASE CONTRACT
- [ ] COUNTERS
- [ ] ADDENDUMS
- [ ] AGENCY DISCLOSURE
- [ ] SPDS
- [ ] BINSR
- [ ] INSURANCE CLAIMS HISTORY
- [ ] EARNEST MONEY RECEIPT
- [ ] PRELIM. TITLE PAPERWORK
- [ ] SCHEDULE B DOCS
- [ ] PRE-QUAL FROM LENDER
- [ ] SELLER FINANCING ADDENDUM
- [ ] FINAL WALKTHROUGH
- [ ] COMMISSION INSTRUCTIONS

- [ ] COMMISSION DISBURSMENT
- [ ] REFERRAL AGREEMENT
- [ ] REFERRING BROKERAGE W9
- [ ] CLOSING PACKAGE
- [ ] LIMITED REPRESENTATION DISC.
- [ ] ON-SITE WASTE WATER ADD.
- [ ] SWIMMING POOL ADD.
- [ ] LEAD BASED PAINT ADDENDUM
- [ ] HOA ADDENDUM
- [ ] WELL SPDS
- [ ] LOAN STATUS UPDATE
- [ ] BUYER CONTINGENCY ADD.
- [ ] BUYER BROKER AGREEMENT
- [ ] MISC.

Pending Sale Tracker

☐ LISTING SIDE   PURCHASE PRICE $ . . . .
☐ BUYERS SIDE   COMMISSION RATE   . . . .%
☐ REFERRAL   COMMISSION $ . . . .

PROPERTY INFORMATION

MLS ID # . . . .
ADDRESS . . . .
CITY . . . .
STATE . . . . ZIP . . . .

CLIENT INFORMATION

NAME . . . .
PHONE . . . .
EMAIL . . . .
CO BUYER/SELLER . . . .

LENDER

NAME . . . .
COMPANY . . . .
PHONE . . . .
EMAIL . . . .

TITLE / ATTORNEY

NAME . . . .
COMPANY . . . .
PHONE . . . .
EMAIL . . . .

COOPERATING AGENT

NAME . . . .
BROKERAGE . . . .
PHONE . . . .
EMAIL . . . .

INSPECTOR

NAME . . . .
COMPANY . . . .
PHONE . . . .
EMAIL . . . .

TIMELINE

CONTRACT DATE . . . .
ACCEPTANCE DATE . . . .
INSPECTION DATE . . . .
INSPECTION END DATE . . . .
APPRAISAL DATE . . . .
FINAL WALK DATE . . . .
SIGNING FINAL DOCS . . . .
CLOSING DATE . . . .
☐ GIVE GIFT TO CLIENT
☐ TAKE DOWN SIGN / LOCKBOX
☐ CLOSE LISTING ON MLS

DOCUMENT CHECKLIST

☐ PURCHASE CONTRACT
☐ COUNTERS
☐ ADDENDUMS
☐ AGENCY DISCLOSURE
☐ SPDS
☐ BINSR
☐ INSURANCE CLAIMS HISTORY
☐ EARNEST MONEY RECEIPT
☐ PRELIM. TITLE PAPERWORK
☐ SCHEDULE B DOCS
☐ PRE-QUAL FROM LENDER
☐ SELLER FINANCING ADDENDUM
☐ FINAL WALKTHROUGH
☐ COMMISSION INSTRUCTIONS

☐ COMMISSION DISBURSMENT
☐ REFERRAL AGREEMENT
☐ REFERRING BROKERAGE W9
☐ CLOSING PACKAGE
☐ LIMITED REPRESENTATION DISC.
☐ ON-SITE WASTE WATER ADD.
☐ SWIMMING POOL ADD.
☐ LEAD BASED PAINT ADDENDUM
☐ HOA ADDENDUM
☐ WELL SPDS
☐ LOAN STATUS UPDATE
☐ BUYER CONTINGENCY ADD.
☐ BUYER BROKER AGREEMENT
☐ MISC.

Pending Sale Tracker

☐ LISTING SIDE   PURCHASE PRICE $ . . . .

☐ BUYERS SIDE   COMMISSION RATE   . . . . %

☐ REFERRAL   COMMISSION $ . . . .

PROPERTY INFORMATION

MLS ID # . . . .

ADDRESS . . . .

CITY . . . .

STATE . . . . ZIP . . . .

CLIENT INFORMATION

NAME . . . .

PHONE . . . .

EMAIL . . . .

CO BUYER/SELLER . . . .

LENDER

NAME . . . .

COMPANY . . . .

PHONE . . . .

EMAIL . . . .

TITLE / ATTORNEY

NAME . . . .

COMPANY . . . .

PHONE . . . .

EMAIL . . . .

COOPERATING AGENT

NAME . . . .

BROKERAGE . . . .

PHONE . . . .

EMAIL . . . .

INSPECTOR

NAME . . . .

COMPANY . . . .

PHONE . . . .

EMAIL . . . .

TIMELINE

CONTRACT DATE . . . .

ACCEPTANCE DATE . . . .

INSPECTION DATE . . . .

INSPECTION END DATE . . . .

APPRAISAL DATE . . . .

FINAL WALK DATE . . . .

SIGNING FINAL DOCS . . . .

CLOSING DATE . . . .

☐ GIVE GIFT TO CLIENT

☐ TAKE DOWN SIGN / LOCKBOX

☐ CLOSE LISTING ON MLS

DOCUMENT CHECKLIST

☐ PURCHASE CONTRACT

☐ COUNTERS

☐ ADDENDUMS

☐ AGENCY DISCLOSURE

☐ SPDS

☐ BINSR

☐ INSURANCE CLAIMS HISTORY

☐ EARNEST MONEY RECEIPT

☐ PRELIM. TITLE PAPERWORK

☐ SCHEDULE B DOCS

☐ PRE-QUAL FROM LENDER

☐ SELLER FINANCING ADDENDUM

☐ FINAL WALKTHROUGH

☐ COMMISSION INSTRUCTIONS

☐ COMMISSION DISBURSMENT

☐ REFERRAL AGREEMENT

☐ REFERRING BROKERAGE W9

☐ CLOSING PACKAGE

☐ LIMITED REPRESENTATION DISC.

☐ ON-SITE WASTE WATER ADD.

☐ SWIMMING POOL ADD.

☐ LEAD BASED PAINT ADDENDUM

☐ HOA ADDENDUM

☐ WELL SPDS

☐ LOAN STATUS UPDATE

☐ BUYER CONTINGENCY ADD.

☐ BUYER BROKER AGREEMENT

☐ MISC.

Pending Sale Tracker

☐ LISTING SIDE   PURCHASE PRICE $ . . . .

☐ BUYERS SIDE   COMMISSION RATE   . . . . %

☐ REFERRAL   COMMISSION $ . . . .

PROPERTY INFORMATION

MLS ID # . . . .

ADDRESS . . . .

CITY . . . .

STATE . . . . ZIP . . . .

CLIENT INFORMATION

NAME . . . .

PHONE . . . .

EMAIL . . . .

CO BUYER/SELLER . . . .

LENDER

NAME . . . .

COMPANY . . . .

PHONE . . . .

EMAIL . . . .

TITLE / ATTORNEY

NAME . . . .

COMPANY . . . .

PHONE . . . .

EMAIL . . . .

COOPERATING AGENT

NAME . . . .

BROKERAGE . . . .

PHONE . . . .

EMAIL . . . .

INSPECTOR

NAME . . . .

COMPANY . . . .

PHONE . . . .

EMAIL . . . .

TIMELINE

CONTRACT DATE . . . .

ACCEPTANCE DATE . . . .

INSPECTION DATE . . . .

INSPECTION END DATE . . . .

APPRAISAL DATE . . . .

FINAL WALK DATE . . . .

SIGNING FINAL DOCS . . . .

CLOSING DATE . . . .

☐ GIVE GIFT TO CLIENT

☐ TAKE DOWN SIGN / LOCKBOX

☐ CLOSE LISTING ON MLS

DOCUMENT CHECKLIST

☐ PURCHASE CONTRACT

☐ COUNTERS

☐ ADDENDUMS

☐ AGENCY DISCLOSURE

☐ SPDS

☐ BINSR

☐ INSURANCE CLAIMS HISTORY

☐ EARNEST MONEY RECEIPT

☐ PRELIM. TITLE PAPERWORK

☐ SCHEDULE B DOCS

☐ PRE-QUAL FROM LENDER

☐ SELLER FINANCING ADDENDUM

☐ FINAL WALKTHROUGH

☐ COMMISSION INSTRUCTIONS

☐ COMMISSION DISBURSMENT

☐ REFERRAL AGREEMENT

☐ REFERRING BROKERAGE W9

☐ CLOSING PACKAGE

☐ LIMITED REPRESENTATION DISC.

☐ ON-SITE WASTE WATER ADD.

☐ SWIMMING POOL ADD.

☐ LEAD BASED PAINT ADDENDUM

☐ HOA ADDENDUM

☐ WELL SPDS

☐ LOAN STATUS UPDATE

☐ BUYER CONTINGENCY ADD.

☐ BUYER BROKER AGREEMENT

☐ MISC.

Pending Sale Tracker

- [ ] LISTING SIDE
- [ ] BUYERS SIDE
- [ ] REFERRAL

PURCHASE PRICE $ . . . .
COMMISSION RATE   . . . . %
COMMISSION $ . . . .

PROPERTY INFORMATION

MLS ID # . . . .
ADDRESS . . . .
CITY . . . .
STATE . . . . ZIP . . . .

CLIENT INFORMATION

NAME . . . .
PHONE . . . .
EMAIL . . . .
CO BUYER/SELLER . . . .

LENDER

NAME . . . .
COMPANY . . . .
PHONE . . . .
EMAIL . . . .

TITLE / ATTORNEY

NAME . . . .
COMPANY . . . .
PHONE . . . .
EMAIL . . . .

COOPERATING AGENT

NAME . . . .
BROKERAGE . . . .
PHONE . . . .
EMAIL . . . .

INSPECTOR

NAME . . . .
COMPANY . . . .
PHONE . . . .
EMAIL . . . .

TIMELINE

CONTRACT DATE . . . .
ACCEPTANCE DATE . . . .
INSPECTION DATE . . . .
INSPECTION END DATE . . . .
APPRAISAL DATE . . . .
FINAL WALK DATE . . . .
SIGNING FINAL DOCS . . . .
CLOSING DATE . . . .

- [ ] GIVE GIFT TO CLIENT
- [ ] TAKE DOWN SIGN / LOCKBOX
- [ ] CLOSE LISTING ON MLS

DOCUMENT CHECKLIST

- [ ] PURCHASE CONTRACT
- [ ] COUNTERS
- [ ] ADDENDUMS
- [ ] AGENCY DISCLOSURE
- [ ] SPDS
- [ ] BINSR
- [ ] INSURANCE CLAIMS HISTORY
- [ ] EARNEST MONEY RECEIPT
- [ ] PRELIM. TITLE PAPERWORK
- [ ] SCHEDULE B DOCS
- [ ] PRE-QUAL FROM LENDER
- [ ] SELLER FINANCING ADDENDUM
- [ ] FINAL WALKTHROUGH
- [ ] COMMISSION INSTRUCTIONS

- [ ] COMMISSION DISBURSMENT
- [ ] REFERRAL AGREEMENT
- [ ] REFERRING BROKERAGE W9
- [ ] CLOSING PACKAGE
- [ ] LIMITED REPRESENTATION DISC.
- [ ] ON-SITE WASTE WATER ADD.
- [ ] SWIMMING POOL ADD.
- [ ] LEAD BASED PAINT ADDENDUM
- [ ] HOA ADDENDUM
- [ ] WELL SPDS
- [ ] LOAN STATUS UPDATE
- [ ] BUYER CONTINGENCY ADD.
- [ ] BUYER BROKER AGREEMENT
- [ ] MISC.

Pending Sale Tracker

☐ LISTING SIDE   PURCHASE PRICE $ . . . .
☐ BUYERS SIDE   COMMISSION RATE   . . . .%
☐ REFERRAL   COMMISSION $ . . . .

PROPERTY INFORMATION

MLS ID # . . . .
ADDRESS . . . .
CITY . . . .
STATE . . . . ZIP . . . .

CLIENT INFORMATION

NAME . . . .
PHONE . . . .
EMAIL . . . .
CO BUYER/SELLER . . . .

LENDER

NAME . . . .
COMPANY . . . .
PHONE . . . .
EMAIL . . . .

TITLE / ATTORNEY

NAME . . . .
COMPANY . . . .
PHONE . . . .
EMAIL . . . .

COOPERATING AGENT

NAME . . . .
BROKERAGE . . . .
PHONE . . . .
EMAIL . . . .

INSPECTOR

NAME . . . .
COMPANY . . . .
PHONE . . . .
EMAIL . . . .

TIMELINE

CONTRACT DATE . . . .
ACCEPTANCE DATE . . . .
INSPECTION DATE . . . .
INSPECTION END DATE . . . .
APPRAISAL DATE . . . .
FINAL WALK DATE . . . .
SIGNING FINAL DOCS . . . .
CLOSING DATE . . . .
☐ GIVE GIFT TO CLIENT
☐ TAKE DOWN SIGN / LOCKBOX
☐ CLOSE LISTING ON MLS

DOCUMENT CHECKLIST

☐ PURCHASE CONTRACT
☐ COUNTERS
☐ ADDENDUMS
☐ AGENCY DISCLOSURE
☐ SPDS
☐ BINSR
☐ INSURANCE CLAIMS HISTORY
☐ EARNEST MONEY RECEIPT
☐ PRELIM. TITLE PAPERWORK
☐ SCHEDULE B DOCS
☐ PRE-QUAL FROM LENDER
☐ SELLER FINANCING ADDENDUM
☐ FINAL WALKTHROUGH
☐ COMMISSION INSTRUCTIONS

☐ COMMISSION DISBURSMENT
☐ REFERRAL AGREEMENT
☐ REFERRING BROKERAGE W9
☐ CLOSING PACKAGE
☐ LIMITED REPRESENTATION DISC.
☐ ON-SITE WASTE WATER ADD.
☐ SWIMMING POOL ADD.
☐ LEAD BASED PAINT ADDENDUM
☐ HOA ADDENDUM
☐ WELL SPDS
☐ LOAN STATUS UPDATE
☐ BUYER CONTINGENCY ADD.
☐ BUYER BROKER AGREEMENT
☐ MISC.

Pending Sale Tracker

- [ ] LISTING SIDE   PURCHASE PRICE $ . . . .
- [ ] BUYERS SIDE   COMMISSION RATE   . . . . %
- [ ] REFERRAL   COMMISSION $ . . . .

PROPERTY INFORMATION

MLS ID # . . . .
ADDRESS . . . .
CITY . . . .
STATE . . . . ZIP . . . .

CLIENT INFORMATION

NAME . . . .
PHONE . . . .
EMAIL . . . .
CO BUYER/SELLER . . . .

LENDER

NAME . . . .
COMPANY . . . .
PHONE . . . .
EMAIL . . . .

TITLE / ATTORNEY

NAME . . . .
COMPANY . . . .
PHONE . . . .
EMAIL . . . .

COOPERATING AGENT

NAME . . . .
BROKERAGE . . . .
PHONE . . . .
EMAIL . . . .

INSPECTOR

NAME . . . .
COMPANY . . . .
PHONE . . . .
EMAIL . . . .

TIMELINE

CONTRACT DATE . . . .
ACCEPTANCE DATE . . . .
INSPECTION DATE . . . .
INSPECTION END DATE . . . .
APPRAISAL DATE . . . .
FINAL WALK DATE . . . .
SIGNING FINAL DOCS . . . .
CLOSING DATE . . . .

- [ ] GIVE GIFT TO CLIENT
- [ ] TAKE DOWN SIGN / LOCKBOX
- [ ] CLOSE LISTING ON MLS

DOCUMENT CHECKLIST

- [ ] PURCHASE CONTRACT
- [ ] COUNTERS
- [ ] ADDENDUMS
- [ ] AGENCY DISCLOSURE
- [ ] SPDS
- [ ] BINSR
- [ ] INSURANCE CLAIMS HISTORY
- [ ] EARNEST MONEY RECEIPT
- [ ] PRELIM. TITLE PAPERWORK
- [ ] SCHEDULE B DOCS
- [ ] PRE-QUAL FROM LENDER
- [ ] SELLER FINANCING ADDENDUM
- [ ] FINAL WALKTHROUGH
- [ ] COMMISSION INSTRUCTIONS

- [ ] COMMISSION DISBURSMENT
- [ ] REFERRAL AGREEMENT
- [ ] REFERRING BROKERAGE W9
- [ ] CLOSING PACKAGE
- [ ] LIMITED REPRESENTATION DISC.
- [ ] ON-SITE WASTE WATER ADD.
- [ ] SWIMMING POOL ADD.
- [ ] LEAD BASED PAINT ADDENDUM
- [ ] HOA ADDENDUM
- [ ] WELL SPDS
- [ ] LOAN STATUS UPDATE
- [ ] BUYER CONTINGENCY ADD.
- [ ] BUYER BROKER AGREEMENT
- [ ] MISC.

Pending Sale Tracker

☐ LISTING SIDE PURCHASE PRICE $ . . . .
☐ BUYERS SIDE COMMISSION RATE . . . . %
☐ REFERRAL COMMISSION $ . . . .

PROPERTY INFORMATION

MLS ID # . . . .
ADDRESS . . . .
CITY . . . .
STATE . . . . ZIP . . . .

CLIENT INFORMATION

NAME . . . .
PHONE . . . .
EMAIL . . . .
CO BUYER/SELLER . . . .

LENDER

NAME . . . .
COMPANY . . . .
PHONE . . . .
EMAIL . . . .

TITLE / ATTORNEY

NAME . . . .
COMPANY . . . .
PHONE . . . .
EMAIL . . . .

COOPERATING AGENT

NAME . . . .
BROKERAGE . . . .
PHONE . . . .
EMAIL . . . .

INSPECTOR

NAME . . . .
COMPANY . . . .
PHONE . . . .
EMAIL . . . .

TIMELINE

CONTRACT DATE . . . .
ACCEPTANCE DATE . . . .
INSPECTION DATE . . . .
INSPECTION END DATE . . . .
APPRAISAL DATE . . . .
FINAL WALK DATE . . . .
SIGNING FINAL DOCS . . . .
CLOSING DATE . . . .
☐ GIVE GIFT TO CLIENT
☐ TAKE DOWN SIGN / LOCKBOX
☐ CLOSE LISTING ON MLS

DOCUMENT CHECKLIST

☐ PURCHASE CONTRACT
☐ COUNTERS
☐ ADDENDUMS
☐ AGENCY DISCLOSURE
☐ SPDS
☐ BINSR
☐ INSURANCE CLAIMS HISTORY
☐ EARNEST MONEY RECEIPT
☐ PRELIM. TITLE PAPERWORK
☐ SCHEDULE B DOCS
☐ PRE-QUAL FROM LENDER
☐ SELLER FINANCING ADDENDUM
☐ FINAL WALKTHROUGH
☐ COMMISSION INSTRUCTIONS

☐ COMMISSION DISBURSMENT
☐ REFERRAL AGREEMENT
☐ REFERRING BROKERAGE W9
☐ CLOSING PACKAGE
☐ LIMITED REPRESENTATION DISC.
☐ ON-SITE WASTE WATER ADD.
☐ SWIMMING POOL ADD.
☐ LEAD BASED PAINT ADDENDUM
☐ HOA ADDENDUM
☐ WELL SPDS
☐ LOAN STATUS UPDATE
☐ BUYER CONTINGENCY ADD.
☐ BUYER BROKER AGREEMENT
☐ MISC.

Pending Sale Tracker

- [ ] LISTING SIDE
- [ ] BUYERS SIDE
- [ ] REFERRAL

PURCHASE PRICE $ . . . .

COMMISSION RATE . . . . %

COMMISSION $ . . . .

PROPERTY INFORMATION

MLS ID # . . . .

ADDRESS . . . .

CITY . . . .

STATE . . . . ZIP . . . .

CLIENT INFORMATION

NAME . . . .

PHONE . . . .

EMAIL . . . .

CO BUYER/SELLER . . . .

LENDER

NAME . . . .

COMPANY . . . .

PHONE . . . .

EMAIL . . . .

TITLE / ATTORNEY

NAME . . . .

COMPANY . . . .

PHONE . . . .

EMAIL . . . .

COOPERATING AGENT

NAME . . . .

BROKERAGE . . . .

PHONE . . . .

EMAIL . . . .

INSPECTOR

NAME . . . .

COMPANY . . . .

PHONE . . . .

EMAIL . . . .

TIMELINE

CONTRACT DATE . . . .

ACCEPTANCE DATE . . . .

INSPECTION DATE . . . .

INSPECTION END DATE . . . .

APPRAISAL DATE . . . .

FINAL WALK DATE . . . .

SIGNING FINAL DOCS . . . .

CLOSING DATE . . . .

- [ ] GIVE GIFT TO CLIENT
- [ ] TAKE DOWN SIGN / LOCKBOX
- [ ] CLOSE LISTING ON MLS

DOCUMENT CHECKLIST

- [ ] PURCHASE CONTRACT
- [ ] COUNTERS
- [ ] ADDENDUMS
- [ ] AGENCY DISCLOSURE
- [ ] SPDS
- [ ] BINSR
- [ ] INSURANCE CLAIMS HISTORY
- [ ] EARNEST MONEY RECEIPT
- [ ] PRELIM. TITLE PAPERWORK
- [ ] SCHEDULE B DOCS
- [ ] PRE-QUAL FROM LENDER
- [ ] SELLER FINANCING ADDENDUM
- [ ] FINAL WALKTHROUGH
- [ ] COMMISSION INSTRUCTIONS

- [ ] COMMISSION DISBURSMENT
- [ ] REFERRAL AGREEMENT
- [ ] REFERRING BROKERAGE W9
- [ ] CLOSING PACKAGE
- [ ] LIMITED REPRESENTATION DISC.
- [ ] ON-SITE WASTE WATER ADD.
- [ ] SWIMMING POOL ADD.
- [ ] LEAD BASED PAINT ADDENDUM
- [ ] HOA ADDENDUM
- [ ] WELL SPDS
- [ ] LOAN STATUS UPDATE
- [ ] BUYER CONTINGENCY ADD.
- [ ] BUYER BROKER AGREEMENT
- [ ] MISC.

Pending Sale Tracker

☐ LISTING SIDE   PURCHASE PRICE $ . . . .

☐ BUYERS SIDE   COMMISSION RATE   . . . . %

☐ REFERRAL   COMMISSION $ . . . .

PROPERTY INFORMATION

MLS ID # . . . .

ADDRESS . . . .

CITY . . . .

STATE . . . . ZIP . . . .

CLIENT INFORMATION

NAME . . . .

PHONE . . . .

EMAIL . . . .

CO BUYER/SELLER . . . .

LENDER

NAME . . . .

COMPANY . . . .

PHONE . . . .

EMAIL . . . .

TITLE / ATTORNEY

NAME . . . .

COMPANY . . . .

PHONE . . . .

EMAIL . . . .

COOPERATING AGENT

NAME . . . .

BROKERAGE . . . .

PHONE . . . .

EMAIL . . . .

INSPECTOR

NAME . . . .

COMPANY . . . .

PHONE . . . .

EMAIL . . . .

TIMELINE

CONTRACT DATE . . . .

ACCEPTANCE DATE . . . .

INSPECTION DATE . . . .

INSPECTION END DATE . . . .

APPRAISAL DATE . . . .

FINAL WALK DATE . . . .

SIGNING FINAL DOCS . . . .

CLOSING DATE . . . .

☐ GIVE GIFT TO CLIENT

☐ TAKE DOWN SIGN / LOCKBOX

☐ CLOSE LISTING ON MLS

DOCUMENT CHECKLIST

☐ PURCHASE CONTRACT

☐ COUNTERS

☐ ADDENDUMS

☐ AGENCY DISCLOSURE

☐ SPDS

☐ BINSR

☐ INSURANCE CLAIMS HISTORY

☐ EARNEST MONEY RECEIPT

☐ PRELIM. TITLE PAPERWORK

☐ SCHEDULE B DOCS

☐ PRE-QUAL FROM LENDER

☐ SELLER FINANCING ADDENDUM

☐ FINAL WALKTHROUGH

☐ COMMISSION INSTRUCTIONS

☐ COMMISSION DISBURSMENT

☐ REFERRAL AGREEMENT

☐ REFERRING BROKERAGE W9

☐ CLOSING PACKAGE

☐ LIMITED REPRESENTATION DISC.

☐ ON-SITE WASTE WATER ADD.

☐ SWIMMING POOL ADD.

☐ LEAD BASED PAINT ADDENDUM

☐ HOA ADDENDUM

☐ WELL SPDS

☐ LOAN STATUS UPDATE

☐ BUYER CONTINGENCY ADD.

☐ BUYER BROKER AGREEMENT

☐ MISC.

Pending Sale Tracker

- [ ] LISTING SIDE
- [ ] BUYERS SIDE
- [ ] REFERRAL

PURCHASE PRICE $ . . . .

COMMISSION RATE . . . . %

COMMISSION $ . . . .

PROPERTY INFORMATION

MLS ID # . . . .

ADDRESS . . . .

CITY . . . .

STATE . . . . ZIP . . . .

CLIENT INFORMATION

NAME . . . .

PHONE . . . .

EMAIL . . . .

CO BUYER/SELLER . . . .

LENDER

NAME . . . .

COMPANY . . . .

PHONE . . . .

EMAIL . . . .

TITLE / ATTORNEY

NAME . . . .

COMPANY . . . .

PHONE . . . .

EMAIL . . . .

COOPERATING AGENT

NAME . . . .

BROKERAGE . . . .

PHONE . . . .

EMAIL . . . .

INSPECTOR

NAME . . . .

COMPANY . . . .

PHONE . . . .

EMAIL . . . .

TIMELINE

CONTRACT DATE . . . .

ACCEPTANCE DATE . . . .

INSPECTION DATE . . . .

INSPECTION END DATE . . . .

APPRAISAL DATE . . . .

FINAL WALK DATE . . . .

SIGNING FINAL DOCS . . . .

CLOSING DATE . . . .

- [ ] GIVE GIFT TO CLIENT
- [ ] TAKE DOWN SIGN / LOCKBOX
- [ ] CLOSE LISTING ON MLS

DOCUMENT CHECKLIST

- [ ] PURCHASE CONTRACT
- [ ] COUNTERS
- [ ] ADDENDUMS
- [ ] AGENCY DISCLOSURE
- [ ] SPDS
- [ ] BINSR
- [ ] INSURANCE CLAIMS HISTORY
- [ ] EARNEST MONEY RECEIPT
- [ ] PRELIM. TITLE PAPERWORK
- [ ] SCHEDULE B DOCS
- [ ] PRE-QUAL FROM LENDER
- [ ] SELLER FINANCING ADDENDUM
- [ ] FINAL WALKTHROUGH
- [ ] COMMISSION INSTRUCTIONS

- [ ] COMMISSION DISBURSMENT
- [ ] REFERRAL AGREEMENT
- [ ] REFERRING BROKERAGE W9
- [ ] CLOSING PACKAGE
- [ ] LIMITED REPRESENTATION DISC.
- [ ] ON-SITE WASTE WATER ADD.
- [ ] SWIMMING POOL ADD.
- [ ] LEAD BASED PAINT ADDENDUM
- [ ] HOA ADDENDUM
- [ ] WELL SPDS
- [ ] LOAN STATUS UPDATE
- [ ] BUYER CONTINGENCY ADD.
- [ ] BUYER BROKER AGREEMENT
- [ ] MISC.

Pending Sale Tracker

▢ LISTING SIDE   PURCHASE PRICE $ . . . .

▢ BUYERS SIDE   COMMISSION RATE   . . . . %

▢ REFERRAL   COMMISSION $ . . . .

PROPERTY INFORMATION

MLS ID # . . . .

ADDRESS . . . .

CITY . . . .

STATE . . . . ZIP . . . .

CLIENT INFORMATION

NAME . . . .

PHONE . . . .

EMAIL . . . .

CO BUYER/SELLER . . . .

LENDER

NAME . . . .

COMPANY . . . .

PHONE . . . .

EMAIL . . . .

TITLE / ATTORNEY

NAME . . . .

COMPANY . . . .

PHONE . . . .

EMAIL . . . .

COOPERATING AGENT

NAME . . . .

BROKERAGE . . . .

PHONE . . . .

EMAIL . . . .

INSPECTOR

NAME . . . .

COMPANY . . . .

PHONE . . . .

EMAIL . . . .

TIMELINE

CONTRACT DATE . . . .

ACCEPTANCE DATE . . . .

INSPECTION DATE . . . .

INSPECTION END DATE . . . .

APPRAISAL DATE . . . .

FINAL WALK DATE . . . .

SIGNING FINAL DOCS . . . .

CLOSING DATE . . . .

▢ GIVE GIFT TO CLIENT

▢ TAKE DOWN SIGN / LOCKBOX

▢ CLOSE LISTING ON MLS

DOCUMENT CHECKLIST

▢ PURCHASE CONTRACT

▢ COUNTERS

▢ ADDENDUMS

▢ AGENCY DISCLOSURE

▢ SPDS

▢ BINSR

▢ INSURANCE CLAIMS HISTORY

▢ EARNEST MONEY RECEIPT

▢ PRELIM. TITLE PAPERWORK

▢ SCHEDULE B DOCS

▢ PRE-QUAL FROM LENDER

▢ SELLER FINANCING ADDENDUM

▢ FINAL WALKTHROUGH

▢ COMMISSION INSTRUCTIONS

▢ COMMISSION DISBURSMENT

▢ REFERRAL AGREEMENT

▢ REFERRING BROKERAGE W9

▢ CLOSING PACKAGE

▢ LIMITED REPRESENTATION DISC.

▢ ON-SITE WASTE WATER ADD.

▢ SWIMMING POOL ADD.

▢ LEAD BASED PAINT ADDENDUM

▢ HOA ADDENDUM

▢ WELL SPDS

▢ LOAN STATUS UPDATE

▢ BUYER CONTINGENCY ADD.

▢ BUYER BROKER AGREEMENT

▢ MISC.

Pending Sale Tracker

- [ ] LISTING SIDE   PURCHASE PRICE $ . . . .
- [ ] BUYERS SIDE   COMMISSION RATE   . . . . %
- [ ] REFERRAL   COMMISSION $ . . . .

PROPERTY INFORMATION

MLS ID # . . . .

ADDRESS . . . .

CITY . . . .

STATE . . . . ZIP . . . .

CLIENT INFORMATION

NAME . . . .

PHONE . . . .

EMAIL . . . .

CO BUYER/SELLER . . . .

LENDER

NAME . . . .

COMPANY . . . .

PHONE . . . .

EMAIL . . . .

TITLE / ATTORNEY

NAME . . . .

COMPANY . . . .

PHONE . . . .

EMAIL . . . .

COOPERATING AGENT

NAME . . . .

BROKERAGE . . . .

PHONE . . . .

EMAIL . . . .

INSPECTOR

NAME . . . .

COMPANY . . . .

PHONE . . . .

EMAIL . . . .

TIMELINE

CONTRACT DATE . . . .

ACCEPTANCE DATE . . . .

INSPECTION DATE . . . .

INSPECTION END DATE . . . .

APPRAISAL DATE . . . .

FINAL WALK DATE . . . .

SIGNING FINAL DOCS . . . .

CLOSING DATE . . . .

- [ ] GIVE GIFT TO CLIENT
- [ ] TAKE DOWN SIGN / LOCKBOX
- [ ] CLOSE LISTING ON MLS

DOCUMENT CHECKLIST

- [ ] PURCHASE CONTRACT
- [ ] COUNTERS
- [ ] ADDENDUMS
- [ ] AGENCY DISCLOSURE
- [ ] SPDS
- [ ] BINSR
- [ ] INSURANCE CLAIMS HISTORY
- [ ] EARNEST MONEY RECEIPT
- [ ] PRELIM. TITLE PAPERWORK
- [ ] SCHEDULE B DOCS
- [ ] PRE-QUAL FROM LENDER
- [ ] SELLER FINANCING ADDENDUM
- [ ] FINAL WALKTHROUGH
- [ ] COMMISSION INSTRUCTIONS

- [ ] COMMISSION DISBURSMENT
- [ ] REFERRAL AGREEMENT
- [ ] REFERRING BROKERAGE W9
- [ ] CLOSING PACKAGE
- [ ] LIMITED REPRESENTATION DISC.
- [ ] ON-SITE WASTE WATER ADD.
- [ ] SWIMMING POOL ADD.
- [ ] LEAD BASED PAINT ADDENDUM
- [ ] HOA ADDENDUM
- [ ] WELL SPDS
- [ ] LOAN STATUS UPDATE
- [ ] BUYER CONTINGENCY ADD.
- [ ] BUYER BROKER AGREEMENT
- [ ] MISC.

Pending Sale Tracker

☐ LISTING SIDE   PURCHASE PRICE $ . . . .

☐ BUYERS SIDE   COMMISSION RATE   . . . . %

☐ REFERRAL   COMMISSION $ . . . .

PROPERTY INFORMATION

MLS ID # . . . .

ADDRESS . . . .

CITY . . . .

STATE . . . . ZIP . . . .

CLIENT INFORMATION

NAME . . . .

PHONE . . . .

EMAIL . . . .

CO BUYER/SELLER . . . .

LENDER

NAME . . . .

COMPANY . . . .

PHONE . . . .

EMAIL . . . .

TITLE / ATTORNEY

NAME . . . .

COMPANY . . . .

PHONE . . . .

EMAIL . . . .

COOPERATING AGENT

NAME . . . .

BROKERAGE . . . .

PHONE . . . .

EMAIL . . . .

INSPECTOR

NAME . . . .

COMPANY . . . .

PHONE . . . .

EMAIL . . . .

TIMELINE

CONTRACT DATE . . . .

ACCEPTANCE DATE . . . .

INSPECTION DATE . . . .

INSPECTION END DATE . . . .

APPRAISAL DATE . . . .

FINAL WALK DATE . . . .

SIGNING FINAL DOCS . . . .

CLOSING DATE . . . .

☐ GIVE GIFT TO CLIENT

☐ TAKE DOWN SIGN / LOCKBOX

☐ CLOSE LISTING ON MLS

DOCUMENT CHECKLIST

☐ PURCHASE CONTRACT

☐ COUNTERS

☐ ADDENDUMS

☐ AGENCY DISCLOSURE

☐ SPDS

☐ BINSR

☐ INSURANCE CLAIMS HISTORY

☐ EARNEST MONEY RECEIPT

☐ PRELIM. TITLE PAPERWORK

☐ SCHEDULE B DOCS

☐ PRE-QUAL FROM LENDER

☐ SELLER FINANCING ADDENDUM

☐ FINAL WALKTHROUGH

☐ COMMISSION INSTRUCTIONS

☐ COMMISSION DISBURSMENT

☐ REFERRAL AGREEMENT

☐ REFERRING BROKERAGE W9

☐ CLOSING PACKAGE

☐ LIMITED REPRESENTATION DISC.

☐ ON-SITE WASTE WATER ADD.

☐ SWIMMING POOL ADD.

☐ LEAD BASED PAINT ADDENDUM

☐ HOA ADDENDUM

☐ WELL SPDS

☐ LOAN STATUS UPDATE

☐ BUYER CONTINGENCY ADD.

☐ BUYER BROKER AGREEMENT

☐ MISC.

Pending Sale Tracker

☐ LISTING SIDE   PURCHASE PRICE $ . . . .
☐ BUYERS SIDE   COMMISSION RATE   . . . .%
☐ REFERRAL   COMMISSION $ . . . .

PROPERTY INFORMATION

MLS ID # . . . .
ADDRESS . . . .
CITY . . . .
STATE . . . . ZIP . . . .

CLIENT INFORMATION

NAME . . . .
PHONE . . . .
EMAIL . . . .
CO BUYER/SELLER . . . .

LENDER

NAME . . . .
COMPANY . . . .
PHONE . . . .
EMAIL . . . .

TITLE / ATTORNEY

NAME . . . .
COMPANY . . . .
PHONE . . . .
EMAIL . . . .

COOPERATING AGENT

NAME . . . .
BROKERAGE . . . .
PHONE . . . .
EMAIL . . . .

INSPECTOR

NAME . . . .
COMPANY . . . .
PHONE . . . .
EMAIL . . . .

TIMELINE

CONTRACT DATE . . . .
ACCEPTANCE DATE . . . .
INSPECTION DATE . . . .
INSPECTION END DATE . . . .
APPRAISAL DATE . . . .
FINAL WALK DATE . . . .
SIGNING FINAL DOCS . . . .
CLOSING DATE . . . .
☐ GIVE GIFT TO CLIENT
☐ TAKE DOWN SIGN / LOCKBOX
☐ CLOSE LISTING ON MLS

DOCUMENT CHECKLIST

☐ PURCHASE CONTRACT
☐ COUNTERS
☐ ADDENDUMS
☐ AGENCY DISCLOSURE
☐ SPDS
☐ BINSR
☐ INSURANCE CLAIMS HISTORY
☐ EARNEST MONEY RECEIPT
☐ PRELIM. TITLE PAPERWORK
☐ SCHEDULE B DOCS
☐ PRE-QUAL FROM LENDER
☐ SELLER FINANCING ADDENDUM
☐ FINAL WALKTHROUGH
☐ COMMISSION INSTRUCTIONS

☐ COMMISSION DISBURSMENT
☐ REFERRAL AGREEMENT
☐ REFERRING BROKERAGE W9
☐ CLOSING PACKAGE
☐ LIMITED REPRESENTATION DISC.
☐ ON-SITE WASTE WATER ADD.
☐ SWIMMING POOL ADD.
☐ LEAD BASED PAINT ADDENDUM
☐ HOA ADDENDUM
☐ WELL SPDS
☐ LOAN STATUS UPDATE
☐ BUYER CONTINGENCY ADD.
☐ BUYER BROKER AGREEMENT
☐ MISC.

Pending Sale Tracker

☐ LISTING SIDE   PURCHASE PRICE $ . . . .

☐ BUYERS SIDE   COMMISSION RATE   . . . . %

☐ REFERRAL   COMMISSION $ . . . .

PROPERTY INFORMATION

MLS ID # . . . .

ADDRESS . . . .

CITY . . . .

STATE . . . . ZIP . . . .

CLIENT INFORMATION

NAME . . . .

PHONE . . . .

EMAIL . . . .

CO BUYER/SELLER . . . .

LENDER

NAME . . . .

COMPANY . . . .

PHONE . . . .

EMAIL . . . .

TITLE / ATTORNEY

NAME . . . .

COMPANY . . . .

PHONE . . . .

EMAIL . . . .

COOPERATING AGENT

NAME . . . .

BROKERAGE . . . .

PHONE . . . .

EMAIL . . . .

INSPECTOR

NAME . . . .

COMPANY . . . .

PHONE . . . .

EMAIL . . . .

TIMELINE

CONTRACT DATE . . . .

ACCEPTANCE DATE . . . .

INSPECTION DATE . . . .

INSPECTION END DATE . . . .

APPRAISAL DATE . . . .

FINAL WALK DATE . . . .

SIGNING FINAL DOCS . . . .

CLOSING DATE . . . .

☐ GIVE GIFT TO CLIENT

☐ TAKE DOWN SIGN / LOCKBOX

☐ CLOSE LISTING ON MLS

DOCUMENT CHECKLIST

☐ PURCHASE CONTRACT

☐ COUNTERS

☐ ADDENDUMS

☐ AGENCY DISCLOSURE

☐ SPDS

☐ BINSR

☐ INSURANCE CLAIMS HISTORY

☐ EARNEST MONEY RECEIPT

☐ PRELIM. TITLE PAPERWORK

☐ SCHEDULE B DOCS

☐ PRE-QUAL FROM LENDER

☐ SELLER FINANCING ADDENDUM

☐ FINAL WALKTHROUGH

☐ COMMISSION INSTRUCTIONS

☐ COMMISSION DISBURSMENT

☐ REFERRAL AGREEMENT

☐ REFERRING BROKERAGE W9

☐ CLOSING PACKAGE

☐ LIMITED REPRESENTATION DISC.

☐ ON-SITE WASTE WATER ADD.

☐ SWIMMING POOL ADD.

☐ LEAD BASED PAINT ADDENDUM

☐ HOA ADDENDUM

☐ WELL SPDS

☐ LOAN STATUS UPDATE

☐ BUYER CONTINGENCY ADD.

☐ BUYER BROKER AGREEMENT

☐ MISC.

Be the kind of person that makes other people want to **up their game.**

Seller Lead Sheets

Seller Lead Sheet

BEDS . . . .   SQ FT . . . .

BATHS . . . .   HOA . . . .

PROPERTY INFORMATION

ADDRESS . . . .

CITY . . . . STATE . . . . ZIP . . . .

COMMUNITY NAME . . . . MANAGEMENT PHONE . . . .

CLIENT

FIRST NAME . . . . LAST NAME . . . .

PHONE . . . . EMAIL . . . .

CO-OWNER NAME . . . . LAST NAME . . . .

PHONE . . . . EMAIL . . . .

CO-OWNER MARRIED? YES ☐ NO ☐ OTHER PARTIES? . . . .

QUESTIONAIRE

ARE YOU WORKING WITH OTHER AGENTS? YES ☐ NO ☐ . . . .

WHY DO YOU WANT TO MOVE? . . . .

WHEN DO YOU WANT TO MOVE BY? . . . .

WHERE WILL YOU BE MOVING TO? . . . .

DO YOU OWE ANYTHING ON THE PROPERTY? YES ☐ NO ☐ . . . .

WHAT PRICE DO YOU WANT TO SELL THE PROPERTY FOR? . . . .

WILL YOU NEED TO MOVE BEFORE YOU SELL? YES ☐ NO ☐ . . . .

WILL YOU NEED FUNDS FROM HOUSE SALE TO PURCHASE NEXT HOME? YES ☐ NO ☐

IS YOUR HOME CURRENTLY RENTED? YES ☐ NO ☐ LEASE END . . . . RENT . . . .

DESCRIPTION (POSITIVES & NEGATIVES): . . . .

. . . .

. . . .

. . . .

ANY MAJOR IMPROVEMENTS MADE TO HOME? . . . .

. . . .

NEIGHBORHOOD AMMENITIES: . . . .

. . . .

WHAT ARE YOU LOOKING FOR IN AN AGENT? . . . .

PREFERRED METHOD OF COMMUNICATION: PHONE ☐ EMAIL ☐ TEXT ☐

Seller Lead Sheet

BEDS . . . .   SQ FT . . . .

BATHS . . . .   HOA . . . .

PROPERTY INFORMATION

ADDRESS . . . .

CITY . . . . STATE . . . . ZIP . . . .

COMMUNITY NAME . . . . MANAGEMENT PHONE . . . .

CLIENT

FIRST NAME . . . . LAST NAME . . . .

PHONE . . . . EMAIL . . . .

CO-OWNER NAME . . . . LAST NAME . . . .

PHONE . . . . EMAIL . . . .

CO-OWNER MARRIED? YES ☐ NO ☐   OTHER PARTIES? . . . .

QUESTIONAIRE

ARE YOU WORKING WITH OTHER AGENTS?   YES ☐ NO ☐ . . . .

WHY DO YOU WANT TO MOVE? . . . .

WHEN DO YOU WANT TO MOVE BY? . . . .

WHERE WILL YOU BE MOVING TO? . . . .

DO YOU OWE ANYTHING ON THE PROPERTY?   YES ☐ NO ☐ . . . .

WHAT PRICE DO YOU WANT TO SELL THE PROPERTY FOR? . . . .

WILL YOU NEED TO MOVE BEFORE YOU SELL?   YES ☐ NO ☐ . . . .

WILL YOU NEED FUNDS FROM HOUSE SALE TO PURCHASE NEXT HOME?   YES ☐ NO ☐

IS YOUR HOME CURRENTLY RENTED? YES ☐ NO ☐ LEASE END . . . . RENT . . . .

DESCRIPTION (POSITIVES & NEGATIVES): . . . .

. . . .

. . . .

. . . .

ANY MAJOR IMPROVEMENTS MADE TO HOME? . . . .

. . . .

NEIGHBORHOOD AMMENITIES: . . . .

. . . .

WHAT ARE YOU LOOKING FOR IN AN AGENT? . . . .

PREFERRED METHOD OF COMMUNICATION: PHONE ☐ EMAIL ☐ TEXT ☐

Seller Lead Sheet

BEDS . . . .　　SQ FT . . . .

PROPERTY INFORMATION

BATHS . . . .　　HOA . . . .

ADDRESS . . . .

CITY . . . . STATE . . . . ZIP . . . .

COMMUNITY NAME . . . . MANAGEMENT PHONE . . . .

CLIENT

FIRST NAME . . . . LAST NAME . . . .

PHONE . . . . EMAIL . . . .

CO-OWNER NAME . . . . LAST NAME . . . .

PHONE . . . . EMAIL . . . .

CO-OWNER MARRIED? YES ▢ NO ▢ OTHER PARTIES? . . . .

QUESTIONAIRE

ARE YOU WORKING WITH OTHER AGENTS? YES ▢ NO ▢ . . . .

WHY DO YOU WANT TO MOVE? . . . .

WHEN DO YOU WANT TO MOVE BY? . . . .

WHERE WILL YOU BE MOVING TO? . . . .

DO YOU OWE ANYTHING ON THE PROPERTY? YES ▢ NO ▢ . . . .

WHAT PRICE DO YOU WANT TO SELL THE PROPERTY FOR? . . . .

WILL YOU NEED TO MOVE BEFORE YOU SELL? YES ▢ NO ▢ . . . .

WILL YOU NEED FUNDS FROM HOUSE SALE TO PURCHASE NEXT HOME? YES ▢ NO ▢

IS YOUR HOME CURRENTLY RENTED? YES ▢ NO ▢ LEASE END . . . . RENT . . . .

DESCRIPTION (POSITIVES & NEGATIVES): . . . .

. . . .

. . . .

. . . .

ANY MAJOR IMPROVEMENTS MADE TO HOME? . . . .

. . . .

NEIGHBORHOOD AMMENITIES: . . . .

. . . .

WHAT ARE YOU LOOKING FOR IN AN AGENT? . . . .

PREFERRED METHOD OF COMMUNICATION: PHONE ▢ EMAIL ▢ TEXT ▢

Seller Lead Sheet

BEDS . . . .   SQ FT . . . .

BATHS . . . .   HOA . . . .

PROPERTY INFORMATION

ADDRESS . . . .

CITY . . . . STATE . . . . ZIP . . . .

COMMUNITY NAME . . . . MANAGEMENT PHONE . . . .

CLIENT

FIRST NAME . . . . LAST NAME . . . .

PHONE . . . . EMAIL . . . .

CO-OWNER NAME . . . . LAST NAME . . . .

PHONE . . . . EMAIL . . . .

CO-OWNER MARRIED? YES ☐ NO ☐   OTHER PARTIES? . . . .

QUESTIONAIRE

ARE YOU WORKING WITH OTHER AGENTS?   YES ☐ NO ☐   . . . .

WHY DO YOU WANT TO MOVE? . . . .

WHEN DO YOU WANT TO MOVE BY? . . . .

WHERE WILL YOU BE MOVING TO? . . . .

DO YOU OWE ANYTHING ON THE PROPERTY?   YES ☐ NO ☐   . . . .

WHAT PRICE DO YOU WANT TO SELL THE PROPERTY FOR? . . . .

WILL YOU NEED TO MOVE BEFORE YOU SELL?   YES ☐ NO ☐   . . . .

WILL YOU NEED FUNDS FROM HOUSE SALE TO PURCHASE NEXT HOME?   YES ☐   NO ☐

IS YOUR HOME CURRENTLY RENTED? YES ☐ NO ☐ LEASE END . . . . RENT . . . .

DESCRIPTION (POSITIVES & NEGATIVES): . . . .

. . . .

. . . .

. . . .

ANY MAJOR IMPROVEMENTS MADE TO HOME? . . . .

. . . .

NEIGHBORHOOD AMMENITIES: . . . .

. . . .

WHAT ARE YOU LOOKING FOR IN AN AGENT? . . . .

PREFERRED METHOD OF COMMUNICATION: PHONE ☐ EMAIL ☐ TEXT ☐

Seller Lead Sheet

BEDS . . . .   SQ FT . . . .

BATHS . . . .   HOA . . . .

PROPERTY INFORMATION

ADDRESS . . . .

CITY . . . . STATE . . . . ZIP . . . .

COMMUNITY NAME . . . . MANAGEMENT PHONE . . . .

CLIENT

FIRST NAME . . . . LAST NAME . . . .

PHONE . . . . EMAIL . . . .

CO-OWNER NAME . . . . LAST NAME . . . .

PHONE . . . . EMAIL . . . .

CO-OWNER MARRIED? YES ▢ NO ▢ OTHER PARTIES? . . . .

QUESTIONAIRE

ARE YOU WORKING WITH OTHER AGENTS?   YES ▢ NO ▢ . . . .

WHY DO YOU WANT TO MOVE? . . . .

WHEN DO YOU WANT TO MOVE BY? . . . .

WHERE WILL YOU BE MOVING TO? . . . .

DO YOU OWE ANYTHING ON THE PROPERTY?   YES ▢ NO ▢ . . . .

WHAT PRICE DO YOU WANT TO SELL THE PROPERTY FOR? . . . .

WILL YOU NEED TO MOVE BEFORE YOU SELL?   YES ▢ NO ▢ . . . .

WILL YOU NEED FUNDS FROM HOUSE SALE TO PURCHASE NEXT HOME?   YES ▢ NO ▢

IS YOUR HOME CURRENTLY RENTED? YES ▢ NO ▢ LEASE END . . . . RENT . . . .

DESCRIPTION (POSITIVES & NEGATIVES): . . . .

. . . .

. . . .

. . . .

ANY MAJOR IMPROVEMENTS MADE TO HOME? . . . .

. . . .

NEIGHBORHOOD AMMENITIES: . . . .

. . . .

WHAT ARE YOU LOOKING FOR IN AN AGENT? . . . .

PREFERRED METHOD OF COMMUNICATION: PHONE ▢ EMAIL ▢ TEXT ▢

Seller Lead Sheet

BEDS . . . . SQ FT . . . .

PROPERTY INFORMATION

BATHS . . . . HOA . . . .

ADDRESS . . . .

CITY . . . . STATE . . . . ZIP . . . .

COMMUNITY NAME . . . . MANAGEMENT PHONE . . . .

CLIENT

FIRST NAME . . . . LAST NAME . . . .

PHONE . . . . EMAIL . . . .

CO-OWNER NAME . . . . LAST NAME . . . .

PHONE . . . . EMAIL . . . .

CO-OWNER MARRIED? YES ☐ NO ☐ OTHER PARTIES? . . . .

QUESTIONAIRE

ARE YOU WORKING WITH OTHER AGENTS? YES ☐ NO ☐ . . . .

WHY DO YOU WANT TO MOVE? . . . .

WHEN DO YOU WANT TO MOVE BY? . . . .

WHERE WILL YOU BE MOVING TO? . . . .

DO YOU OWE ANYTHING ON THE PROPERTY? YES ☐ NO ☐ . . . .

WHAT PRICE DO YOU WANT TO SELL THE PROPERTY FOR? . . . .

WILL YOU NEED TO MOVE BEFORE YOU SELL? YES ☐ NO ☐ . . . .

WILL YOU NEED FUNDS FROM HOUSE SALE TO PURCHASE NEXT HOME? YES ☐ NO ☐

IS YOUR HOME CURRENTLY RENTED? YES ☐ NO ☐ LEASE END . . . . RENT . . . .

DESCRIPTION (POSITIVES & NEGATIVES): . . . .

. . . .

. . . .

. . . .

ANY MAJOR IMPROVEMENTS MADE TO HOME? . . . .

. . . .

NEIGHBORHOOD AMMENITIES: . . . .

. . . .

WHAT ARE YOU LOOKING FOR IN AN AGENT? . . . .

PREFERRED METHOD OF COMMUNICATION: PHONE ☐ EMAIL ☐ TEXT ☐

Seller Lead Sheet

BEDS . . . .   SQ FT . . . .

BATHS . . . .   HOA . . . .

PROPERTY INFORMATION

ADDRESS . . . .

CITY . . . . STATE . . . . ZIP . . . .

COMMUNITY NAME . . . . MANAGEMENT PHONE . . . .

CLIENT

FIRST NAME . . . . LAST NAME . . . .

PHONE . . . . EMAIL . . . .

CO-OWNER NAME . . . . LAST NAME . . . .

PHONE . . . . EMAIL . . . .

CO-OWNER MARRIED? YES ☐ NO ☐ OTHER PARTIES? . . . .

QUESTIONAIRE

ARE YOU WORKING WITH OTHER AGENTS?   YES ☐ NO ☐ . . . .

WHY DO YOU WANT TO MOVE? . . . .

WHEN DO YOU WANT TO MOVE BY? . . . .

WHERE WILL YOU BE MOVING TO? . . . .

DO YOU OWE ANYTHING ON THE PROPERTY?   YES ☐ NO ☐ . . . .

WHAT PRICE DO YOU WANT TO SELL THE PROPERTY FOR? . . . .

WILL YOU NEED TO MOVE BEFORE YOU SELL?   YES ☐ NO ☐ . . . .

WILL YOU NEED FUNDS FROM HOUSE SALE TO PURCHASE NEXT HOME?   YES ☐ NO ☐

IS YOUR HOME CURRENTLY RENTED? YES ☐ NO ☐ LEASE END . . . . RENT . . . .

DESCRIPTION (POSITIVES & NEGATIVES): . . . .

. . . .

. . . .

. . . .

ANY MAJOR IMPROVEMENTS MADE TO HOME? . . . .

. . . .

NEIGHBORHOOD AMMENITIES: . . . .

. . . .

WHAT ARE YOU LOOKING FOR IN AN AGENT? . . . .

PREFERRED METHOD OF COMMUNICATION: PHONE ☐ EMAIL ☐ TEXT ☐

Seller Lead Sheet

BEDS . . . . SQ FT . . . .

PROPERTY INFORMATION

BATHS . . . . HOA . . . .

ADDRESS . . . .

CITY . . . . STATE . . . . ZIP . . . .

COMMUNITY NAME . . . . MANAGEMENT PHONE . . . .

CLIENT

FIRST NAME . . . . LAST NAME . . . .

PHONE . . . . EMAIL . . . .

CO-OWNER NAME . . . . LAST NAME . . . .

PHONE . . . . EMAIL . . . .

CO-OWNER MARRIED? YES ☐ NO ☐ OTHER PARTIES? . . . .

QUESTIONAIRE

ARE YOU WORKING WITH OTHER AGENTS?   YES ☐ NO ☐ . . . .

WHY DO YOU WANT TO MOVE? . . . .

WHEN DO YOU WANT TO MOVE BY? . . . .

WHERE WILL YOU BE MOVING TO? . . . .

DO YOU OWE ANYTHING ON THE PROPERTY?   YES ☐ NO ☐ . . . .

WHAT PRICE DO YOU WANT TO SELL THE PROPERTY FOR? . . . .

WILL YOU NEED TO MOVE BEFORE YOU SELL?   YES ☐ NO ☐ . . . .

WILL YOU NEED FUNDS FROM HOUSE SALE TO PURCHASE NEXT HOME?   YES ☐ NO ☐

IS YOUR HOME CURRENTLY RENTED? YES ☐ NO ☐ LEASE END . . . . RENT . . . .

DESCRIPTION (POSITIVES & NEGATIVES): . . . .

. . . .

. . . .

. . . .

ANY MAJOR IMPROVEMENTS MADE TO HOME? . . . .

. . . .

NEIGHBORHOOD AMMENITIES: . . . .

. . . .

WHAT ARE YOU LOOKING FOR IN AN AGENT? . . . .

PREFERRED METHOD OF COMMUNICATION: PHONE ☐ EMAIL ☐ TEXT ☐

Seller Lead Sheet

BEDS . . . .   SQ FT . . . .

BATHS . . . .   HOA . . . .

PROPERTY INFORMATION

ADDRESS . . . .

CITY . . . . STATE . . . . ZIP . . . .

COMMUNITY NAME . . . . MANAGEMENT PHONE . . . .

CLIENT

FIRST NAME . . . . LAST NAME . . . .

PHONE . . . . EMAIL . . . .

CO-OWNER NAME . . . . LAST NAME . . . .

PHONE . . . . EMAIL . . . .

CO-OWNER MARRIED? YES ☐ NO ☐ OTHER PARTIES? . . . .

QUESTIONAIRE

ARE YOU WORKING WITH OTHER AGENTS? YES ☐ NO ☐ . . . .

WHY DO YOU WANT TO MOVE? . . . .

WHEN DO YOU WANT TO MOVE BY? . . . .

WHERE WILL YOU BE MOVING TO? . . . .

DO YOU OWE ANYTHING ON THE PROPERTY? YES ☐ NO ☐ . . . .

WHAT PRICE DO YOU WANT TO SELL THE PROPERTY FOR? . . . .

WILL YOU NEED TO MOVE BEFORE YOU SELL? YES ☐ NO ☐ . . . .

WILL YOU NEED FUNDS FROM HOUSE SALE TO PURCHASE NEXT HOME? YES ☐ NO ☐

IS YOUR HOME CURRENTLY RENTED? YES ☐ NO ☐ LEASE END . . . . RENT . . . .

DESCRIPTION (POSITIVES & NEGATIVES): . . . .

. . . .

. . . .

. . . .

ANY MAJOR IMPROVEMENTS MADE TO HOME? . . . .

. . . .

NEIGHBORHOOD AMMENITIES: . . . .

. . . .

WHAT ARE YOU LOOKING FOR IN AN AGENT? . . . .

PREFERRED METHOD OF COMMUNICATION: PHONE ☐ EMAIL ☐ TEXT ☐

Seller Lead Sheet

BEDS . . . .   SQ FT . . . .

PROPERTY INFORMATION

BATHS . . . .   HOA . . . .

ADDRESS . . . .

CITY . . . . STATE . . . . ZIP . . . .

COMMUNITY NAME . . . . MANAGEMENT PHONE . . . .

CLIENT

FIRST NAME . . . . LAST NAME . . . .

PHONE . . . . EMAIL . . . .

CO-OWNER NAME . . . . LAST NAME . . . .

PHONE . . . . EMAIL . . . .

CO-OWNER MARRIED? YES ☐ NO ☐ OTHER PARTIES? . . . .

QUESTIONAIRE

ARE YOU WORKING WITH OTHER AGENTS? YES ☐ NO ☐ . . . .

WHY DO YOU WANT TO MOVE? . . . .

WHEN DO YOU WANT TO MOVE BY? . . . .

WHERE WILL YOU BE MOVING TO? . . . .

DO YOU OWE ANYTHING ON THE PROPERTY? YES ☐ NO ☐ . . . .

WHAT PRICE DO YOU WANT TO SELL THE PROPERTY FOR? . . . .

WILL YOU NEED TO MOVE BEFORE YOU SELL? YES ☐ NO ☐ . . . .

WILL YOU NEED FUNDS FROM HOUSE SALE TO PURCHASE NEXT HOME? YES ☐ NO ☐

IS YOUR HOME CURRENTLY RENTED? YES ☐ NO ☐ LEASE END . . . . RENT . . . .

DESCRIPTION (POSITIVES & NEGATIVES): . . . .

. . . .

. . . .

. . . .

ANY MAJOR IMPROVEMENTS MADE TO HOME? . . . .

. . . .

NEIGHBORHOOD AMMENITIES: . . . .

. . . .

WHAT ARE YOU LOOKING FOR IN AN AGENT? . . . .

PREFERRED METHOD OF COMMUNICATION: PHONE ☐ EMAIL ☐ TEXT ☐

Seller Lead Sheet

BEDS . . . .   SQ FT . . . .

BATHS . . . .   HOA . . . .

PROPERTY INFORMATION

ADDRESS . . . .

CITY . . . . STATE . . . . ZIP . . . .

COMMUNITY NAME . . . . MANAGEMENT PHONE . . . .

CLIENT

FIRST NAME . . . . LAST NAME . . . .

PHONE . . . . EMAIL . . . .

CO-OWNER NAME . . . . LAST NAME . . . .

PHONE . . . . EMAIL . . . .

CO-OWNER MARRIED? YES ☐ NO ☐ OTHER PARTIES? . . . .

QUESTIONAIRE

ARE YOU WORKING WITH OTHER AGENTS? YES ☐ NO ☐ . . . .

WHY DO YOU WANT TO MOVE? . . . .

WHEN DO YOU WANT TO MOVE BY? . . . .

WHERE WILL YOU BE MOVING TO? . . . .

DO YOU OWE ANYTHING ON THE PROPERTY? YES ☐ NO ☐ . . . .

WHAT PRICE DO YOU WANT TO SELL THE PROPERTY FOR? . . . .

WILL YOU NEED TO MOVE BEFORE YOU SELL? YES ☐ NO ☐ . . . .

WILL YOU NEED FUNDS FROM HOUSE SALE TO PURCHASE NEXT HOME? YES ☐ NO ☐

IS YOUR HOME CURRENTLY RENTED? YES ☐ NO ☐ LEASE END . . . . RENT . . . .

DESCRIPTION (POSITIVES & NEGATIVES): . . . .

. . . .

. . . .

. . . .

ANY MAJOR IMPROVEMENTS MADE TO HOME? . . . .

. . . .

NEIGHBORHOOD AMMENITIES: . . . .

. . . .

WHAT ARE YOU LOOKING FOR IN AN AGENT? . . . .

PREFERRED METHOD OF COMMUNICATION: PHONE ☐ EMAIL ☐ TEXT ☐

Seller Lead Sheet

BEDS . . . .   SQ FT . . . .

BATHS . . . .   HOA . . . .

PROPERTY INFORMATION

ADDRESS . . . .

CITY . . . . STATE . . . . ZIP . . . .

COMMUNITY NAME . . . . MANAGEMENT PHONE . . . .

CLIENT

FIRST NAME . . . . LAST NAME . . . .

PHONE . . . . EMAIL

CO-OWNER NAME . . . . LAST NAME . . . .

PHONE . . . . EMAIL

CO-OWNER MARRIED? YES [ ] NO [ ] OTHER PARTIES? . . . .

QUESTIONAIRE

ARE YOU WORKING WITH OTHER AGENTS? YES [ ] NO [ ] . . . .

WHY DO YOU WANT TO MOVE? . . . .

WHEN DO YOU WANT TO MOVE BY? . . . .

WHERE WILL YOU BE MOVING TO? . . . .

DO YOU OWE ANYTHING ON THE PROPERTY? YES [ ] NO [ ] . . . .

WHAT PRICE DO YOU WANT TO SELL THE PROPERTY FOR? . . . .

WILL YOU NEED TO MOVE BEFORE YOU SELL? YES [ ] NO [ ] . . . .

WILL YOU NEED FUNDS FROM HOUSE SALE TO PURCHASE NEXT HOME? YES [ ] NO [ ]

IS YOUR HOME CURRENTLY RENTED? YES [ ] NO [ ] LEASE END . . . . RENT . . . .

DESCRIPTION (POSITIVES & NEGATIVES): . . . .

. . . .

. . . .

. . . .

ANY MAJOR IMPROVEMENTS MADE TO HOME? . . . .

. . . .

NEIGHBORHOOD AMMENITIES: . . . .

. . . .

WHAT ARE YOU LOOKING FOR IN AN AGENT? . . . .

PREFERRED METHOD OF COMMUNICATION: PHONE [ ] EMAIL [ ] TEXT [ ]

Seller Lead Sheet

BEDS . . . .   SQ FT . . . .

PROPERTY INFORMATION

BATHS . . . .   HOA . . . .

ADDRESS . . . .

CITY . . . . STATE . . . . ZIP . . . .

COMMUNITY NAME . . . . MANAGEMENT PHONE . . . .

CLIENT

FIRST NAME . . . . LAST NAME . . . .

PHONE . . . . EMAIL . . . .

CO-OWNER NAME . . . . LAST NAME . . . .

PHONE . . . . EMAIL . . . .

CO-OWNER MARRIED? YES ▢ NO ▢ OTHER PARTIES? . . . .

QUESTIONAIRE

ARE YOU WORKING WITH OTHER AGENTS?   YES ▢ NO ▢ . . . .

WHY DO YOU WANT TO MOVE? . . . .

WHEN DO YOU WANT TO MOVE BY? . . . .

WHERE WILL YOU BE MOVING TO? . . . .

DO YOU OWE ANYTHING ON THE PROPERTY?   YES ▢ NO ▢ . . . .

WHAT PRICE DO YOU WANT TO SELL THE PROPERTY FOR? . . . .

WILL YOU NEED TO MOVE BEFORE YOU SELL?   YES ▢ NO ▢ . . . .

WILL YOU NEED FUNDS FROM HOUSE SALE TO PURCHASE NEXT HOME?   YES ▢ NO ▢

IS YOUR HOME CURRENTLY RENTED? YES ▢ NO ▢ LEASE END . . . . RENT . . . .

DESCRIPTION (POSITIVES & NEGATIVES): . . . .

. . . .

. . . .

. . . .

ANY MAJOR IMPROVEMENTS MADE TO HOME? . . . .

. . . .

NEIGHBORHOOD AMMENITIES: . . . .

. . . .

WHAT ARE YOU LOOKING FOR IN AN AGENT? . . . .

PREFERRED METHOD OF COMMUNICATION: PHONE ▢ EMAIL ▢ TEXT ▢

Seller Lead Sheet

BEDS . . . .　　SQ FT . . . .

BATHS . . . .　　HOA . . . .

PROPERTY INFORMATION

ADDRESS . . . .

CITY . . . . STATE . . . . ZIP . . . .

COMMUNITY NAME . . . . MANAGEMENT PHONE . . . .

CLIENT

FIRST NAME . . . . LAST NAME . . . .

PHONE . . . . EMAIL . . . .

CO-OWNER NAME . . . . LAST NAME . . . .

PHONE . . . . EMAIL . . . .

CO-OWNER MARRIED? YES ▢ NO ▢ OTHER PARTIES? . . . .

QUESTIONAIRE

ARE YOU WORKING WITH OTHER AGENTS? YES ▢ NO ▢ . . . .

WHY DO YOU WANT TO MOVE? . . . .

WHEN DO YOU WANT TO MOVE BY? . . . .

WHERE WILL YOU BE MOVING TO? . . . .

DO YOU OWE ANYTHING ON THE PROPERTY? YES ▢ NO ▢ . . . .

WHAT PRICE DO YOU WANT TO SELL THE PROPERTY FOR? . . . .

WILL YOU NEED TO MOVE BEFORE YOU SELL? YES ▢ NO ▢ . . . .

WILL YOU NEED FUNDS FROM HOUSE SALE TO PURCHASE NEXT HOME? YES ▢ NO ▢

IS YOUR HOME CURRENTLY RENTED? YES ▢ NO ▢ LEASE END . . . . RENT . . . .

DESCRIPTION (POSITIVES & NEGATIVES): . . . .

. . . .

. . . .

. . . .

ANY MAJOR IMPROVEMENTS MADE TO HOME? . . . .

. . . .

NEIGHBORHOOD AMMENITIES: . . . .

. . . .

WHAT ARE YOU LOOKING FOR IN AN AGENT? . . . .

PREFERRED METHOD OF COMMUNICATION: PHONE ▢ EMAIL ▢ TEXT ▢

Seller Lead Sheet

BEDS . . . .   SQ FT . . . .

BATHS . . . .   HOA . . . .

PROPERTY INFORMATION

ADDRESS . . . .

CITY . . . . STATE . . . . ZIP . . . .

COMMUNITY NAME . . . . MANAGEMENT PHONE . . . .

CLIENT

FIRST NAME . . . . LAST NAME . . . .

PHONE . . . . EMAIL . . . .

CO-OWNER NAME . . . . LAST NAME . . . .

PHONE . . . . EMAIL . . . .

CO-OWNER MARRIED? YES ▢ NO ▢ OTHER PARTIES? . . . .

QUESTIONAIRE

ARE YOU WORKING WITH OTHER AGENTS? YES ▢ NO ▢ . . . .

WHY DO YOU WANT TO MOVE? . . . .

WHEN DO YOU WANT TO MOVE BY? . . . .

WHERE WILL YOU BE MOVING TO? . . . .

DO YOU OWE ANYTHING ON THE PROPERTY? YES ▢ NO ▢ . . . .

WHAT PRICE DO YOU WANT TO SELL THE PROPERTY FOR? . . . .

WILL YOU NEED TO MOVE BEFORE YOU SELL? YES ▢ NO ▢ . . . .

WILL YOU NEED FUNDS FROM HOUSE SALE TO PURCHASE NEXT HOME? YES ▢ NO ▢

IS YOUR HOME CURRENTLY RENTED? YES ▢ NO ▢ LEASE END . . . . RENT . . . .

DESCRIPTION (POSITIVES & NEGATIVES): . . . .

. . . .

. . . .

. . . .

ANY MAJOR IMPROVEMENTS MADE TO HOME? . . . .

. . . .

NEIGHBORHOOD AMMENITIES: . . . .

. . . .

WHAT ARE YOU LOOKING FOR IN AN AGENT? . . . .

PREFERRED METHOD OF COMMUNICATION: PHONE ▢ EMAIL ▢ TEXT ▢

Seller Lead Sheet

BEDS . . . . SQ FT . . . .

PROPERTY INFORMATION

BATHS . . . . HOA . . . .

ADDRESS . . . .

CITY . . . . STATE . . . . ZIP . . . .

COMMUNITY NAME . . . . MANAGEMENT PHONE . . . .

CLIENT

FIRST NAME . . . . LAST NAME . . . .

PHONE . . . . EMAIL . . . .

CO-OWNER NAME . . . . LAST NAME . . . .

PHONE . . . . EMAIL . . . .

CO-OWNER MARRIED? YES ☐ NO ☐ OTHER PARTIES? . . . .

QUESTIONAIRE

ARE YOU WORKING WITH OTHER AGENTS? YES ☐ NO ☐ . . . .

WHY DO YOU WANT TO MOVE? . . . .

WHEN DO YOU WANT TO MOVE BY? . . . .

WHERE WILL YOU BE MOVING TO? . . . .

DO YOU OWE ANYTHING ON THE PROPERTY? YES ☐ NO ☐ . . . .

WHAT PRICE DO YOU WANT TO SELL THE PROPERTY FOR? . . . .

WILL YOU NEED TO MOVE BEFORE YOU SELL? YES ☐ NO ☐ . . . .

WILL YOU NEED FUNDS FROM HOUSE SALE TO PURCHASE NEXT HOME? YES ☐ NO ☐

IS YOUR HOME CURRENTLY RENTED? YES ☐ NO ☐ LEASE END . . . . RENT . . . .

DESCRIPTION (POSITIVES & NEGATIVES): . . . .

. . . .

. . . .

. . . .

ANY MAJOR IMPROVEMENTS MADE TO HOME? . . . .

. . . .

NEIGHBORHOOD AMMENITIES: . . . .

. . . .

WHAT ARE YOU LOOKING FOR IN AN AGENT? . . . .

PREFERRED METHOD OF COMMUNICATION: PHONE ☐ EMAIL ☐ TEXT ☐

Seller Lead Sheet

BEDS . . . .   SQ FT . . . .

PROPERTY INFORMATION

BATHS . . . .   HOA . . . .

ADDRESS . . . .

CITY . . . . STATE . . . . ZIP . . . .

COMMUNITY NAME . . . . MANAGEMENT PHONE . . . .

CLIENT

FIRST NAME . . . . LAST NAME . . . .

PHONE . . . . EMAIL . . . .

CO-OWNER NAME . . . . LAST NAME . . . .

PHONE . . . . EMAIL . . . .

CO-OWNER MARRIED? YES ☐ NO ☐   OTHER PARTIES? . . . .

QUESTIONAIRE

ARE YOU WORKING WITH OTHER AGENTS?   YES ☐ NO ☐ . . . .

WHY DO YOU WANT TO MOVE? . . . .

WHEN DO YOU WANT TO MOVE BY? . . . .

WHERE WILL YOU BE MOVING TO? . . . .

DO YOU OWE ANYTHING ON THE PROPERTY?   YES ☐ NO ☐ . . . .

WHAT PRICE DO YOU WANT TO SELL THE PROPERTY FOR? . . . .

WILL YOU NEED TO MOVE BEFORE YOU SELL?   YES ☐ NO ☐ . . . .

WILL YOU NEED FUNDS FROM HOUSE SALE TO PURCHASE NEXT HOME?   YES ☐ NO ☐

IS YOUR HOME CURRENTLY RENTED? YES ☐ NO ☐ LEASE END . . . . RENT . . . .

DESCRIPTION (POSITIVES & NEGATIVES): . . . .

. . . .

. . . .

. . . .

ANY MAJOR IMPROVEMENTS MADE TO HOME? . . . .

. . . .

NEIGHBORHOOD AMMENITIES: . . . .

. . . .

WHAT ARE YOU LOOKING FOR IN AN AGENT? . . . .

PREFERRED METHOD OF COMMUNICATION: PHONE ☐ EMAIL ☐ TEXT ☐

Seller Lead Sheet

BEDS . . . .   SQ FT . . . .

BATHS . . . .   HOA . . . .

PROPERTY INFORMATION

ADDRESS . . . .

CITY . . . . STATE . . . . ZIP . . . .

COMMUNITY NAME . . . . MANAGEMENT PHONE . . . .

CLIENT

FIRST NAME . . . . LAST NAME . . . .

PHONE . . . . EMAIL . . . .

CO-OWNER NAME . . . . LAST NAME . . . .

PHONE . . . . EMAIL . . . .

CO-OWNER MARRIED? YES ▢ NO ▢ OTHER PARTIES? . . . .

QUESTIONAIRE

ARE YOU WORKING WITH OTHER AGENTS?   YES ▢ NO ▢ . . . .

WHY DO YOU WANT TO MOVE? . . . .

WHEN DO YOU WANT TO MOVE BY? . . . .

WHERE WILL YOU BE MOVING TO? . . . .

DO YOU OWE ANYTHING ON THE PROPERTY?   YES ▢ NO ▢ . . . .

WHAT PRICE DO YOU WANT TO SELL THE PROPERTY FOR? . . . .

WILL YOU NEED TO MOVE BEFORE YOU SELL?   YES ▢ NO ▢ . . . .

WILL YOU NEED FUNDS FROM HOUSE SALE TO PURCHASE NEXT HOME?   YES ▢ NO ▢

IS YOUR HOME CURRENTLY RENTED? YES ▢ NO ▢ LEASE END . . . . RENT . . . .

DESCRIPTION (POSITIVES & NEGATIVES): . . . .

. . . .

. . . .

. . . .

ANY MAJOR IMPROVEMENTS MADE TO HOME? . . . .

. . . .

NEIGHBORHOOD AMMENITIES: . . . .

. . . .

WHAT ARE YOU LOOKING FOR IN AN AGENT? . . . .

PREFERRED METHOD OF COMMUNICATION: PHONE ▢ EMAIL ▢ TEXT ▢

Seller Lead Sheet

BEDS . . . .   SQ FT . . . .

BATHS . . . .   HOA . . . .

PROPERTY INFORMATION

ADDRESS . . . .

CITY . . . . STATE . . . . ZIP . . . .

COMMUNITY NAME . . . . MANAGEMENT PHONE . . . .

CLIENT

FIRST NAME . . . . LAST NAME . . . .

PHONE . . . . EMAIL . . . .

CO-OWNER NAME . . . . LAST NAME . . . .

PHONE . . . . EMAIL . . . .

CO-OWNER MARRIED? YES ☐ NO ☐ OTHER PARTIES? . . . .

QUESTIONAIRE

ARE YOU WORKING WITH OTHER AGENTS? YES ☐ NO ☐ . . . .

WHY DO YOU WANT TO MOVE? . . . .

WHEN DO YOU WANT TO MOVE BY? . . . .

WHERE WILL YOU BE MOVING TO? . . . .

DO YOU OWE ANYTHING ON THE PROPERTY? YES ☐ NO ☐ . . . .

WHAT PRICE DO YOU WANT TO SELL THE PROPERTY FOR? . . . .

WILL YOU NEED TO MOVE BEFORE YOU SELL? YES ☐ NO ☐ . . . .

WILL YOU NEED FUNDS FROM HOUSE SALE TO PURCHASE NEXT HOME? YES ☐ NO ☐

IS YOUR HOME CURRENTLY RENTED? YES ☐ NO ☐ LEASE END . . . . RENT . . . .

DESCRIPTION (POSITIVES & NEGATIVES): . . . .

. . . .

. . . .

. . . .

ANY MAJOR IMPROVEMENTS MADE TO HOME? . . . .

. . . .

NEIGHBORHOOD AMMENITIES: . . . .

. . . .

WHAT ARE YOU LOOKING FOR IN AN AGENT? . . . .

PREFERRED METHOD OF COMMUNICATION: PHONE ☐ EMAIL ☐ TEXT ☐

Seller Lead Sheet

BEDS . . . .   SQ FT . . . .

PROPERTY INFORMATION

BATHS . . . .   HOA . . . .

ADDRESS . . . .

CITY . . . . STATE . . . . ZIP . . . .

COMMUNITY NAME . . . . MANAGEMENT PHONE . . . .

CLIENT

FIRST NAME . . . . LAST NAME . . . .

PHONE . . . . EMAIL . . . .

CO-OWNER NAME . . . . LAST NAME . . . .

PHONE . . . . EMAIL . . . .

CO-OWNER MARRIED? YES ☐ NO ☐   OTHER PARTIES? . . . .

QUESTIONAIRE

ARE YOU WORKING WITH OTHER AGENTS?   YES ☐ NO ☐ . . . .

WHY DO YOU WANT TO MOVE? . . . .

WHEN DO YOU WANT TO MOVE BY? . . . .

WHERE WILL YOU BE MOVING TO? . . . .

DO YOU OWE ANYTHING ON THE PROPERTY?   YES ☐ NO ☐ . . . .

WHAT PRICE DO YOU WANT TO SELL THE PROPERTY FOR? . . . .

WILL YOU NEED TO MOVE BEFORE YOU SELL?   YES ☐ NO ☐ . . . .

WILL YOU NEED FUNDS FROM HOUSE SALE TO PURCHASE NEXT HOME?   YES ☐ NO ☐

IS YOUR HOME CURRENTLY RENTED? YES ☐ NO ☐ LEASE END . . . . RENT . . . .

DESCRIPTION (POSITIVES & NEGATIVES): . . . .

. . . .

. . . .

. . . .

ANY MAJOR IMPROVEMENTS MADE TO HOME? . . . .

. . . .

NEIGHBORHOOD AMMENITIES: . . . .

. . . .

WHAT ARE YOU LOOKING FOR IN AN AGENT? . . . .

PREFERRED METHOD OF COMMUNICATION: PHONE ☐ EMAIL ☐ TEXT ☐

Be that person who decided to go for it.

Buyer Consultation Sheets

BUYER CONSULTATION

CLIENT

FIRST NAME . . . . LAST NAME . . . .

PHONE . . . . EMAIL

ALTERNATIVE . . . . PETS   YES   NO   . . . .

MARRIED? YES ☐ NO ☐   MARRIED TO CO-BUYER? YES ☐ NO ☐

EMPLOYER . . . . WORK PHONE . . . .

CO-BUYER

FIRST NAME . . . . LAST NAME . . . .

PHONE . . . . EMAIL

ALTERNATIVE . . . . PETS   YES ☐ NO ☐ . . . .

MARRIED? YES ☐ NO ☐   MARRIED TO CO-BUYER? YES ☐ NO ☐

EMPLOYER . . . . WORK PHONE . . . .

QUESTIONAIRE

HOW WILL YOU BE PAYING FOR YOUR HOME? CASH ☐ FINANCE ☐ LOAN TYPE . . . .

LENDER . . . . PHONE . . . . EMAIL . . . .

WHAT TYPE OF HOME ARE YOU LOOKING FOR? ☐ TOWNHOME ☐ SINGLE FAMILY ☐ CONDO

WHAT IS YOUR MONTHLY BUDGET FOR YOUR MORTGAGE PAYMENT? . . . .

HOW MANY BEDS/BATHS? . . . . BEDS . . . . BATHS

WHAT AREAS DO YOU WANT TO PURCHASE IN? . . . .

ARE YOU LOOKING TO BE IN A SPECIFIC SCHOOL DISTRICT? . . . .

WHAT SPECIFIC FEATURES ARE YOU LOOKING FOR? . . . .

. . . .

. . . .

. . . .

DO YOU OWN A HOME? YES ☐ NO ☐   DO YOU NEED TO SELL? YES ☐ NO ☐

ARE YOU IN A LEASE? YES ☐ NO ☐   WHEN DOES IT EXPIRE? . . . .

HOW SOON DO YOU WANT TO PURCHASE YOUR NEW HOME? . . . .

WHAT DAYS / TIMES ARE BEST TO VIEW HOMES?   MON . . . . TUE . . . .

WED . . . . THU . . . . FRI . . . . SAT . . . . SUN . . . .

PREFERRED METHOD OF COMMUNICATION: ☐ CALL ☐ TEXT ☐ EMAIL

IF YOU FIND A HOME YOU LOVE ARE YOU PREPARED TO MAKE AN OFFER? YES ☐ NO ☐

BUYER CONSULTATION

CLIENT

FIRST NAME . . . . LAST NAME . . . .

PHONE . . . . EMAIL . . . .

ALTERNATIVE . . . . PETS   YES   NO   . . . .

MARRIED?   YES ☐   NO ☐   MARRIED TO CO-BUYER?   YES ☐   NO ☐

EMPLOYER . . . . WORK PHONE . . . .

CO-BUYER

FIRST NAME . . . . LAST NAME . . . .

PHONE . . . . EMAIL . . . .

ALTERNATIVE . . . . PETS   YES ☐   NO ☐   . . . .

MARRIED?   YES ☐   NO ☐   MARRIED TO CO-BUYER?   YES ☐   NO ☐

EMPLOYER . . . . WORK PHONE . . . .

QUESTIONAIRE

HOW WILL YOU BE PAYING FOR YOUR HOME? CASH ☐   FINANCE ☐   LOAN TYPE . . . .

LENDER . . . . PHONE . . . . EMAIL . . . .

WHAT TYPE OF HOME ARE YOU LOOKING FOR? ☐ TOWNHOME   ☐ SINGLE FAMILY   ☐ CONDO

WHAT IS YOUR MONTHLY BUDGET FOR YOUR MORTGAGE PAYMENT? . . . .

HOW MANY BEDS/BATHS? . . . . BEDS . . . . BATHS

WHAT AREAS DO YOU WANT TO PURCHASE IN? . . . .

ARE YOU LOOKING TO BE IN A SPECIFIC SCHOOL DISTRICT? . . . .

WHAT SPECIFIC FEATURES ARE YOU LOOKING FOR? . . . .

. . . .

. . . .

. . . .

DO YOU OWN A HOME?   YES ☐   NO ☐   DO YOU NEED TO SELL?   YES ☐   NO ☐

ARE YOU IN A LEASE?   YES ☐   NO ☐   WHEN DOES IT EXPIRE? . . . .

HOW SOON DO YOU WANT TO PURCHASE YOUR NEW HOME? . . . .

WHAT DAYS / TIMES ARE BEST TO VIEW HOMES?   MON . . . . TUE . . . .

WED . . . . THU . . . . FRI . . . . SAT . . . . SUN . . . .

PREFERRED METHOD OF COMMUNICATION: ☐ CALL   ☐ TEXT   ☐ EMAIL

IF YOU FIND A HOME YOU LOVE ARE YOU PREPARED TO MAKE AN OFFER?   YES ☐   NO ☐

BUYER CONSULTATION

CLIENT

FIRST NAME . . . . LAST NAME . . . .

PHONE . . . . EMAIL

ALTERNATIVE . . . . PETS   YES   NO   . . . .

MARRIED?   YES ▢   NO ▢   MARRIED TO CO-BUYER?   YES ▢   NO ▢

EMPLOYER . . . . WORK PHONE . . . .

CO-BUYER

FIRST NAME . . . . LAST NAME . . . .

PHONE . . . . EMAIL

ALTERNATIVE . . . . PETS   YES ▢   NO ▢   . . . .

MARRIED?   YES ▢   NO ▢   MARRIED TO CO-BUYER?   YES ▢   NO ▢

EMPLOYER . . . . WORK PHONE . . . .

QUESTIONAIRE

HOW WILL YOU BE PAYING FOR YOUR HOME? CASH ▢   FINANCE ▢   LOAN TYPE . . . .

LENDER . . . . PHONE . . . . EMAIL . . . .

WHAT TYPE OF HOME ARE YOU LOOKING FOR? ▢ TOWNHOME   ▢ SINGLE FAMILY   ▢ CONDO

WHAT IS YOUR MONTHLY BUDGET FOR YOUR MORTGAGE PAYMENT? . . . .

HOW MANY BEDS/BATHS? . . . . BEDS . . . . BATHS

WHAT AREAS DO YOU WANT TO PURCHASE IN? . . . .

ARE YOU LOOKING TO BE IN A SPECIFIC SCHOOL DISTRICT? . . . .

WHAT SPECIFIC FEATURES ARE YOU LOOKING FOR? . . . .

. . . .

. . . .

. . . .

DO YOU OWN A HOME? YES ▢   NO ▢   DO YOU NEED TO SELL?   YES ▢   NO ▢

ARE YOU IN A LEASE?   YES ▢   NO ▢   WHEN DOES IT EXPIRE? . . . .

HOW SOON DO YOU WANT TO PURCHASE YOUR NEW HOME? . . . .

WHAT DAYS / TIMES ARE BEST TO VIEW HOMES?   MON . . . . TUE . . . .

WED . . . . THU . . . . FRI . . . . SAT . . . . SUN . . . .

PREFERRED METHOD OF COMMUNICATION: ▢ CALL   ▢ TEXT   ▢ EMAIL

IF YOU FIND A HOME YOU LOVE ARE YOU PREPARED TO MAKE AN OFFER?   YES ▢   NO ▢

BUYER CONSULTATION

CLIENT

FIRST NAME . . . . LAST NAME . . . .

PHONE . . . . EMAIL . . . .

ALTERNATIVE . . . . PETS   YES   NO   . . . .

MARRIED? YES ☐ NO ☐   MARRIED TO CO-BUYER? YES ☐   NO ☐

EMPLOYER . . . . WORK PHONE

CO-BUYER

FIRST NAME . . . . LAST NAME . . . .

PHONE . . . . EMAIL . . . .

ALTERNATIVE . . . . PETS   YES ☐   NO ☐   . . . .

MARRIED? YES ☐ NO ☐   MARRIED TO CO-BUYER? YES ☐   NO ☐

EMPLOYER . . . . WORK PHONE . . . .

QUESTIONAIRE

HOW WILL YOU BE PAYING FOR YOUR HOME? CASH ☐   FINANCE ☐   LOAN TYPE . . . .

LENDER . . . . PHONE . . . . EMAIL . . . .

WHAT TYPE OF HOME ARE YOU LOOKING FOR? ☐ TOWNHOME   ☐ SINGLE FAMILY   ☐ CONDO

WHAT IS YOUR MONTHLY BUDGET FOR YOUR MORTGAGE PAYMENT? . . . .

HOW MANY BEDS/BATHS? . . . . BEDS . . . . BATHS

WHAT AREAS DO YOU WANT TO PURCHASE IN? . . . .

ARE YOU LOOKING TO BE IN A SPECIFIC SCHOOL DISTRICT? . . . .

WHAT SPECIFIC FEATURES ARE YOU LOOKING FOR? . . . .

. . . .

. . . .

. . . .

DO YOU OWN A HOME? YES ☐   NO ☐   DO YOU NEED TO SELL? YES ☐   NO ☐

ARE YOU IN A LEASE? YES ☐   NO ☐   WHEN DOES IT EXPIRE? . . . .

HOW SOON DO YOU WANT TO PURCHASE YOUR NEW HOME? . . . .

WHAT DAYS / TIMES ARE BEST TO VIEW HOMES?   MON . . . . TUE . . . .

WED . . . . THU . . . . FRI . . . . SAT . . . . SUN . . . .

PREFERRED METHOD OF COMMUNICATION: ☐ CALL ☐ TEXT ☐ EMAIL

IF YOU FIND A HOME YOU LOVE ARE YOU PREPARED TO MAKE AN OFFER? YES ☐   NO ☐

BUYER CONSULTATION

CLIENT

FIRST NAME . . . . LAST NAME . . . .

PHONE . . . . EMAIL . . . .

ALTERNATIVE . . . . PETS   YES   NO   . . . .

MARRIED? YES ☐   NO ☐   MARRIED TO CO-BUYER? YES ☐   NO ☐

EMPLOYER . . . . WORK PHONE . . . .

CO-BUYER

FIRST NAME . . . . LAST NAME . . . .

PHONE . . . . EMAIL . . . .

ALTERNATIVE . . . . PETS   YES ☐   NO ☐   . . . .

MARRIED? YES ☐   NO ☐   MARRIED TO CO-BUYER? YES ☐   NO ☐

EMPLOYER . . . . WORK PHONE . . . .

QUESTIONAIRE

HOW WILL YOU BE PAYING FOR YOUR HOME? CASH ☐   FINANCE ☐   LOAN TYPE . . . .

LENDER . . . .   PHONE . . . .   EMAIL . . . .

WHAT TYPE OF HOME ARE YOU LOOKING FOR? ☐ TOWNHOME   ☐ SINGLE FAMILY   ☐ CONDO

WHAT IS YOUR MONTHLY BUDGET FOR YOUR MORTGAGE PAYMENT? . . . .

HOW MANY BEDS/BATHS? . . . . BEDS . . . . BATHS

WHAT AREAS DO YOU WANT TO PURCHASE IN? . . . .

ARE YOU LOOKING TO BE IN A SPECIFIC SCHOOL DISTRICT? . . . .

WHAT SPECIFIC FEATURES ARE YOU LOOKING FOR? . . . .

. . . .

. . . .

. . . .

DO YOU OWN A HOME? YES ☐   NO ☐   DO YOU NEED TO SELL? YES ☐   NO ☐

ARE YOU IN A LEASE? YES ☐   NO ☐   WHEN DOES IT EXPIRE? . . . .

HOW SOON DO YOU WANT TO PURCHASE YOUR NEW HOME? . . . .

WHAT DAYS / TIMES ARE BEST TO VIEW HOMES?   MON . . . . TUE . . . .

WED . . . . THU . . . . FRI . . . . SAT . . . . SUN . . . .

PREFERRED METHOD OF COMMUNICATION: ☐ CALL ☐ TEXT ☐ EMAIL

IF YOU FIND A HOME YOU LOVE ARE YOU PREPARED TO MAKE AN OFFER? YES ☐   NO ☐

BUYER CONSULTATION

CLIENT

FIRST NAME . . . . LAST NAME . . . .

PHONE . . . . EMAIL . . . .

ALTERNATIVE . . . . PETS   YES   NO   . . . .

MARRIED? YES ☐ NO ☐   MARRIED TO CO-BUYER? YES ☐ NO ☐

EMPLOYER . . . . WORK PHONE

CO-BUYER

FIRST NAME . . . . LAST NAME . . . .

PHONE . . . . EMAIL . . . .

ALTERNATIVE . . . . PETS   YES ☐ NO ☐ . . . .

MARRIED? YES ☐ NO ☐   MARRIED TO CO-BUYER? YES ☐ NO ☐

EMPLOYER . . . . WORK PHONE . . . .

QUESTIONAIRE

HOW WILL YOU BE PAYING FOR YOUR HOME? CASH ☐ FINANCE ☐ LOAN TYPE . . . .

LENDER . . . . PHONE . . . . EMAIL . . . .

WHAT TYPE OF HOME ARE YOU LOOKING FOR? ☐ TOWNHOME ☐ SINGLE FAMILY ☐ CONDO

WHAT IS YOUR MONTHLY BUDGET FOR YOUR MORTGAGE PAYMENT? . . . .

HOW MANY BEDS/BATHS? . . . . BEDS . . . . BATHS

WHAT AREAS DO YOU WANT TO PURCHASE IN? . . . .

ARE YOU LOOKING TO BE IN A SPECIFIC SCHOOL DISTRICT? . . . .

WHAT SPECIFIC FEATURES ARE YOU LOOKING FOR? . . . .

. . . .

. . . .

. . . .

DO YOU OWN A HOME? YES ☐ NO ☐   DO YOU NEED TO SELL? YES ☐ NO ☐

ARE YOU IN A LEASE? YES ☐ NO ☐   WHEN DOES IT EXPIRE? . . . .

HOW SOON DO YOU WANT TO PURCHASE YOUR NEW HOME? . . . .

WHAT DAYS / TIMES ARE BEST TO VIEW HOMES?   MON . . . . TUE . . . .

WED . . . . THU . . . . FRI . . . . SAT . . . . SUN . . . .

PREFERRED METHOD OF COMMUNICATION: ☐ CALL ☐ TEXT ☐ EMAIL

IF YOU FIND A HOME YOU LOVE ARE YOU PREPARED TO MAKE AN OFFER? YES ☐ NO ☐

BUYER CONSULTATION

CLIENT

FIRST NAME . . . . LAST NAME . . . .

PHONE . . . . EMAIL

ALTERNATIVE . . . . PETS   YES   NO   . . . .

MARRIED? YES ⬜ NO ⬜   MARRIED TO CO-BUYER? YES ⬜ NO ⬜

EMPLOYER . . . . WORK PHONE . . . .

CO-BUYER

FIRST NAME . . . . LAST NAME . . . .

PHONE . . . . EMAIL

ALTERNATIVE . . . . PETS   YES ⬜ NO ⬜ . . . .

MARRIED? YES ⬜ NO ⬜   MARRIED TO CO-BUYER? YES ⬜ NO ⬜

EMPLOYER . . . . WORK PHONE . . . .

QUESTIONAIRE

HOW WILL YOU BE PAYING FOR YOUR HOME? CASH ⬜   FINANCE ⬜   LOAN TYPE . . . .

LENDER . . . .   PHONE . . . .   EMAIL . . . .

WHAT TYPE OF HOME ARE YOU LOOKING FOR? ⬜ TOWNHOME   ⬜ SINGLE FAMILY   ⬜ CONDO

WHAT IS YOUR MONTHLY BUDGET FOR YOUR MORTGAGE PAYMENT? . . . .

HOW MANY BEDS/BATHS? . . . . BEDS . . . . BATHS

WHAT AREAS DO YOU WANT TO PURCHASE IN? . . . .

ARE YOU LOOKING TO BE IN A SPECIFIC SCHOOL DISTRICT? . . . .

WHAT SPECIFIC FEATURES ARE YOU LOOKING FOR? . . . .

. . . .

. . . .

. . . .

DO YOU OWN A HOME? YES ⬜   NO ⬜   DO YOU NEED TO SELL? YES ⬜   NO ⬜

ARE YOU IN A LEASE? YES ⬜   NO ⬜   WHEN DOES IT EXPIRE? . . . .

HOW SOON DO YOU WANT TO PURCHASE YOUR NEW HOME? . . . .

WHAT DAYS / TIMES ARE BEST TO VIEW HOMES?   MON . . . .   TUE . . . .

WED . . . .   THU . . . .   FRI . . . .   SAT . . . .   SUN . . . .

PREFERRED METHOD OF COMMUNICATION: ⬜ CALL   ⬜ TEXT   ⬜ EMAIL

IF YOU FIND A HOME YOU LOVE ARE YOU PREPARED TO MAKE AN OFFER? YES ⬜   NO ⬜

BUYER CONSULTATION

CLIENT

FIRST NAME . . . . LAST NAME . . . .

PHONE . . . . EMAIL . . . .

ALTERNATIVE . . . . PETS   YES   NO   . . . .

MARRIED? YES   NO   MARRIED TO CO-BUYER? YES   NO

EMPLOYER . . . . WORK PHONE

CO-BUYER

FIRST NAME . . . . LAST NAME . . . .

PHONE . . . . EMAIL . . . .

ALTERNATIVE . . . . PETS   YES   NO   . . . .

MARRIED? YES   NO   MARRIED TO CO-BUYER? YES   NO

EMPLOYER . . . . WORK PHONE . . . .

QUESTIONAIRE

HOW WILL YOU BE PAYING FOR YOUR HOME? CASH   FINANCE   LOAN TYPE . . . .

LENDER . . . . PHONE . . . . EMAIL . . . .

WHAT TYPE OF HOME ARE YOU LOOKING FOR?   TOWNHOME   SINGLE FAMILY   CONDO

WHAT IS YOUR MONTHLY BUDGET FOR YOUR MORTGAGE PAYMENT? . . . .

HOW MANY BEDS/BATHS? . . . . BEDS . . . . BATHS

WHAT AREAS DO YOU WANT TO PURCHASE IN? . . . .

ARE YOU LOOKING TO BE IN A SPECIFIC SCHOOL DISTRICT? . . . .

WHAT SPECIFIC FEATURES ARE YOU LOOKING FOR? . . . .

. . . .

. . . .

. . . .

DO YOU OWN A HOME? YES   NO   DO YOU NEED TO SELL? YES   NO

ARE YOU IN A LEASE? YES   NO   WHEN DOES IT EXPIRE? . . . .

HOW SOON DO YOU WANT TO PURCHASE YOUR NEW HOME? . . . .

WHAT DAYS / TIMES ARE BEST TO VIEW HOMES?   MON . . . . TUE . . . .

WED . . . . THU . . . . FRI . . . . SAT . . . . SUN . . . .

PREFERRED METHOD OF COMMUNICATION: CALL   TEXT   EMAIL

IF YOU FIND A HOME YOU LOVE ARE YOU PREPARED TO MAKE AN OFFER? YES   NO

BUYER CONSULTATION

CLIENT

FIRST NAME . . . . LAST NAME . . . .

PHONE . . . . EMAIL . . . .

ALTERNATIVE . . . . PETS   YES   NO   . . . .

MARRIED? YES ☐ NO ☐   MARRIED TO CO-BUYER? YES ☐   NO ☐

EMPLOYER . . . . WORK PHONE . . . .

CO-BUYER

FIRST NAME . . . . LAST NAME . . . .

PHONE . . . . EMAIL . . . .

ALTERNATIVE . . . . PETS   YES ☐   NO ☐   . . . .

MARRIED? YES ☐ NO ☐   MARRIED TO CO-BUYER? YES ☐   NO ☐

EMPLOYER . . . . WORK PHONE . . . .

QUESTIONAIRE

HOW WILL YOU BE PAYING FOR YOUR HOME? CASH ☐   FINANCE ☐   LOAN TYPE . . . .

LENDER . . . . PHONE . . . . EMAIL . . . .

WHAT TYPE OF HOME ARE YOU LOOKING FOR? ☐ TOWNHOME ☐ SINGLE FAMILY ☐ CONDO

WHAT IS YOUR MONTHLY BUDGET FOR YOUR MORTGAGE PAYMENT? . . . .

HOW MANY BEDS/BATHS? . . . . BEDS . . . . BATHS

WHAT AREAS DO YOU WANT TO PURCHASE IN? . . . .

ARE YOU LOOKING TO BE IN A SPECIFIC SCHOOL DISTRICT? . . . .

WHAT SPECIFIC FEATURES ARE YOU LOOKING FOR? . . . .

. . . .

. . . .

. . . .

DO YOU OWN A HOME? YES ☐   NO ☐   DO YOU NEED TO SELL? YES ☐   NO ☐

ARE YOU IN A LEASE? YES ☐   NO ☐   WHEN DOES IT EXPIRE? . . . .

HOW SOON DO YOU WANT TO PURCHASE YOUR NEW HOME? . . . .

WHAT DAYS / TIMES ARE BEST TO VIEW HOMES?   MON . . . . TUE . . . .

WED . . . . THU . . . . FRI . . . . SAT . . . . SUN . . . .

PREFERRED METHOD OF COMMUNICATION: ☐ CALL ☐ TEXT ☐ EMAIL

IF YOU FIND A HOME YOU LOVE ARE YOU PREPARED TO MAKE AN OFFER? YES ☐   NO ☐

BUYER CONSULTATION

CLIENT

FIRST NAME . . . . LAST NAME . . . .

PHONE . . . . EMAIL . . . .

ALTERNATIVE . . . . PETS   YES   NO   . . . .

MARRIED? YES ☐ NO ☐   MARRIED TO CO-BUYER? YES ☐   NO ☐

EMPLOYER . . . . WORK PHONE . . . .

CO-BUYER

FIRST NAME . . . . LAST NAME . . . .

PHONE . . . . EMAIL . . . .

ALTERNATIVE . . . . PETS   YES ☐   NO ☐   . . . .

MARRIED? YES ☐ NO ☐   MARRIED TO CO-BUYER? YES ☐   NO ☐

EMPLOYER . . . . WORK PHONE . . . .

QUESTIONAIRE

HOW WILL YOU BE PAYING FOR YOUR HOME? CASH ☐ FINANCE ☐ LOAN TYPE . . . .

LENDER . . . . PHONE . . . . EMAIL . . . .

WHAT TYPE OF HOME ARE YOU LOOKING FOR? ☐ TOWNHOME   ☐ SINGLE FAMILY   ☐ CONDO

WHAT IS YOUR MONTHLY BUDGET FOR YOUR MORTGAGE PAYMENT? . . . .

HOW MANY BEDS/BATHS? . . . . BEDS . . . . BATHS

WHAT AREAS DO YOU WANT TO PURCHASE IN? . . . .

ARE YOU LOOKING TO BE IN A SPECIFIC SCHOOL DISTRICT? . . . .

WHAT SPECIFIC FEATURES ARE YOU LOOKING FOR? . . . .

. . . .

. . . .

. . . .

DO YOU OWN A HOME? YES ☐   NO ☐   DO YOU NEED TO SELL? YES ☐   NO ☐

ARE YOU IN A LEASE? YES ☐   NO ☐   WHEN DOES IT EXPIRE? . . . .

HOW SOON DO YOU WANT TO PURCHASE YOUR NEW HOME? . . . .

WHAT DAYS / TIMES ARE BEST TO VIEW HOMES?   MON . . . . TUE . . . .

WED . . . . THU . . . . FRI . . . . SAT . . . . SUN . . . .

PREFERRED METHOD OF COMMUNICATION: ☐ CALL   ☐ TEXT   ☐ EMAIL

IF YOU FIND A HOME YOU LOVE ARE YOU PREPARED TO MAKE AN OFFER? YES ☐   NO ☐

BUYER CONSULTATION

CLIENT

FIRST NAME . . . . LAST NAME . . . .

PHONE . . . . EMAIL . . . .

ALTERNATIVE . . . . PETS   YES   NO   . . . .

MARRIED? YES [ ] NO [ ]   MARRIED TO CO-BUYER? YES [ ]   NO [ ]

EMPLOYER . . . . WORK PHONE . . . .

CO-BUYER

FIRST NAME . . . . LAST NAME . . . .

PHONE . . . . EMAIL . . . .

ALTERNATIVE . . . . PETS   YES [ ]   NO [ ] . . . .

MARRIED? YES [ ] NO [ ]   MARRIED TO CO-BUYER? YES [ ]   NO [ ]

EMPLOYER . . . . WORK PHONE . . . .

QUESTIONAIRE

HOW WILL YOU BE PAYING FOR YOUR HOME? CASH [ ]   FINANCE [ ] LOAN TYPE . . . .

LENDER . . . . PHONE . . . . EMAIL . . . .

WHAT TYPE OF HOME ARE YOU LOOKING FOR? [ ] TOWNHOME   [ ] SINGLE FAMILY   [ ] CONDO

WHAT IS YOUR MONTHLY BUDGET FOR YOUR MORTGAGE PAYMENT? . . . .

HOW MANY BEDS/BATHS? . . . . BEDS . . . . BATHS

WHAT AREAS DO YOU WANT TO PURCHASE IN? . . . .

ARE YOU LOOKING TO BE IN A SPECIFIC SCHOOL DISTRICT? . . . .

WHAT SPECIFIC FEATURES ARE YOU LOOKING FOR? . . . .

. . . .

. . . .

. . . .

DO YOU OWN A HOME? YES [ ]   NO [ ]   DO YOU NEED TO SELL? YES [ ]   NO [ ]

ARE YOU IN A LEASE? YES [ ]   NO [ ]   WHEN DOES IT EXPIRE? . . . .

HOW SOON DO YOU WANT TO PURCHASE YOUR NEW HOME? . . . .

WHAT DAYS / TIMES ARE BEST TO VIEW HOMES?   MON . . . . TUE . . . .

WED . . . . THU . . . . FRI . . . . SAT . . . . SUN . . . .

PREFERRED METHOD OF COMMUNICATION: [ ] CALL [ ] TEXT [ ] EMAIL

IF YOU FIND A HOME YOU LOVE ARE YOU PREPARED TO MAKE AN OFFER? YES [ ]   NO [ ]

BUYER CONSULTATION

CLIENT

FIRST NAME . . . . LAST NAME . . . .

PHONE . . . . EMAIL . . . .

ALTERNATIVE . . . . PETS   YES   NO   . . . .

MARRIED?   YES ☐   NO ☐   MARRIED TO CO-BUYER?   YES ☐   NO ☐

EMPLOYER . . . . WORK PHONE . . . .

CO-BUYER

FIRST NAME . . . . LAST NAME . . . .

PHONE . . . . EMAIL . . . .

ALTERNATIVE . . . . PETS   YES ☐   NO ☐   . . . .

MARRIED?   YES ☐   NO ☐   MARRIED TO CO-BUYER?   YES ☐   NO ☐

EMPLOYER . . . . WORK PHONE . . . .

QUESTIONAIRE

HOW WILL YOU BE PAYING FOR YOUR HOME? CASH ☐   FINANCE ☐ LOAN TYPE . . . .

LENDER . . . . PHONE . . . . EMAIL . . . .

WHAT TYPE OF HOME ARE YOU LOOKING FOR? ☐ TOWNHOME ☐ SINGLE FAMILY ☐ CONDO

WHAT IS YOUR MONTHLY BUDGET FOR YOUR MORTGAGE PAYMENT? . . . .

HOW MANY BEDS/BATHS? . . . . BEDS . . . . BATHS

WHAT AREAS DO YOU WANT TO PURCHASE IN? . . . .

ARE YOU LOOKING TO BE IN A SPECIFIC SCHOOL DISTRICT? . . . .

WHAT SPECIFIC FEATURES ARE YOU LOOKING FOR? . . . .

. . . .

. . . .

. . . .

DO YOU OWN A HOME?   YES ☐   NO ☐   DO YOU NEED TO SELL?   YES ☐   NO ☐

ARE YOU IN A LEASE?   YES ☐   NO ☐   WHEN DOES IT EXPIRE? . . . .

HOW SOON DO YOU WANT TO PURCHASE YOUR NEW HOME? . . . .

WHAT DAYS / TIMES ARE BEST TO VIEW HOMES?   MON . . . . TUE . . . .

WED . . . . THU . . . . FRI . . . . SAT . . . . SUN . . . .

PREFERRED METHOD OF COMMUNICATION: ☐ CALL ☐ TEXT ☐ EMAIL

IF YOU FIND A HOME YOU LOVE ARE YOU PREPARED TO MAKE AN OFFER?   YES ☐   NO ☐

BUYER CONSULTATION

CLIENT

FIRST NAME . . . . LAST NAME . . . .

PHONE . . . . EMAIL

ALTERNATIVE . . . . PETS   YES   NO   . . . .

MARRIED?   YES ▢   NO ▢   MARRIED TO CO-BUYER?   YES ▢   NO ▢

EMPLOYER . . . . WORK PHONE . . . .

CO-BUYER

FIRST NAME . . . . LAST NAME . . . .

PHONE . . . . EMAIL

ALTERNATIVE . . . . PETS   YES ▢   NO ▢   . . . .

MARRIED?   YES ▢   NO ▢   MARRIED TO CO-BUYER?   YES ▢   NO ▢

EMPLOYER . . . . WORK PHONE . . . .

QUESTIONAIRE

HOW WILL YOU BE PAYING FOR YOUR HOME? CASH ▢   FINANCE ▢   LOAN TYPE . . . .

LENDER . . . . PHONE . . . . EMAIL . . . .

WHAT TYPE OF HOME ARE YOU LOOKING FOR? ▢ TOWNHOME   ▢ SINGLE FAMILY   ▢ CONDO

WHAT IS YOUR MONTHLY BUDGET FOR YOUR MORTGAGE PAYMENT? . . . .

HOW MANY BEDS/BATHS? . . . . BEDS . . . . BATHS

WHAT AREAS DO YOU WANT TO PURCHASE IN? . . . .

ARE YOU LOOKING TO BE IN A SPECIFIC SCHOOL DISTRICT? . . . .

WHAT SPECIFIC FEATURES ARE YOU LOOKING FOR? . . . .

. . . .

. . . .

. . . .

DO YOU OWN A HOME? YES ▢   NO ▢   DO YOU NEED TO SELL? YES ▢   NO ▢

ARE YOU IN A LEASE? YES ▢   NO ▢   WHEN DOES IT EXPIRE? . . . .

HOW SOON DO YOU WANT TO PURCHASE YOUR NEW HOME? . . . .

WHAT DAYS / TIMES ARE BEST TO VIEW HOMES?   MON . . . . TUE . . . .

WED . . . . THU . . . . FRI . . . . SAT . . . . SUN . . . .

PREFERRED METHOD OF COMMUNICATION: ▢ CALL   ▢ TEXT   ▢ EMAIL

IF YOU FIND A HOME YOU LOVE ARE YOU PREPARED TO MAKE AN OFFER? YES ▢   NO ▢

BUYER CONSULTATION

CLIENT

FIRST NAME . . . . LAST NAME . . . .

PHONE . . . . EMAIL . . . .

ALTERNATIVE . . . . PETS   YES   NO   . . . .

MARRIED? YES ☐ NO ☐   MARRIED TO CO-BUYER? YES ☐   NO ☐

EMPLOYER . . . . WORK PHONE . . . .

CO-BUYER

FIRST NAME . . . . LAST NAME . . . .

PHONE . . . . EMAIL . . . .

ALTERNATIVE . . . . PETS   YES ☐   NO ☐   . . . .

MARRIED? YES ☐ NO ☐   MARRIED TO CO-BUYER? YES ☐   NO ☐

EMPLOYER . . . . WORK PHONE . . . .

QUESTIONAIRE

HOW WILL YOU BE PAYING FOR YOUR HOME? CASH ☐   FINANCE ☐   LOAN TYPE . . . .

LENDER . . . .   PHONE . . . .   EMAIL . . . .

WHAT TYPE OF HOME ARE YOU LOOKING FOR? ☐ TOWNHOME   ☐ SINGLE FAMILY   ☐ CONDO

WHAT IS YOUR MONTHLY BUDGET FOR YOUR MORTGAGE PAYMENT? . . . .

HOW MANY BEDS/BATHS? . . . . BEDS . . . . BATHS

WHAT AREAS DO YOU WANT TO PURCHASE IN? . . . .

ARE YOU LOOKING TO BE IN A SPECIFIC SCHOOL DISTRICT? . . . .

WHAT SPECIFIC FEATURES ARE YOU LOOKING FOR? . . . .

. . . .

. . . .

. . . .

DO YOU OWN A HOME? YES ☐   NO ☐   DO YOU NEED TO SELL? YES ☐   NO ☐

ARE YOU IN A LEASE? YES ☐   NO ☐   WHEN DOES IT EXPIRE? . . . .

HOW SOON DO YOU WANT TO PURCHASE YOUR NEW HOME? . . . .

WHAT DAYS / TIMES ARE BEST TO VIEW HOMES?   MON . . . .   TUE . . . .

WED . . . .   THU . . . .   FRI . . . .   SAT . . . .   SUN . . . .

PREFERRED METHOD OF COMMUNICATION: ☐ CALL ☐ TEXT ☐ EMAIL

IF YOU FIND A HOME YOU LOVE ARE YOU PREPARED TO MAKE AN OFFER? YES ☐   NO ☐

BUYER CONSULTATION

CLIENT

FIRST NAME . . . . LAST NAME . . . .

PHONE . . . . EMAIL

ALTERNATIVE . . . . PETS   YES   NO   . . . .

MARRIED? YES ☐   NO ☐   MARRIED TO CO-BUYER? YES ☐   NO ☐

EMPLOYER . . . . WORK PHONE . . . .

CO-BUYER

FIRST NAME . . . . LAST NAME . . . .

PHONE . . . . EMAIL

ALTERNATIVE . . . . PETS   YES ☐   NO ☐   . . . .

MARRIED? YES ☐   NO ☐   MARRIED TO CO-BUYER? YES ☐   NO ☐

EMPLOYER . . . . WORK PHONE . . . .

QUESTIONAIRE

HOW WILL YOU BE PAYING FOR YOUR HOME? CASH ☐   FINANCE ☐   LOAN TYPE . . . .

LENDER . . . .   PHONE . . . .   EMAIL . . . .

WHAT TYPE OF HOME ARE YOU LOOKING FOR? ☐ TOWNHOME   ☐ SINGLE FAMILY   ☐ CONDO

WHAT IS YOUR MONTHLY BUDGET FOR YOUR MORTGAGE PAYMENT? . . . .

HOW MANY BEDS/BATHS? . . . . BEDS . . . . BATHS

WHAT AREAS DO YOU WANT TO PURCHASE IN? . . . .

ARE YOU LOOKING TO BE IN A SPECIFIC SCHOOL DISTRICT? . . . .

WHAT SPECIFIC FEATURES ARE YOU LOOKING FOR? . . . .

. . . .

. . . .

. . . .

DO YOU OWN A HOME? YES ☐   NO ☐   DO YOU NEED TO SELL? YES ☐   NO ☐

ARE YOU IN A LEASE? YES ☐   NO ☐   WHEN DOES IT EXPIRE? . . . .

HOW SOON DO YOU WANT TO PURCHASE YOUR NEW HOME? . . . .

WHAT DAYS / TIMES ARE BEST TO VIEW HOMES?   MON . . . .   TUE . . . .

WED . . . .   THU . . . .   FRI . . . .   SAT . . . .   SUN . . . .

PREFERRED METHOD OF COMMUNICATION: ☐ CALL   ☐ TEXT   ☐ EMAIL

IF YOU FIND A HOME YOU LOVE ARE YOU PREPARED TO MAKE AN OFFER? YES ☐   NO ☐

BUYER CONSULTATION

CLIENT

FIRST NAME . . . . LAST NAME . . . .

PHONE . . . . EMAIL . . . .

ALTERNATIVE . . . . PETS   YES   NO   . . . .

MARRIED? YES ▢ NO ▢   MARRIED TO CO-BUYER? YES ▢   NO ▢

EMPLOYER . . . . WORK PHONE . . . .

CO-BUYER

FIRST NAME . . . . LAST NAME . . . .

PHONE . . . . EMAIL . . . .

ALTERNATIVE . . . . PETS   YES ▢   NO ▢   . . . .

MARRIED? YES ▢ NO ▢   MARRIED TO CO-BUYER? YES ▢   NO ▢

EMPLOYER . . . . WORK PHONE . . . .

QUESTIONAIRE

HOW WILL YOU BE PAYING FOR YOUR HOME? CASH ▢   FINANCE ▢ LOAN TYPE . . . .

LENDER . . . .   PHONE . . . . EMAIL . . . .

WHAT TYPE OF HOME ARE YOU LOOKING FOR? ▢ TOWNHOME   ▢ SINGLE FAMILY   ▢ CONDO

WHAT IS YOUR MONTHLY BUDGET FOR YOUR MORTGAGE PAYMENT? . . . .

HOW MANY BEDS/BATHS? . . . . BEDS . . . . BATHS

WHAT AREAS DO YOU WANT TO PURCHASE IN? . . . .

ARE YOU LOOKING TO BE IN A SPECIFIC SCHOOL DISTRICT? . . . .

WHAT SPECIFIC FEATURES ARE YOU LOOKING FOR? . . . .

. . . .

. . . .

. . . .

DO YOU OWN A HOME? YES ▢   NO ▢   DO YOU NEED TO SELL? YES ▢   NO ▢

ARE YOU IN A LEASE? YES ▢   NO ▢   WHEN DOES IT EXPIRE? . . . .

HOW SOON DO YOU WANT TO PURCHASE YOUR NEW HOME? . . . .

WHAT DAYS / TIMES ARE BEST TO VIEW HOMES?   MON . . . . TUE . . . .

WED . . . . THU . . . . FRI . . . . SAT . . . . SUN . . . .

PREFERRED METHOD OF COMMUNICATION: ▢ CALL   ▢ TEXT   ▢ EMAIL

IF YOU FIND A HOME YOU LOVE ARE YOU PREPARED TO MAKE AN OFFER? YES ▢   NO ▢

BUYER CONSULTATION

CLIENT

FIRST NAME . . . . LAST NAME . . . .

PHONE . . . . EMAIL

ALTERNATIVE . . . . PETS   YES   NO   . . . .

MARRIED? YES ☐ NO ☐   MARRIED TO CO-BUYER? YES ☐   NO ☐

EMPLOYER . . . . WORK PHONE . . . .

CO-BUYER

FIRST NAME . . . . LAST NAME . . . .

PHONE . . . . EMAIL

ALTERNATIVE . . . . PETS   YES ☐   NO ☐   . . . .

MARRIED? YES ☐ NO ☐   MARRIED TO CO-BUYER? YES ☐   NO ☐

EMPLOYER . . . . WORK PHONE . . . .

QUESTIONAIRE

HOW WILL YOU BE PAYING FOR YOUR HOME? CASH ☐   FINANCE ☐ LOAN TYPE . . . .

LENDER . . . .   PHONE . . . .   EMAIL . . . .

WHAT TYPE OF HOME ARE YOU LOOKING FOR? ☐ TOWNHOME   ☐ SINGLE FAMILY   ☐ CONDO

WHAT IS YOUR MONTHLY BUDGET FOR YOUR MORTGAGE PAYMENT? . . . .

HOW MANY BEDS/BATHS? . . . . BEDS . . . . BATHS

WHAT AREAS DO YOU WANT TO PURCHASE IN? . . . .

ARE YOU LOOKING TO BE IN A SPECIFIC SCHOOL DISTRICT? . . . .

WHAT SPECIFIC FEATURES ARE YOU LOOKING FOR? . . . .

. . . .

. . . .

. . . .

DO YOU OWN A HOME? YES ☐   NO ☐   DO YOU NEED TO SELL? YES ☐   NO ☐

ARE YOU IN A LEASE? YES ☐   NO ☐   WHEN DOES IT EXPIRE? . . . .

HOW SOON DO YOU WANT TO PURCHASE YOUR NEW HOME? . . . .

WHAT DAYS / TIMES ARE BEST TO VIEW HOMES?   MON . . . .   TUE . . . .

WED . . . .   THU . . . .   FRI . . . .   SAT . . . .   SUN . . . .

PREFERRED METHOD OF COMMUNICATION: ☐ CALL ☐ TEXT ☐ EMAIL

IF YOU FIND A HOME YOU LOVE ARE YOU PREPARED TO MAKE AN OFFER? YES ☐   NO ☐

BUYER CONSULTATION

CLIENT

FIRST NAME . . . . LAST NAME . . . .

PHONE . . . . EMAIL . . . .

ALTERNATIVE . . . . PETS   YES   NO   . . . .

MARRIED? YES   NO   MARRIED TO CO-BUYER? YES   NO

EMPLOYER . . . . WORK PHONE . . . .

CO-BUYER

FIRST NAME . . . . LAST NAME . . . .

PHONE . . . . EMAIL . . . .

ALTERNATIVE . . . . PETS   YES   NO   . . . .

MARRIED? YES   NO   MARRIED TO CO-BUYER? YES   NO

EMPLOYER . . . . WORK PHONE . . . .

QUESTIONAIRE

HOW WILL YOU BE PAYING FOR YOUR HOME? CASH   FINANCE   LOAN TYPE . . . .

LENDER . . . . PHONE . . . . EMAIL . . . .

WHAT TYPE OF HOME ARE YOU LOOKING FOR?   TOWNHOME   SINGLE FAMILY   CONDO

WHAT IS YOUR MONTHLY BUDGET FOR YOUR MORTGAGE PAYMENT? . . . .

HOW MANY BEDS/BATHS? . . . . BEDS . . . . BATHS

WHAT AREAS DO YOU WANT TO PURCHASE IN? . . . .

ARE YOU LOOKING TO BE IN A SPECIFIC SCHOOL DISTRICT? . . . .

WHAT SPECIFIC FEATURES ARE YOU LOOKING FOR? . . . .

. . . .

. . . .

. . . .

DO YOU OWN A HOME? YES   NO   DO YOU NEED TO SELL? YES   NO

ARE YOU IN A LEASE? YES   NO   WHEN DOES IT EXPIRE? . . . .

HOW SOON DO YOU WANT TO PURCHASE YOUR NEW HOME? . . . .

WHAT DAYS / TIMES ARE BEST TO VIEW HOMES?   MON . . . . TUE . . . .

WED . . . . THU . . . . FRI . . . . SAT . . . . SUN . . . .

PREFERRED METHOD OF COMMUNICATION: CALL   TEXT   EMAIL

IF YOU FIND A HOME YOU LOVE ARE YOU PREPARED TO MAKE AN OFFER? YES   NO

BUYER CONSULTATION

CLIENT

FIRST NAME . . . . LAST NAME . . . .

PHONE . . . . EMAIL

ALTERNATIVE . . . . PETS   YES   NO   . . . .

MARRIED?   YES   NO   MARRIED TO CO-BUYER?   YES   NO

EMPLOYER . . . . WORK PHONE . . . .

CO-BUYER

FIRST NAME . . . . LAST NAME . . . .

PHONE . . . . EMAIL

ALTERNATIVE . . . . PETS   YES   NO   . . . .

MARRIED?   YES   NO   MARRIED TO CO-BUYER?   YES   NO

EMPLOYER . . . . WORK PHONE . . . .

QUESTIONAIRE

HOW WILL YOU BE PAYING FOR YOUR HOME? CASH   FINANCE   LOAN TYPE . . . .

LENDER . . . .   PHONE . . . .   EMAIL . . . .

WHAT TYPE OF HOME ARE YOU LOOKING FOR?   TOWNHOME   SINGLE FAMILY   CONDO

WHAT IS YOUR MONTHLY BUDGET FOR YOUR MORTGAGE PAYMENT? . . . .

HOW MANY BEDS/BATHS? . . . . BEDS . . . . BATHS

WHAT AREAS DO YOU WANT TO PURCHASE IN? . . . .

ARE YOU LOOKING TO BE IN A SPECIFIC SCHOOL DISTRICT? . . . .

WHAT SPECIFIC FEATURES ARE YOU LOOKING FOR? . . . .

. . . .

. . . .

. . . .

DO YOU OWN A HOME? YES   NO   DO YOU NEED TO SELL?   YES   NO

ARE YOU IN A LEASE?   YES   NO   WHEN DOES IT EXPIRE? . . . .

HOW SOON DO YOU WANT TO PURCHASE YOUR NEW HOME? . . . .

WHAT DAYS / TIMES ARE BEST TO VIEW HOMES?   MON . . . . TUE . . . .

WED . . . . THU . . . . FRI . . . . SAT . . . . SUN . . . .

PREFERRED METHOD OF COMMUNICATION: CALL   TEXT   EMAIL

IF YOU FIND A HOME YOU LOVE ARE YOU PREPARED TO MAKE AN OFFER?   YES   NO

BUYER CONSULTATION

CLIENT

FIRST NAME . . . . LAST NAME . . . .

PHONE . . . . EMAIL . . . .

ALTERNATIVE . . . . PETS   YES   NO   . . . .

MARRIED? YES ☐ NO ☐   MARRIED TO CO-BUYER? YES ☐   NO ☐

EMPLOYER . . . . WORK PHONE . . . .

CO-BUYER

FIRST NAME . . . . LAST NAME . . . .

PHONE . . . . EMAIL . . . .

ALTERNATIVE . . . . PETS   YES ☐   NO ☐   . . . .

MARRIED? YES ☐ NO ☐   MARRIED TO CO-BUYER? YES ☐   NO ☐

EMPLOYER . . . . WORK PHONE

QUESTIONAIRE

HOW WILL YOU BE PAYING FOR YOUR HOME? CASH ☐   FINANCE ☐ LOAN TYPE . . . .

LENDER . . . . PHONE . . . . EMAIL . . . .

WHAT TYPE OF HOME ARE YOU LOOKING FOR? ☐ TOWNHOME ☐ SINGLE FAMILY ☐ CONDO

WHAT IS YOUR MONTHLY BUDGET FOR YOUR MORTGAGE PAYMENT? . . . .

HOW MANY BEDS/BATHS? . . . . BEDS . . . . BATHS

WHAT AREAS DO YOU WANT TO PURCHASE IN? . . . .

ARE YOU LOOKING TO BE IN A SPECIFIC SCHOOL DISTRICT? . . . .

WHAT SPECIFIC FEATURES ARE YOU LOOKING FOR? . . . .

. . . .

. . . .

. . . .

DO YOU OWN A HOME? YES ☐   NO ☐   DO YOU NEED TO SELL? YES ☐   NO ☐

ARE YOU IN A LEASE? YES ☐   NO ☐   WHEN DOES IT EXPIRE? . . . .

HOW SOON DO YOU WANT TO PURCHASE YOUR NEW HOME? . . . .

WHAT DAYS / TIMES ARE BEST TO VIEW HOMES?   MON . . . . TUE . . . .

WED . . . . THU . . . . FRI . . . . SAT . . . . SUN . . . .

PREFERRED METHOD OF COMMUNICATION: ☐ CALL ☐ TEXT ☐ EMAIL

IF YOU FIND A HOME YOU LOVE ARE YOU PREPARED TO MAKE AN OFFER? YES ☐   NO ☐

Either
you run the day,
or the day
runs you.

You Choose.

New Lead
Trackers

FIRST NAME . . . . LAST NAME . . . .

PHONE . . . . EMAIL . . . .

LENDER . . . . PURCHASE PRICE . . . .

PROPERTY TYPE: ☐ TOWNHOME ☐ SINGLE FAMILY ☐ CONDO

PUT IN DATABASE ☐ SEARCH PORTAL CREATED ☐

DETAILS / INFO TO KNOW:. . . . .

. . . .

. . . .

FOLLOW UP DATE:. . . . . PUT FOLLOW UP REMINDER IN CALENDAR ☐

FOLLOW UP DATE:. . . . . PUT FOLLOW UP REMINDER IN CALENDAR ☐

FOLLOW UP DATE:. . . . . PUT FOLLOW UP REMINDER IN CALENDAR ☐

FIRST NAME . . . . LAST NAME . . . .

PHONE . . . . EMAIL . . . .

LENDER . . . . PURCHASE PRICE . . . .

PROPERTY TYPE: ☐ TOWNHOME ☐ SINGLE FAMILY ☐ CONDO

PUT IN DATABASE ☐ SEARCH PORTAL CREATED ☐

DETAILS / INFO TO KNOW:. . . . .

. . . .

. . . .

FOLLOW UP DATE:. . . . . PUT FOLLOW UP REMINDER IN CALENDAR ☐

FOLLOW UP DATE:. . . . . PUT FOLLOW UP REMINDER IN CALENDAR ☐

FOLLOW UP DATE:. . . . . PUT FOLLOW UP REMINDER IN CALENDAR ☐

FIRST NAME . . . . LAST NAME . . . .

PHONE . . . . EMAIL . . . .

LENDER . . . . PURCHASE PRICE . . . .

PROPERTY TYPE: ☐ TOWNHOME ☐ SINGLE FAMILY ☐ CONDO

PUT IN DATABASE ☐ SEARCH PORTAL CREATED ☐

DETAILS / INFO TO KNOW:. . . . .

. . . .

. . . .

FOLLOW UP DATE:. . . . . PUT FOLLOW UP REMINDER IN CALENDAR ☐

FOLLOW UP DATE:. . . . . PUT FOLLOW UP REMINDER IN CALENDAR ☐

FOLLOW UP DATE:. . . . . PUT FOLLOW UP REMINDER IN CALENDAR ☐

NEW LEAD TRACKERS

FIRST NAME . . . . LAST NAME . . . .

PHONE . . . . EMAIL . . . .

LENDER . . . . PURCHASE PRICE . . . .

PROPERTY TYPE: ☐ TOWNHOME ☐ SINGLE FAMILY ☐ CONDO

PUT IN DATABASE ☐ SEARCH PORTAL CREATED ☐

DETAILS / INFO TO KNOW: . . . .

. . . .

. . . .

FOLLOW UP DATE: . . . . PUT FOLLOW UP REMINDER IN CALENDAR ☐

FOLLOW UP DATE: . . . . PUT FOLLOW UP REMINDER IN CALENDAR ☐

FOLLOW UP DATE: . . . . PUT FOLLOW UP REMINDER IN CALENDAR ☐

FIRST NAME . . . . LAST NAME . . . .

PHONE . . . . EMAIL . . . .

LENDER . . . . PURCHASE PRICE . . . .

PROPERTY TYPE: ☐ TOWNHOME ☐ SINGLE FAMILY ☐ CONDO

PUT IN DATABASE ☐ SEARCH PORTAL CREATED ☐

DETAILS / INFO TO KNOW: . . . .

. . . .

. . . .

FOLLOW UP DATE: . . . . PUT FOLLOW UP REMINDER IN CALENDAR ☐

FOLLOW UP DATE: . . . . PUT FOLLOW UP REMINDER IN CALENDAR ☐

FOLLOW UP DATE: . . . . PUT FOLLOW UP REMINDER IN CALENDAR ☐

FIRST NAME . . . . LAST NAME . . . .

PHONE . . . . EMAIL . . . .

LENDER . . . . PURCHASE PRICE . . . .

PROPERTY TYPE: ☐ TOWNHOME ☐ SINGLE FAMILY ☐ CONDO

PUT IN DATABASE ☐ SEARCH PORTAL CREATED ☐

DETAILS / INFO TO KNOW: . . . .

. . . .

. . . .

FOLLOW UP DATE: . . . . PUT FOLLOW UP REMINDER IN CALENDAR ☐

FOLLOW UP DATE: . . . . PUT FOLLOW UP REMINDER IN CALENDAR ☐

FOLLOW UP DATE: . . . . PUT FOLLOW UP REMINDER IN CALENDAR ☐

NEW LEAD TRACKERS

FIRST NAME . . . . LAST NAME . . . .

PHONE . . . . EMAIL . . . .

LENDER . . . . PURCHASE PRICE . . . .

PROPERTY TYPE: ☐ TOWNHOME ☐ SINGLE FAMILY ☐ CONDO

PUT IN DATABASE ☐ SEARCH PORTAL CREATED ☐

DETAILS / INFO TO KNOW: . . . .

. . . .

. . . .

FOLLOW UP DATE: . . . . PUT FOLLOW UP REMINDER IN CALENDAR ☐

FOLLOW UP DATE: . . . . PUT FOLLOW UP REMINDER IN CALENDAR ☐

FOLLOW UP DATE: . . . . PUT FOLLOW UP REMINDER IN CALENDAR ☐

FIRST NAME . . . . LAST NAME . . . .

PHONE . . . . EMAIL . . . .

LENDER . . . . PURCHASE PRICE . . . .

PROPERTY TYPE: ☐ TOWNHOME ☐ SINGLE FAMILY ☐ CONDO

PUT IN DATABASE ☐ SEARCH PORTAL CREATED ☐

DETAILS / INFO TO KNOW: . . . .

. . . .

. . . .

FOLLOW UP DATE: . . . . PUT FOLLOW UP REMINDER IN CALENDAR ☐

FOLLOW UP DATE: . . . . PUT FOLLOW UP REMINDER IN CALENDAR ☐

FOLLOW UP DATE: . . . . PUT FOLLOW UP REMINDER IN CALENDAR ☐

FIRST NAME . . . . LAST NAME . . . .

PHONE . . . . EMAIL . . . .

LENDER . . . . PURCHASE PRICE . . . .

PROPERTY TYPE: ☐ TOWNHOME ☐ SINGLE FAMILY ☐ CONDO

PUT IN DATABASE ☐ SEARCH PORTAL CREATED ☐

DETAILS / INFO TO KNOW: . . . .

. . . .

. . . .

FOLLOW UP DATE: . . . . PUT FOLLOW UP REMINDER IN CALENDAR ☐

FOLLOW UP DATE: . . . . PUT FOLLOW UP REMINDER IN CALENDAR ☐

FOLLOW UP DATE: . . . . PUT FOLLOW UP REMINDER IN CALENDAR ☐

NEW LEAD TRACKERS

FIRST NAME . . . . LAST NAME . . . .

PHONE . . . . EMAIL . . . .

LENDER . . . . PURCHASE PRICE . . . .

PROPERTY TYPE: ☐ TOWNHOME ☐ SINGLE FAMILY ☐ CONDO

PUT IN DATABASE ☐   SEARCH PORTAL CREATED ☐

DETAILS / INFO TO KNOW: . . . .

. . . .

. . . .

FOLLOW UP DATE: . . . . PUT FOLLOW UP REMINDER IN CALENDAR ☐

FOLLOW UP DATE: . . . . PUT FOLLOW UP REMINDER IN CALENDAR ☐

FOLLOW UP DATE: . . . . PUT FOLLOW UP REMINDER IN CALENDAR ☐

FIRST NAME . . . . LAST NAME . . . .

PHONE . . . . EMAIL . . . .

LENDER . . . . PURCHASE PRICE . . . .

PROPERTY TYPE: ☐ TOWNHOME ☐ SINGLE FAMILY ☐ CONDO

PUT IN DATABASE ☐   SEARCH PORTAL CREATED ☐

DETAILS / INFO TO KNOW: . . . .

. . . .

. . . .

FOLLOW UP DATE: . . . . PUT FOLLOW UP REMINDER IN CALENDAR ☐

FOLLOW UP DATE: . . . . PUT FOLLOW UP REMINDER IN CALENDAR ☐

FOLLOW UP DATE: . . . . PUT FOLLOW UP REMINDER IN CALENDAR ☐

FIRST NAME . . . . LAST NAME . . . .

PHONE . . . . EMAIL . . . .

LENDER . . . . PURCHASE PRICE . . . .

PROPERTY TYPE: ☐ TOWNHOME ☐ SINGLE FAMILY ☐ CONDO

PUT IN DATABASE ☐   SEARCH PORTAL CREATED ☐

DETAILS / INFO TO KNOW: . . . .

. . . .

. . . .

FOLLOW UP DATE: . . . . PUT FOLLOW UP REMINDER IN CALENDAR ☐

FOLLOW UP DATE: . . . . PUT FOLLOW UP REMINDER IN CALENDAR ☐

FOLLOW UP DATE: . . . . PUT FOLLOW UP REMINDER IN CALENDAR ☐

NEW LEAD TRACKERS

FIRST NAME . . . . LAST NAME . . . .

PHONE . . . . EMAIL

LENDER . . . . PURCHASE PRICE . . . .

PROPERTY TYPE: ☐ TOWNHOME ☐ SINGLE FAMILY ☐ CONDO

PUT IN DATABASE ☐   SEARCH PORTAL CREATED ☐

DETAILS / INFO TO KNOW: . . . .

. . . .

. . . .

FOLLOW UP DATE: . . . . PUT FOLLOW UP REMINDER IN CALENDAR ☐

FOLLOW UP DATE: . . . . PUT FOLLOW UP REMINDER IN CALENDAR ☐

FOLLOW UP DATE: . . . . PUT FOLLOW UP REMINDER IN CALENDAR ☐

FIRST NAME . . . . LAST NAME . . . .

PHONE . . . . EMAIL

LENDER . . . . PURCHASE PRICE

PROPERTY TYPE: ☐ TOWNHOME ☐ SINGLE FAMILY ☐ CONDO

PUT IN DATABASE ☐   SEARCH PORTAL CREATED ☐

DETAILS / INFO TO KNOW: . . . .

. . . .

. . . .

FOLLOW UP DATE: . . . . PUT FOLLOW UP REMINDER IN CALENDAR ☐

FOLLOW UP DATE: . . . . PUT FOLLOW UP REMINDER IN CALENDAR ☐

FOLLOW UP DATE: . . . . PUT FOLLOW UP REMINDER IN CALENDAR ☐

FIRST NAME . . . . LAST NAME . . . .

PHONE . . . . EMAIL

LENDER . . . . PURCHASE PRICE . . . .

PROPERTY TYPE: ☐ TOWNHOME ☐ SINGLE FAMILY ☐ CONDO

PUT IN DATABASE ☐   SEARCH PORTAL CREATED ☐

DETAILS / INFO TO KNOW: . . . .

. . . .

. . . .

FOLLOW UP DATE: . . . . PUT FOLLOW UP REMINDER IN CALENDAR ☐

FOLLOW UP DATE: . . . . PUT FOLLOW UP REMINDER IN CALENDAR ☐

FOLLOW UP DATE: . . . . PUT FOLLOW UP REMINDER IN CALENDAR ☐

NEW LEAD TRACKERS

FIRST NAME . . . . LAST NAME . . . .

PHONE . . . . EMAIL . . . .

LENDER . . . . PURCHASE PRICE . . . .

PROPERTY TYPE: ☐ TOWNHOME ☐ SINGLE FAMILY ☐ CONDO

PUT IN DATABASE ☐ SEARCH PORTAL CREATED ☐

DETAILS / INFO TO KNOW: . . . .

. . . .

. . . .

FOLLOW UP DATE: . . . . PUT FOLLOW UP REMINDER IN CALENDAR ☐

FOLLOW UP DATE: . . . . PUT FOLLOW UP REMINDER IN CALENDAR ☐

FOLLOW UP DATE: . . . . PUT FOLLOW UP REMINDER IN CALENDAR ☐

FIRST NAME . . . . LAST NAME . . . .

PHONE . . . . EMAIL . . . .

LENDER . . . . PURCHASE PRICE . . . .

PROPERTY TYPE: ☐ TOWNHOME ☐ SINGLE FAMILY ☐ CONDO

PUT IN DATABASE ☐ SEARCH PORTAL CREATED ☐

DETAILS / INFO TO KNOW: . . . .

. . . .

. . . .

FOLLOW UP DATE: . . . . PUT FOLLOW UP REMINDER IN CALENDAR ☐

FOLLOW UP DATE: . . . . PUT FOLLOW UP REMINDER IN CALENDAR ☐

FOLLOW UP DATE: . . . . PUT FOLLOW UP REMINDER IN CALENDAR ☐

FIRST NAME . . . . LAST NAME . . . .

PHONE . . . . EMAIL . . . .

LENDER . . . . PURCHASE PRICE . . . .

PROPERTY TYPE: ☐ TOWNHOME ☐ SINGLE FAMILY ☐ CONDO

PUT IN DATABASE ☐ SEARCH PORTAL CREATED ☐

DETAILS / INFO TO KNOW: . . . .

. . . .

. . . .

FOLLOW UP DATE: . . . . PUT FOLLOW UP REMINDER IN CALENDAR ☐

FOLLOW UP DATE: . . . . PUT FOLLOW UP REMINDER IN CALENDAR ☐

FOLLOW UP DATE: . . . . PUT FOLLOW UP REMINDER IN CALENDAR ☐

NEW LEAD TRACKERS

FIRST NAME . . . . LAST NAME . . . .

PHONE . . . . EMAIL

LENDER . . . . PURCHASE PRICE . . . .

PROPERTY TYPE: ☐ TOWNHOME ☐ SINGLE FAMILY ☐ CONDO

PUT IN DATABASE ☐ SEARCH PORTAL CREATED ☐

DETAILS / INFO TO KNOW: . . . .

. . . .

. . . .

FOLLOW UP DATE: . . . . PUT FOLLOW UP REMINDER IN CALENDAR ☐

FOLLOW UP DATE: . . . . PUT FOLLOW UP REMINDER IN CALENDAR ☐

FOLLOW UP DATE: . . . . PUT FOLLOW UP REMINDER IN CALENDAR ☐

FIRST NAME . . . . LAST NAME . . . .

PHONE . . . . EMAIL

LENDER . . . . PURCHASE PRICE

PROPERTY TYPE: ☐ TOWNHOME ☐ SINGLE FAMILY ☐ CONDO

PUT IN DATABASE ☐ SEARCH PORTAL CREATED ☐

DETAILS / INFO TO KNOW: . . . .

. . . .

. . . .

FOLLOW UP DATE: . . . . PUT FOLLOW UP REMINDER IN CALENDAR ☐

FOLLOW UP DATE: . . . . PUT FOLLOW UP REMINDER IN CALENDAR ☐

FOLLOW UP DATE: . . . . PUT FOLLOW UP REMINDER IN CALENDAR ☐

FIRST NAME . . . . LAST NAME . . . .

PHONE . . . . EMAIL

LENDER . . . . PURCHASE PRICE . . . .

PROPERTY TYPE: ☐ TOWNHOME ☐ SINGLE FAMILY ☐ CONDO

PUT IN DATABASE ☐ SEARCH PORTAL CREATED ☐

DETAILS / INFO TO KNOW: . . . .

. . . .

. . . .

FOLLOW UP DATE: . . . . PUT FOLLOW UP REMINDER IN CALENDAR ☐

FOLLOW UP DATE: . . . . PUT FOLLOW UP REMINDER IN CALENDAR ☐

FOLLOW UP DATE: . . . . PUT FOLLOW UP REMINDER IN CALENDAR ☐

NEW LEAD TRACKERS

FIRST NAME . . . . LAST NAME . . . .

PHONE . . . . EMAIL . . . .

LENDER . . . . PURCHASE PRICE . . . .

PROPERTY TYPE: ☐ TOWNHOME ☐ SINGLE FAMILY ☐ CONDO

PUT IN DATABASE ☐ SEARCH PORTAL CREATED ☐

DETAILS / INFO TO KNOW: . . . .

. . . .

. . . .

FOLLOW UP DATE: . . . . PUT FOLLOW UP REMINDER IN CALENDAR ☐

FOLLOW UP DATE: . . . . PUT FOLLOW UP REMINDER IN CALENDAR ☐

FOLLOW UP DATE: . . . . PUT FOLLOW UP REMINDER IN CALENDAR ☐

FIRST NAME . . . . LAST NAME . . . .

PHONE . . . . EMAIL . . . .

LENDER . . . . PURCHASE PRICE . . . .

PROPERTY TYPE: ☐ TOWNHOME ☐ SINGLE FAMILY ☐ CONDO

PUT IN DATABASE ☐ SEARCH PORTAL CREATED ☐

DETAILS / INFO TO KNOW: . . . .

. . . .

. . . .

FOLLOW UP DATE: . . . . PUT FOLLOW UP REMINDER IN CALENDAR ☐

FOLLOW UP DATE: . . . . PUT FOLLOW UP REMINDER IN CALENDAR ☐

FOLLOW UP DATE: . . . . PUT FOLLOW UP REMINDER IN CALENDAR ☐

FIRST NAME . . . . LAST NAME . . . .

PHONE . . . . EMAIL . . . .

LENDER . . . . PURCHASE PRICE . . . .

PROPERTY TYPE: ☐ TOWNHOME ☐ SINGLE FAMILY ☐ CONDO

PUT IN DATABASE ☐ SEARCH PORTAL CREATED ☐

DETAILS / INFO TO KNOW: . . . .

. . . .

. . . .

FOLLOW UP DATE: . . . . PUT FOLLOW UP REMINDER IN CALENDAR ☐

FOLLOW UP DATE: . . . . PUT FOLLOW UP REMINDER IN CALENDAR ☐

FOLLOW UP DATE: . . . . PUT FOLLOW UP REMINDER IN CALENDAR

NEW LEAD TRACKERS

FIRST NAME . . . . LAST NAME . . . .

PHONE . . . . EMAIL . . . .

LENDER . . . . PURCHASE PRICE . . . .

PROPERTY TYPE: ☐ TOWNHOME ☐ SINGLE FAMILY ☐ CONDO

PUT IN DATABASE ☐ SEARCH PORTAL CREATED ☐

DETAILS / INFO TO KNOW: . . . .

. . . .

. . . .

FOLLOW UP DATE: . . . . PUT FOLLOW UP REMINDER IN CALENDAR ☐

FOLLOW UP DATE: . . . . PUT FOLLOW UP REMINDER IN CALENDAR ☐

FOLLOW UP DATE: . . . . PUT FOLLOW UP REMINDER IN CALENDAR ☐

FIRST NAME . . . . LAST NAME . . . .

PHONE . . . . EMAIL . . . .

LENDER . . . . PURCHASE PRICE . . . .

PROPERTY TYPE: ☐ TOWNHOME ☐ SINGLE FAMILY ☐ CONDO

PUT IN DATABASE ☐ SEARCH PORTAL CREATED ☐

DETAILS / INFO TO KNOW: . . . .

. . . .

. . . .

FOLLOW UP DATE: . . . . PUT FOLLOW UP REMINDER IN CALENDAR ☐

FOLLOW UP DATE: . . . . PUT FOLLOW UP REMINDER IN CALENDAR ☐

FOLLOW UP DATE: . . . . PUT FOLLOW UP REMINDER IN CALENDAR ☐

FIRST NAME . . . . LAST NAME . . . .

PHONE . . . . EMAIL . . . .

LENDER . . . . PURCHASE PRICE . . . .

PROPERTY TYPE: ☐ TOWNHOME ☐ SINGLE FAMILY ☐ CONDO

PUT IN DATABASE ☐ SEARCH PORTAL CREATED ☐

DETAILS / INFO TO KNOW: . . . .

. . . .

. . . .

FOLLOW UP DATE: . . . . PUT FOLLOW UP REMINDER IN CALENDAR ☐

FOLLOW UP DATE: . . . . PUT FOLLOW UP REMINDER IN CALENDAR ☐

FOLLOW UP DATE: . . . . PUT FOLLOW UP REMINDER IN CALENDAR ☐

NEW LEAD TRACKERS

FIRST NAME . . . . LAST NAME . . . .

PHONE . . . . EMAIL . . . .

LENDER . . . . PURCHASE PRICE . . . .

PROPERTY TYPE: ☐ TOWNHOME ☐ SINGLE FAMILY ☐ CONDO

PUT IN DATABASE ☐ SEARCH PORTAL CREATED ☐

DETAILS / INFO TO KNOW: . . . .

. . . .

. . . .

FOLLOW UP DATE: . . . . PUT FOLLOW UP REMINDER IN CALENDAR ☐

FOLLOW UP DATE: . . . . PUT FOLLOW UP REMINDER IN CALENDAR ☐

FOLLOW UP DATE: . . . . PUT FOLLOW UP REMINDER IN CALENDAR ☐

FIRST NAME . . . . LAST NAME . . . .

PHONE . . . . EMAIL . . . .

LENDER . . . . PURCHASE PRICE . . . .

PROPERTY TYPE: ☐ TOWNHOME ☐ SINGLE FAMILY ☐ CONDO

PUT IN DATABASE ☐ SEARCH PORTAL CREATED ☐

DETAILS / INFO TO KNOW: . . . .

. . . .

. . . .

FOLLOW UP DATE: . . . . PUT FOLLOW UP REMINDER IN CALENDAR ☐

FOLLOW UP DATE: . . . . PUT FOLLOW UP REMINDER IN CALENDAR ☐

FOLLOW UP DATE: . . . . PUT FOLLOW UP REMINDER IN CALENDAR ☐

FIRST NAME . . . . LAST NAME . . . .

PHONE . . . . EMAIL . . . .

LENDER . . . . PURCHASE PRICE . . . .

PROPERTY TYPE: ☐ TOWNHOME ☐ SINGLE FAMILY ☐ CONDO

PUT IN DATABASE ☐ SEARCH PORTAL CREATED ☐

DETAILS / INFO TO KNOW: . . . .

. . . .

. . . .

FOLLOW UP DATE: . . . . PUT FOLLOW UP REMINDER IN CALENDAR ☐

FOLLOW UP DATE: . . . . PUT FOLLOW UP REMINDER IN CALENDAR ☐

FOLLOW UP DATE: . . . . PUT FOLLOW UP REMINDER IN CALENDAR ☐

FIRST NAME . . . . LAST NAME . . . .

PHONE . . . . EMAIL . . . .

LENDER . . . . PURCHASE PRICE . . . .

PROPERTY TYPE: ☐ TOWNHOME ☐ SINGLE FAMILY ☐ CONDO

PUT IN DATABASE ☐ SEARCH PORTAL CREATED ☐

DETAILS / INFO TO KNOW: . . . .

. . . .

. . . .

FOLLOW UP DATE: . . . . PUT FOLLOW UP REMINDER IN CALENDAR ☐

FOLLOW UP DATE: . . . . PUT FOLLOW UP REMINDER IN CALENDAR ☐

FOLLOW UP DATE: . . . . PUT FOLLOW UP REMINDER IN CALENDAR ☐

FIRST NAME . . . . LAST NAME . . . .

PHONE . . . . EMAIL . . . .

LENDER . . . . PURCHASE PRICE . . . .

PROPERTY TYPE: ☐ TOWNHOME ☐ SINGLE FAMILY ☐ CONDO

PUT IN DATABASE ☐ SEARCH PORTAL CREATED ☐

DETAILS / INFO TO KNOW: . . . .

. . . .

. . . .

FOLLOW UP DATE: . . . . PUT FOLLOW UP REMINDER IN CALENDAR ☐

FOLLOW UP DATE: . . . . PUT FOLLOW UP REMINDER IN CALENDAR ☐

FOLLOW UP DATE: . . . . PUT FOLLOW UP REMINDER IN CALENDAR ☐

FIRST NAME . . . . LAST NAME . . . .

PHONE . . . . EMAIL . . . .

LENDER . . . . PURCHASE PRICE . . . .

PROPERTY TYPE: ☐ TOWNHOME ☐ SINGLE FAMILY ☐ CONDO

PUT IN DATABASE ☐ SEARCH PORTAL CREATED ☐

DETAILS / INFO TO KNOW: . . . .

. . . .

. . . .

FOLLOW UP DATE: . . . . PUT FOLLOW UP REMINDER IN CALENDAR ☐

FOLLOW UP DATE: . . . . PUT FOLLOW UP REMINDER IN CALENDAR ☐

FOLLOW UP DATE: . . . . PUT FOLLOW UP REMINDER IN CALENDAR ☐

NEW LEAD TRACKERS

FIRST NAME . . . . LAST NAME . . . .

PHONE . . . . EMAIL . . . .

LENDER . . . . PURCHASE PRICE . . . .

PROPERTY TYPE: ☐ TOWNHOME ☐ SINGLE FAMILY ☐ CONDO

PUT IN DATABASE ☐   SEARCH PORTAL CREATED ☐

DETAILS / INFO TO KNOW: . . . .

. . . .

. . . .

FOLLOW UP DATE: . . . . PUT FOLLOW UP REMINDER IN CALENDAR ☐

FOLLOW UP DATE: . . . . PUT FOLLOW UP REMINDER IN CALENDAR ☐

FOLLOW UP DATE: . . . . PUT FOLLOW UP REMINDER IN CALENDAR ☐

FIRST NAME . . . . LAST NAME . . . .

PHONE . . . . EMAIL . . . .

LENDER . . . . PURCHASE PRICE . . . .

PROPERTY TYPE: ☐ TOWNHOME ☐ SINGLE FAMILY ☐ CONDO

PUT IN DATABASE ☐   SEARCH PORTAL CREATED ☐

DETAILS / INFO TO KNOW: . . . .

. . . .

. . . .

FOLLOW UP DATE: . . . . PUT FOLLOW UP REMINDER IN CALENDAR ☐

FOLLOW UP DATE: . . . . PUT FOLLOW UP REMINDER IN CALENDAR ☐

FOLLOW UP DATE: . . . . PUT FOLLOW UP REMINDER IN CALENDAR ☐

FIRST NAME . . . . LAST NAME . . . .

PHONE . . . . EMAIL . . . .

LENDER . . . . PURCHASE PRICE . . . .

PROPERTY TYPE: ☐ TOWNHOME ☐ SINGLE FAMILY ☐ CONDO

PUT IN DATABASE ☐   SEARCH PORTAL CREATED ☐

DETAILS / INFO TO KNOW: . . . .

. . . .

. . . .

FOLLOW UP DATE: . . . . PUT FOLLOW UP REMINDER IN CALENDAR ☐

FOLLOW UP DATE: . . . . PUT FOLLOW UP REMINDER IN CALENDAR ☐

FOLLOW UP DATE: . . . . PUT FOLLOW UP REMINDER IN CALENDAR ☐

NEW LEAD TRACKERS

FIRST NAME . . . . LAST NAME . . . .

PHONE . . . . EMAIL . . . .

LENDER . . . . PURCHASE PRICE . . . .

PROPERTY TYPE: ☐ TOWNHOME   ☐ SINGLE FAMILY   ☐ CONDO

PUT IN DATABASE ☐   SEARCH PORTAL CREATED ☐

DETAILS / INFO TO KNOW: . . . .

. . . .

. . . .

FOLLOW UP DATE: . . . . PUT FOLLOW UP REMINDER IN CALENDAR ☐

FOLLOW UP DATE: . . . . PUT FOLLOW UP REMINDER IN CALENDAR ☐

FOLLOW UP DATE: . . . . PUT FOLLOW UP REMINDER IN CALENDAR ☐

FIRST NAME . . . . LAST NAME . . . .

PHONE . . . . EMAIL . . . .

LENDER . . . . PURCHASE PRICE . . . .

PROPERTY TYPE: ☐ TOWNHOME   ☐ SINGLE FAMILY   ☐ CONDO

PUT IN DATABASE ☐   SEARCH PORTAL CREATED ☐

DETAILS / INFO TO KNOW: . . . .

. . . .

. . . .

FOLLOW UP DATE: . . . . PUT FOLLOW UP REMINDER IN CALENDAR ☐

FOLLOW UP DATE: . . . . PUT FOLLOW UP REMINDER IN CALENDAR ☐

FOLLOW UP DATE: . . . . PUT FOLLOW UP REMINDER IN CALENDAR ☐

FIRST NAME . . . . LAST NAME . . . .

PHONE . . . . EMAIL . . . .

LENDER . . . . PURCHASE PRICE . . . .

PROPERTY TYPE: ☐ TOWNHOME   ☐ SINGLE FAMILY   ☐ CONDO

PUT IN DATABASE ☐   SEARCH PORTAL CREATED ☐

DETAILS / INFO TO KNOW: . . . .

. . . .

. . . .

FOLLOW UP DATE: . . . . PUT FOLLOW UP REMINDER IN CALENDAR ☐

FOLLOW UP DATE: . . . . PUT FOLLOW UP REMINDER IN CALENDAR ☐

FOLLOW UP DATE: . . . . PUT FOLLOW UP REMINDER IN CALENDAR ☐

NEW LEAD TRACKERS

FIRST NAME . . . . LAST NAME . . . .

PHONE . . . . EMAIL . . . .

LENDER . . . . PURCHASE PRICE . . . .

PROPERTY TYPE: ☐ TOWNHOME ☐ SINGLE FAMILY ☐ CONDO

PUT IN DATABASE ☐ SEARCH PORTAL CREATED ☐

DETAILS / INFO TO KNOW: . . . .

. . . .

. . . .

FOLLOW UP DATE: . . . . PUT FOLLOW UP REMINDER IN CALENDAR ☐

FOLLOW UP DATE: . . . . PUT FOLLOW UP REMINDER IN CALENDAR ☐

FOLLOW UP DATE: . . . . PUT FOLLOW UP REMINDER IN CALENDAR ☐

FIRST NAME . . . . LAST NAME . . . .

PHONE . . . . EMAIL . . . .

LENDER . . . . PURCHASE PRICE . . . .

PROPERTY TYPE: ☐ TOWNHOME ☐ SINGLE FAMILY ☐ CONDO

PUT IN DATABASE ☐ SEARCH PORTAL CREATED ☐

DETAILS / INFO TO KNOW: . . . .

. . . .

. . . .

FOLLOW UP DATE: . . . . PUT FOLLOW UP REMINDER IN CALENDAR ☐

FOLLOW UP DATE: . . . . PUT FOLLOW UP REMINDER IN CALENDAR ☐

FOLLOW UP DATE: . . . . PUT FOLLOW UP REMINDER IN CALENDAR ☐

FIRST NAME . . . . LAST NAME . . . .

PHONE . . . . EMAIL . . . .

LENDER . . . . PURCHASE PRICE . . . .

PROPERTY TYPE: ☐ TOWNHOME ☐ SINGLE FAMILY ☐ CONDO

PUT IN DATABASE ☐ SEARCH PORTAL CREATED ☐

DETAILS / INFO TO KNOW: . . . .

. . . .

. . . .

FOLLOW UP DATE: . . . . PUT FOLLOW UP REMINDER IN CALENDAR ☐

FOLLOW UP DATE: . . . . PUT FOLLOW UP REMINDER IN CALENDAR ☐

FOLLOW UP DATE: . . . . PUT FOLLOW UP REMINDER IN CALENDAR ☐

NEW LEAD TRACKERS

FIRST NAME . . . . LAST NAME . . . .

PHONE . . . . EMAIL . . . .

LENDER . . . . PURCHASE PRICE . . . .

PROPERTY TYPE: ☐ TOWNHOME ☐ SINGLE FAMILY ☐ CONDO

PUT IN DATABASE ☐   SEARCH PORTAL CREATED ☐

DETAILS / INFO TO KNOW: . . . .

. . . .

. . . .

FOLLOW UP DATE: . . . . PUT FOLLOW UP REMINDER IN CALENDAR ☐

FOLLOW UP DATE: . . . . PUT FOLLOW UP REMINDER IN CALENDAR ☐

FOLLOW UP DATE: . . . . PUT FOLLOW UP REMINDER IN CALENDAR ☐

FIRST NAME . . . . LAST NAME . . . .

PHONE . . . . EMAIL . . . .

LENDER . . . . PURCHASE PRICE . . . .

PROPERTY TYPE: ☐ TOWNHOME ☐ SINGLE FAMILY ☐ CONDO

PUT IN DATABASE ☐   SEARCH PORTAL CREATED ☐

DETAILS / INFO TO KNOW: . . . .

. . . .

. . . .

FOLLOW UP DATE: . . . . PUT FOLLOW UP REMINDER IN CALENDAR ☐

FOLLOW UP DATE: . . . . PUT FOLLOW UP REMINDER IN CALENDAR ☐

FOLLOW UP DATE: . . . . PUT FOLLOW UP REMINDER IN CALENDAR ☐

FIRST NAME . . . . LAST NAME . . . .

PHONE . . . . EMAIL . . . .

LENDER . . . . PURCHASE PRICE . . . .

PROPERTY TYPE: ☐ TOWNHOME ☐ SINGLE FAMILY ☐ CONDO

PUT IN DATABASE ☐   SEARCH PORTAL CREATED ☐

DETAILS / INFO TO KNOW: . . . .

. . . .

. . . .

FOLLOW UP DATE: . . . . PUT FOLLOW UP REMINDER IN CALENDAR ☐

FOLLOW UP DATE: . . . . PUT FOLLOW UP REMINDER IN CALENDAR ☐

FOLLOW UP DATE: . . . . PUT FOLLOW UP REMINDER IN CALENDAR ☐

NEW LEAD TRACKERS

FIRST NAME . . . . LAST NAME . . . .

PHONE . . . . EMAIL . . . .

LENDER . . . . PURCHASE PRICE . . . .

PROPERTY TYPE: ☐ TOWNHOME ☐ SINGLE FAMILY ☐ CONDO

PUT IN DATABASE ☐ SEARCH PORTAL CREATED ☐

DETAILS / INFO TO KNOW: . . . .

. . . .

. . . .

FOLLOW UP DATE: . . . . PUT FOLLOW UP REMINDER IN CALENDAR ☐

FOLLOW UP DATE: . . . . PUT FOLLOW UP REMINDER IN CALENDAR ☐

FOLLOW UP DATE: . . . . PUT FOLLOW UP REMINDER IN CALENDAR ☐

FIRST NAME . . . . LAST NAME . . . .

PHONE . . . . EMAIL . . . .

LENDER . . . . PURCHASE PRICE . . . .

PROPERTY TYPE: ☐ TOWNHOME ☐ SINGLE FAMILY ☐ CONDO

PUT IN DATABASE ☐ SEARCH PORTAL CREATED ☐

DETAILS / INFO TO KNOW: . . . .

. . . .

. . . .

FOLLOW UP DATE: . . . . PUT FOLLOW UP REMINDER IN CALENDAR ☐

FOLLOW UP DATE: . . . . PUT FOLLOW UP REMINDER IN CALENDAR ☐

FOLLOW UP DATE: . . . . PUT FOLLOW UP REMINDER IN CALENDAR ☐

FIRST NAME . . . . LAST NAME . . . .

PHONE . . . . EMAIL . . . .

LENDER . . . . PURCHASE PRICE . . . .

PROPERTY TYPE: ☐ TOWNHOME ☐ SINGLE FAMILY ☐ CONDO

PUT IN DATABASE ☐ SEARCH PORTAL CREATED ☐

DETAILS / INFO TO KNOW: . . . .

. . . .

. . . .

FOLLOW UP DATE: . . . . PUT FOLLOW UP REMINDER IN CALENDAR ☐

FOLLOW UP DATE: . . . . PUT FOLLOW UP REMINDER IN CALENDAR ☐

FOLLOW UP DATE: . . . . PUT FOLLOW UP REMINDER IN CALENDAR ☐

NEW LEAD TRACKERS

FIRST NAME . . . . LAST NAME . . . .

PHONE . . . . EMAIL . . . .

LENDER . . . . PURCHASE PRICE . . . .

PROPERTY TYPE: ☐ TOWNHOME ☐ SINGLE FAMILY ☐ CONDO

PUT IN DATABASE ☐ SEARCH PORTAL CREATED ☐

DETAILS / INFO TO KNOW: . . . .

. . . .

. . . .

FOLLOW UP DATE: . . . . PUT FOLLOW UP REMINDER IN CALENDAR ☐

FOLLOW UP DATE: . . . . PUT FOLLOW UP REMINDER IN CALENDAR ☐

FOLLOW UP DATE: . . . . PUT FOLLOW UP REMINDER IN CALENDAR ☐

FIRST NAME . . . . LAST NAME . . . .

PHONE . . . . EMAIL . . . .

LENDER . . . . PURCHASE PRICE . . . .

PROPERTY TYPE: ☐ TOWNHOME ☐ SINGLE FAMILY ☐ CONDO

PUT IN DATABASE ☐ SEARCH PORTAL CREATED ☐

DETAILS / INFO TO KNOW: . . . .

. . . .

. . . .

FOLLOW UP DATE: . . . . PUT FOLLOW UP REMINDER IN CALENDAR ☐

FOLLOW UP DATE: . . . . PUT FOLLOW UP REMINDER IN CALENDAR ☐

FOLLOW UP DATE: . . . . PUT FOLLOW UP REMINDER IN CALENDAR ☐

FIRST NAME . . . . LAST NAME . . . .

PHONE . . . . EMAIL . . . .

LENDER . . . . PURCHASE PRICE . . . .

PROPERTY TYPE: ☐ TOWNHOME ☐ SINGLE FAMILY ☐ CONDO

PUT IN DATABASE ☐ SEARCH PORTAL CREATED ☐

DETAILS / INFO TO KNOW: . . . .

. . . .

. . . .

FOLLOW UP DATE: . . . . PUT FOLLOW UP REMINDER IN CALENDAR ☐

FOLLOW UP DATE: . . . . PUT FOLLOW UP REMINDER IN CALENDAR ☐

FOLLOW UP DATE: . . . . PUT FOLLOW UP REMINDER IN CALENDAR ☐

FIRST NAME . . . . LAST NAME . . . .

PHONE . . . . EMAIL . . . .

LENDER . . . . PURCHASE PRICE . . . .

PROPERTY TYPE: ☐ TOWNHOME ☐ SINGLE FAMILY ☐ CONDO

PUT IN DATABASE ☐ SEARCH PORTAL CREATED ☐

DETAILS / INFO TO KNOW: . . . .

. . . .

. . . .

FOLLOW UP DATE: . . . . PUT FOLLOW UP REMINDER IN CALENDAR ☐

FOLLOW UP DATE: . . . . PUT FOLLOW UP REMINDER IN CALENDAR ☐

FOLLOW UP DATE: . . . . PUT FOLLOW UP REMINDER IN CALENDAR ☐

FIRST NAME . . . . LAST NAME . . . .

PHONE . . . . EMAIL . . . .

LENDER . . . . PURCHASE PRICE . . . .

PROPERTY TYPE: ☐ TOWNHOME ☐ SINGLE FAMILY ☐ CONDO

PUT IN DATABASE ☐ SEARCH PORTAL CREATED ☐

DETAILS / INFO TO KNOW: . . . .

. . . .

. . . .

FOLLOW UP DATE: . . . . PUT FOLLOW UP REMINDER IN CALENDAR ☐

FOLLOW UP DATE: . . . . PUT FOLLOW UP REMINDER IN CALENDAR ☐

FOLLOW UP DATE: . . . . PUT FOLLOW UP REMINDER IN CALENDAR ☐

FIRST NAME . . . . LAST NAME . . . .

PHONE . . . . EMAIL . . . .

LENDER . . . . PURCHASE PRICE . . . .

PROPERTY TYPE: ☐ TOWNHOME ☐ SINGLE FAMILY ☐ CONDO

PUT IN DATABASE ☐ SEARCH PORTAL CREATED ☐

DETAILS / INFO TO KNOW: . . . .

. . . .

. . . .

FOLLOW UP DATE: . . . . PUT FOLLOW UP REMINDER IN CALENDAR ☐

FOLLOW UP DATE: . . . . PUT FOLLOW UP REMINDER IN CALENDAR ☐

FOLLOW UP DATE: . . . . PUT FOLLOW UP REMINDER IN CALENDAR ☐

NEW LEAD TRACKERS

FIRST NAME . . . . LAST NAME . . . .

PHONE . . . . EMAIL . . . .

LENDER . . . . PURCHASE PRICE . . . .

PROPERTY TYPE: ☐ TOWNHOME ☐ SINGLE FAMILY ☐ CONDO

PUT IN DATABASE ☐   SEARCH PORTAL CREATED ☐

DETAILS / INFO TO KNOW: . . . .

. . . .

. . . .

FOLLOW UP DATE: . . . . PUT FOLLOW UP REMINDER IN CALENDAR ☐

FOLLOW UP DATE: . . . . PUT FOLLOW UP REMINDER IN CALENDAR ☐

FOLLOW UP DATE: . . . . PUT FOLLOW UP REMINDER IN CALENDAR ☐

FIRST NAME . . . . LAST NAME . . . .

PHONE . . . . EMAIL . . . .

LENDER . . . . PURCHASE PRICE . . . .

PROPERTY TYPE: ☐ TOWNHOME ☐ SINGLE FAMILY ☐ CONDO

PUT IN DATABASE ☐   SEARCH PORTAL CREATED ☐

DETAILS / INFO TO KNOW: . . . .

. . . .

. . . .

FOLLOW UP DATE: . . . . PUT FOLLOW UP REMINDER IN CALENDAR ☐

FOLLOW UP DATE: . . . . PUT FOLLOW UP REMINDER IN CALENDAR ☐

FOLLOW UP DATE: . . . . PUT FOLLOW UP REMINDER IN CALENDAR ☐

FIRST NAME . . . . LAST NAME . . . .

PHONE . . . . EMAIL . . . .

LENDER . . . . PURCHASE PRICE . . . .

PROPERTY TYPE: ☐ TOWNHOME ☐ SINGLE FAMILY ☐ CONDO

PUT IN DATABASE ☐   SEARCH PORTAL CREATED ☐

DETAILS / INFO TO KNOW: . . . .

. . . .

. . . .

FOLLOW UP DATE: . . . . PUT FOLLOW UP REMINDER IN CALENDAR ☐

FOLLOW UP DATE: . . . . PUT FOLLOW UP REMINDER IN CALENDAR ☐

FOLLOW UP DATE: . . . . PUT FOLLOW UP REMINDER IN CALENDAR ☐

FIRST NAME . . . . LAST NAME . . . .

PHONE . . . . EMAIL . . . .

LENDER . . . . PURCHASE PRICE . . . .

PROPERTY TYPE: ☐ TOWNHOME ☐ SINGLE FAMILY ☐ CONDO

PUT IN DATABASE ☐ SEARCH PORTAL CREATED ☐

DETAILS / INFO TO KNOW: . . . .

. . . .

. . . .

FOLLOW UP DATE: . . . . PUT FOLLOW UP REMINDER IN CALENDAR ☐

FOLLOW UP DATE: . . . . PUT FOLLOW UP REMINDER IN CALENDAR ☐

FOLLOW UP DATE: . . . . PUT FOLLOW UP REMINDER IN CALENDAR ☐

FIRST NAME . . . . LAST NAME . . . .

PHONE . . . . EMAIL . . . .

LENDER . . . . PURCHASE PRICE . . . .

PROPERTY TYPE: ☐ TOWNHOME ☐ SINGLE FAMILY ☐ CONDO

PUT IN DATABASE ☐ SEARCH PORTAL CREATED ☐

DETAILS / INFO TO KNOW: . . . .

. . . .

. . . .

FOLLOW UP DATE: . . . . PUT FOLLOW UP REMINDER IN CALENDAR ☐

FOLLOW UP DATE: . . . . PUT FOLLOW UP REMINDER IN CALENDAR ☐

FOLLOW UP DATE: . . . . PUT FOLLOW UP REMINDER IN CALENDAR ☐

FIRST NAME . . . . LAST NAME . . . .

PHONE . . . . EMAIL . . . .

LENDER . . . . PURCHASE PRICE . . . .

PROPERTY TYPE: ☐ TOWNHOME ☐ SINGLE FAMILY ☐ CONDO

PUT IN DATABASE ☐ SEARCH PORTAL CREATED ☐

DETAILS / INFO TO KNOW: . . . .

. . . .

. . . .

FOLLOW UP DATE: . . . . PUT FOLLOW UP REMINDER IN CALENDAR ☐

FOLLOW UP DATE: . . . . PUT FOLLOW UP REMINDER IN CALENDAR ☐

FOLLOW UP DATE: . . . . PUT FOLLOW UP REMINDER IN CALENDAR ☐

Become the hardest working person you know.

Listing Management Checklists

Listing Management Checklist

PRE-LISTING

- LISTING APPOINTMENT SET
- PREVIEW COMPARABLES
- RUN COMPARABLES
- CREATE CMA
- EDIT LISTING PRESENTATION
- PREPARE LISTING PAPERWORK
- PREPARE LISTING FOLDER FOR CLIENT

CREATE LISTING

- SCHEDULE PHOTOGRAPHER
- CREATE VIDEO TOUR
- INPUT DATA IN MLS
- SCAN / UPLOAD DOCUMENTS INTO MLS
- INSTALL YARD SIGN
- CREATE "JUST LISTED" SOCIAL MEDIA POST
- CREATE "JUST LISTED" POSTCARDS
- EMAIL LISTING TO DATABASE

OPEN HOUSE

- SCHEDULE OPEN HOUSE
- SCHEDULE BROKERS OPEN HOUSE
- PREPARE PROPERTY MARKETING MATERIALS
- PROMOTE OPEN HOUSE TO OTHER AGENTS
- PROMOTE OPEN HOUSE ON SOCIAL MEDIA

ON THE MARKET

- MONITOR NEIGHBORHOOD MARKET CHANGES
- COMMUNICATE CHANGES TO CLIENTS
- GATHER SHOWING FEEDBACK
- CREATE SHOWING FEEDBACK REPORT
- REVIEW PRICING STRATEGY

SETTING CLIENT EXPECTATIONS

- DISCUSS CLIENTS GOALS
- IDENTIFY AREAS OF PROPERTY THAT NEED IMPROVING
- ADDRESS DECLUTTERING, DEPERSONALIZING, REPAIRS
- DISCUSS PRICING AND TIMING STRATEGY
- DISCUSS SHOWING PREFERENCES & APPROVALS
- PRELIMINARY NET SHEET

NOTES

Listing Management Checklist

PRE-LISTING

- [ ] LISTING APPOINTMENT SET
- [ ] PREVIEW COMPARABLES
- [ ] RUN COMPARABLES
- [ ] CREATE CMA
- [ ] EDIT LISTING PRESENTATION
- [ ] PREPARE LISTING PAPERWORK
- [ ] PREPARE LISTING FOLDER FOR CLIENT

CREATE LISTING

- [ ] SCHEDULE PHOTOGRAPHER
- [ ] CREATE VIDEO TOUR
- [ ] INPUT DATA IN MLS
- [ ] SCAN / UPLOAD DOCUMENTS INTO MLS
- [ ] INSTALL YARD SIGN
- [ ] CREATE "JUST LISTED" SOCIAL MEDIA POST
- [ ] CREATE "JUST LISTED" POSTCARDS
- [ ] EMAIL LISTING TO DATABASE

OPEN HOUSE

- [ ] SCHEDULE OPEN HOUSE
- [ ] SCHEDULE BROKERS OPEN HOUSE
- [ ] PREPARE PROPERTY MARKETING MATERIALS
- [ ] PROMOTE OPEN HOUSE TO OTHER AGENTS
- [ ] PROMOTE OPEN HOUSE ON SOCIAL MEDIA

ON THE MARKET

- [ ] MONITOR NEIGHBORHOOD MARKET CHANGES
- [ ] COMMUNICATE CHANGES TO CLIENTS
- [ ] GATHER SHOWING FEEDBACK
- [ ] CREATE SHOWING FEEDBACK REPORT
- [ ] REVIEW PRICING STRATEGY

SETTING CLIENT EXPECTATIONS

- [ ] DISCUSS CLIENTS GOALS
- [ ] IDENTIFY AREAS OF PROPERTY THAT NEED IMPROVING
- [ ] ADDRESS DECLUTTERING, DEPERSONALIZING, REPAIRS
- [ ] DISCUSS PRICING AND TIMING STRATEGY
- [ ] DISCUSS SHOWING PREFERENCES & APPROVALS
- [ ] PRELIMINARY NET SHEET

NOTES

Listing Management Checklist

PRE-LISTING

- [ ] LISTING APPOINTMENT SET
- [ ] PREVIEW COMPARABLES
- [ ] RUN COMPARABLES
- [ ] CREATE CMA
- [ ] EDIT LISTING PRESENTATION
- [ ] PREPARE LISTING PAPERWORK
- [ ] PREPARE LISTING FOLDER FOR CLIENT

CREATE LISTING

- [ ] SCHEDULE PHOTOGRAPHER
- [ ] CREATE VIDEO TOUR
- [ ] INPUT DATA IN MLS
- [ ] SCAN / UPLOAD DOCUMENTS INTO MLS
- [ ] INSTALL YARD SIGN
- [ ] CREATE "JUST LISTED" SOCIAL MEDIA POST
- [ ] CREATE "JUST LISTED" POSTCARDS
- [ ] EMAIL LISTING TO DATABASE

OPEN HOUSE

- [ ] SCHEDULE OPEN HOUSE
- [ ] SCHEDULE BROKERS OPEN HOUSE
- [ ] PREPARE PROPERTY MARKETING MATERIALS
- [ ] PROMOTE OPEN HOUSE TO OTHER AGENTS
- [ ] PROMOTE OPEN HOUSE ON SOCIAL MEDIA

ON THE MARKET

- [ ] MONITOR NEIGHBORHOOD MARKET CHANGES
- [ ] COMMUNICATE CHANGES TO CLIENTS
- [ ] GATHER SHOWING FEEDBACK
- [ ] CREATE SHOWING FEEDBACK REPORT
- [ ] REVIEW PRICING STRATEGY

SETTING CLIENT EXPECTATIONS

- [ ] DISCUSS CLIENTS GOALS
- [ ] IDENTIFY AREAS OF PROPERTY THAT NEED IMPROVING
- [ ] ADDRESS DECLUTTERING, DEPERSONALIZING, REPAIRS
- [ ] DISCUSS PRICING AND TIMING STRATEGY
- [ ] DISCUSS SHOWING PREFERENCES & APPROVALS
- [ ] PRELIMINARY NET SHEET

NOTES

Listing Management
Checklist

PRE-LISTING

- [ ] LISTING APPOINTMENT SET
- [ ] PREVIEW COMPARABLES
- [ ] RUN COMPARABLES
- [ ] CREATE CMA
- [ ] EDIT LISTING PRESENTATION
- [ ] PREPARE LISTING PAPERWORK
- [ ] PREPARE LISTING FOLDER FOR CLIENT

CREATE LISTING

- [ ] SCHEDULE PHOTOGRAPHER
- [ ] CREATE VIDEO TOUR
- [ ] INPUT DATA IN MLS
- [ ] SCAN / UPLOAD DOCUMENTS INTO MLS
- [ ] INSTALL YARD SIGN
- [ ] CREATE "JUST LISTED" SOCIAL MEDIA POST
- [ ] CREATE "JUST LISTED" POSTCARDS
- [ ] EMAIL LISTING TO DATABASE

OPEN HOUSE

- [ ] SCHEDULE OPEN HOUSE
- [ ] SCHEDULE BROKERS OPEN HOUSE
- [ ] PREPARE PROPERTY MARKETING MATERIALS
- [ ] PROMOTE OPEN HOUSE TO OTHER AGENTS
- [ ] PROMOTE OPEN HOUSE ON SOCIAL MEDIA

ON THE MARKET

- [ ] MONITOR NEIGHBORHOOD MARKET CHANGES
- [ ] COMMUNICATE CHANGES TO CLIENTS
- [ ] GATHER SHOWING FEEDBACK
- [ ] CREATE SHOWING FEEDBACK REPORT
- [ ] REVIEW PRICING STRATEGY

SETTING CLIENT EXPECTATIONS

- [ ] DISCUSS CLIENTS GOALS
- [ ] IDENTIFY AREAS OF PROPERTY THAT NEED IMPROVING
- [ ] ADDRESS DECLUTTERING, DEPERSONALIZING, REPAIRS
- [ ] DISCUSS PRICING AND TIMING STRATEGY
- [ ] DISCUSS SHOWING PREFERENCES & APPROVALS
- [ ] PRELIMINARY NET SHEET

NOTES

Listing Management Checklist

PRE-LISTING

- [ ] LISTING APPOINTMENT SET
- [ ] PREVIEW COMPARABLES
- [ ] RUN COMPARABLES
- [ ] CREATE CMA
- [ ] EDIT LISTING PRESENTATION
- [ ] PREPARE LISTING PAPERWORK
- [ ] PREPARE LISTING FOLDER FOR CLIENT

CREATE LISTING

- [ ] SCHEDULE PHOTOGRAPHER
- [ ] CREATE VIDEO TOUR
- [ ] INPUT DATA IN MLS
- [ ] SCAN / UPLOAD DOCUMENTS INTO MLS
- [ ] INSTALL YARD SIGN
- [ ] CREATE "JUST LISTED" SOCIAL MEDIA POST
- [ ] CREATE "JUST LISTED" POSTCARDS
- [ ] EMAIL LISTING TO DATABASE

OPEN HOUSE

- [ ] SCHEDULE OPEN HOUSE
- [ ] SCHEDULE BROKERS OPEN HOUSE
- [ ] PREPARE PROPERTY MARKETING MATERIALS
- [ ] PROMOTE OPEN HOUSE TO OTHER AGENTS
- [ ] PROMOTE OPEN HOUSE ON SOCIAL MEDIA

ON THE MARKET

- [ ] MONITOR NEIGHBORHOOD MARKET CHANGES
- [ ] COMMUNICATE CHANGES TO CLIENTS
- [ ] GATHER SHOWING FEEDBACK
- [ ] CREATE SHOWING FEEDBACK REPORT
- [ ] REVIEW PRICING STRATEGY

SETTING CLIENT EXPECTATIONS

- [ ] DISCUSS CLIENTS GOALS
- [ ] IDENTIFY AREAS OF PROPERTY THAT NEED IMPROVING
- [ ] ADDRESS DECLUTTERING, DEPERSONALIZING, REPAIRS
- [ ] DISCUSS PRICING AND TIMING STRATEGY
- [ ] DISCUSS SHOWING PREFERENCES & APPROVALS
- [ ] PRELIMINARY NET SHEET

NOTES

Listing Management Checklist

PRE-LISTING

- [ ] LISTING APPOINTMENT SET
- [ ] PREVIEW COMPARABLES
- [ ] RUN COMPARABLES
- [ ] CREATE CMA
- [ ] EDIT LISTING PRESENTATION
- [ ] PREPARE LISTING PAPERWORK
- [ ] PREPARE LISTING FOLDER FOR CLIENT

CREATE LISTING

- [ ] SCHEDULE PHOTOGRAPHER
- [ ] CREATE VIDEO TOUR
- [ ] INPUT DATA IN MLS
- [ ] SCAN / UPLOAD DOCUMENTS INTO MLS
- [ ] INSTALL YARD SIGN
- [ ] CREATE "JUST LISTED" SOCIAL MEDIA POST
- [ ] CREATE "JUST LISTED" POSTCARDS
- [ ] EMAIL LISTING TO DATABASE

OPEN HOUSE

- [ ] SCHEDULE OPEN HOUSE
- [ ] SCHEDULE BROKERS OPEN HOUSE
- [ ] PREPARE PROPERTY MARKETING MATERIALS
- [ ] PROMOTE OPEN HOUSE TO OTHER AGENTS
- [ ] PROMOTE OPEN HOUSE ON SOCIAL MEDIA

ON THE MARKET

- [ ] MONITOR NEIGHBORHOOD MARKET CHANGES
- [ ] COMMUNICATE CHANGES TO CLIENTS
- [ ] GATHER SHOWING FEEDBACK
- [ ] CREATE SHOWING FEEDBACK REPORT
- [ ] REVIEW PRICING STRATEGY

SETTING CLIENT EXPECTATIONS

- [ ] DISCUSS CLIENTS GOALS
- [ ] IDENTIFY AREAS OF PROPERTY THAT NEED IMPROVING
- [ ] ADDRESS DECLUTTERING, DEPERSONALIZING, REPAIRS
- [ ] DISCUSS PRICING AND TIMING STRATEGY
- [ ] DISCUSS SHOWING PREFERENCES & APPROVALS
- [ ] PRELIMINARY NET SHEET

NOTES

Listing Management Checklist

PRE-LISTING

- [ ] LISTING APPOINTMENT SET
- [ ] PREVIEW COMPARABLES
- [ ] RUN COMPARABLES
- [ ] CREATE CMA
- [ ] EDIT LISTING PRESENTATION
- [ ] PREPARE LISTING PAPERWORK
- [ ] PREPARE LISTING FOLDER FOR CLIENT

CREATE LISTING

- [ ] SCHEDULE PHOTOGRAPHER
- [ ] CREATE VIDEO TOUR
- [ ] INPUT DATA IN MLS
- [ ] SCAN / UPLOAD DOCUMENTS INTO MLS
- [ ] INSTALL YARD SIGN
- [ ] CREATE "JUST LISTED" SOCIAL MEDIA POST
- [ ] CREATE "JUST LISTED" POSTCARDS
- [ ] EMAIL LISTING TO DATABASE

OPEN HOUSE

- [ ] SCHEDULE OPEN HOUSE
- [ ] SCHEDULE BROKERS OPEN HOUSE
- [ ] PREPARE PROPERTY MARKETING MATERIALS
- [ ] PROMOTE OPEN HOUSE TO OTHER AGENTS
- [ ] PROMOTE OPEN HOUSE ON SOCIAL MEDIA

ON THE MARKET

- [ ] MONITOR NEIGHBORHOOD MARKET CHANGES
- [ ] COMMUNICATE CHANGES TO CLIENTS
- [ ] GATHER SHOWING FEEDBACK
- [ ] CREATE SHOWING FEEDBACK REPORT
- [ ] REVIEW PRICING STRATEGY

SETTING CLIENT EXPECTATIONS

- [ ] DISCUSS CLIENTS GOALS
- [ ] IDENTIFY AREAS OF PROPERTY THAT NEED IMPROVING
- [ ] ADDRESS DECLUTTERING, DEPERSONALIZING, REPAIRS
- [ ] DISCUSS PRICING AND TIMING STRATEGY
- [ ] DISCUSS SHOWING PREFERENCES & APPROVALS
- [ ] PRELIMINARY NET SHEET

NOTES

Listing Management Checklist

PRE-LISTING

- LISTING APPOINTMENT SET
- PREVIEW COMPARABLES
- RUN COMPARABLES
- CREATE CMA
- EDIT LISTING PRESENTATION
- PREPARE LISTING PAPERWORK
- PREPARE LISTING FOLDER FOR CLIENT

CREATE LISTING

- SCHEDULE PHOTOGRAPHER
- CREATE VIDEO TOUR
- INPUT DATA IN MLS
- SCAN / UPLOAD DOCUMENTS INTO MLS
- INSTALL YARD SIGN
- CREATE "JUST LISTED" SOCIAL MEDIA POST
- CREATE "JUST LISTED" POSTCARDS
- EMAIL LISTING TO DATABASE

OPEN HOUSE

- SCHEDULE OPEN HOUSE
- SCHEDULE BROKERS OPEN HOUSE
- PREPARE PROPERTY MARKETING MATERIALS
- PROMOTE OPEN HOUSE TO OTHER AGENTS
- PROMOTE OPEN HOUSE ON SOCIAL MEDIA

ON THE MARKET

- MONITOR NEIGHBORHOOD MARKET CHANGES
- COMMUNICATE CHANGES TO CLIENTS
- GATHER SHOWING FEEDBACK
- CREATE SHOWING FEEDBACK REPORT
- REVIEW PRICING STRATEGY

SETTING CLIENT EXPECTATIONS

- DISCUSS CLIENTS GOALS
- IDENTIFY AREAS OF PROPERTY THAT NEED IMPROVING
- ADDRESS DECLUTTERING, DEPERSONALIZING, REPAIRS
- DISCUSS PRICING AND TIMING STRATEGY
- DISCUSS SHOWING PREFERENCES & APPROVALS
- PRELIMINARY NET SHEET

NOTES

Listing Management Checklist

PRE-LISTING

- [ ] LISTING APPOINTMENT SET
- [ ] PREVIEW COMPARABLES
- [ ] RUN COMPARABLES
- [ ] CREATE CMA
- [ ] EDIT LISTING PRESENTATION
- [ ] PREPARE LISTING PAPERWORK
- [ ] PREPARE LISTING FOLDER FOR CLIENT

CREATE LISTING

- [ ] SCHEDULE PHOTOGRAPHER
- [ ] CREATE VIDEO TOUR
- [ ] INPUT DATA IN MLS
- [ ] SCAN / UPLOAD DOCUMENTS INTO MLS
- [ ] INSTALL YARD SIGN
- [ ] CREATE "JUST LISTED" SOCIAL MEDIA POST
- [ ] CREATE "JUST LISTED" POSTCARDS
- [ ] EMAIL LISTING TO DATABASE

OPEN HOUSE

- [ ] SCHEDULE OPEN HOUSE
- [ ] SCHEDULE BROKERS OPEN HOUSE
- [ ] PREPARE PROPERTY MARKETING MATERIALS
- [ ] PROMOTE OPEN HOUSE TO OTHER AGENTS
- [ ] PROMOTE OPEN HOUSE ON SOCIAL MEDIA

ON THE MARKET

- [ ] MONITOR NEIGHBORHOOD MARKET CHANGES
- [ ] COMMUNICATE CHANGES TO CLIENTS
- [ ] GATHER SHOWING FEEDBACK
- [ ] CREATE SHOWING FEEDBACK REPORT
- [ ] REVIEW PRICING STRATEGY

SETTING CLIENT EXPECTATIONS

- [ ] DISCUSS CLIENTS GOALS
- [ ] IDENTIFY AREAS OF PROPERTY THAT NEED IMPROVING
- [ ] ADDRESS DECLUTTERING, DEPERSONALIZING, REPAIRS
- [ ] DISCUSS PRICING AND TIMING STRATEGY
- [ ] DISCUSS SHOWING PREFERENCES & APPROVALS
- [ ] PRELIMINARY NET SHEET

NOTES

Listing Management Checklist

PRE-LISTING

- [ ] LISTING APPOINTMENT SET
- [ ] PREVIEW COMPARABLES
- [ ] RUN COMPARABLES
- [ ] CREATE CMA
- [ ] EDIT LISTING PRESENTATION
- [ ] PREPARE LISTING PAPERWORK
- [ ] PREPARE LISTING FOLDER FOR CLIENT

CREATE LISTING

- [ ] SCHEDULE PHOTOGRAPHER
- [ ] CREATE VIDEO TOUR
- [ ] INPUT DATA IN MLS
- [ ] SCAN / UPLOAD DOCUMENTS INTO MLS
- [ ] INSTALL YARD SIGN
- [ ] CREATE "JUST LISTED" SOCIAL MEDIA POST
- [ ] CREATE "JUST LISTED" POSTCARDS
- [ ] EMAIL LISTING TO DATABASE

OPEN HOUSE

- [ ] SCHEDULE OPEN HOUSE
- [ ] SCHEDULE BROKERS OPEN HOUSE
- [ ] PREPARE PROPERTY MARKETING MATERIALS
- [ ] PROMOTE OPEN HOUSE TO OTHER AGENTS
- [ ] PROMOTE OPEN HOUSE ON SOCIAL MEDIA

ON THE MARKET

- [ ] MONITOR NEIGHBORHOOD MARKET CHANGES
- [ ] COMMUNICATE CHANGES TO CLIENTS
- [ ] GATHER SHOWING FEEDBACK
- [ ] CREATE SHOWING FEEDBACK REPORT
- [ ] REVIEW PRICING STRATEGY

SETTING CLIENT EXPECTATIONS

- [ ] DISCUSS CLIENTS GOALS
- [ ] IDENTIFY AREAS OF PROPERTY THAT NEED IMPROVING
- [ ] ADDRESS DECLUTTERING, DEPERSONALIZING, REPAIRS
- [ ] DISCUSS PRICING AND TIMING STRATEGY
- [ ] DISCUSS SHOWING PREFERENCES & APPROVALS
- [ ] PRELIMINARY NET SHEET

NOTES

Listing Management Checklist

PRE-LISTING

- [ ] LISTING APPOINTMENT SET
- [ ] PREVIEW COMPARABLES
- [ ] RUN COMPARABLES
- [ ] CREATE CMA
- [ ] EDIT LISTING PRESENTATION
- [ ] PREPARE LISTING PAPERWORK
- [ ] PREPARE LISTING FOLDER FOR CLIENT

CREATE LISTING

- [ ] SCHEDULE PHOTOGRAPHER
- [ ] CREATE VIDEO TOUR
- [ ] INPUT DATA IN MLS
- [ ] SCAN / UPLOAD DOCUMENTS INTO MLS
- [ ] INSTALL YARD SIGN
- [ ] CREATE "JUST LISTED" SOCIAL MEDIA POST
- [ ] CREATE "JUST LISTED" POSTCARDS
- [ ] EMAIL LISTING TO DATABASE

OPEN HOUSE

- [ ] SCHEDULE OPEN HOUSE
- [ ] SCHEDULE BROKERS OPEN HOUSE
- [ ] PREPARE PROPERTY MARKETING MATERIALS
- [ ] PROMOTE OPEN HOUSE TO OTHER AGENTS
- [ ] PROMOTE OPEN HOUSE ON SOCIAL MEDIA

ON THE MARKET

- [ ] MONITOR NEIGHBORHOOD MARKET CHANGES
- [ ] COMMUNICATE CHANGES TO CLIENTS
- [ ] GATHER SHOWING FEEDBACK
- [ ] CREATE SHOWING FEEDBACK REPORT
- [ ] REVIEW PRICING STRATEGY

SETTING CLIENT EXPECTATIONS

- [ ] DISCUSS CLIENTS GOALS
- [ ] IDENTIFY AREAS OF PROPERTY THAT NEED IMPROVING
- [ ] ADDRESS DECLUTTERING, DEPERSONALIZING, REPAIRS
- [ ] DISCUSS PRICING AND TIMING STRATEGY
- [ ] DISCUSS SHOWING PREFERENCES & APPROVALS
- [ ] PRELIMINARY NET SHEET

NOTES

Listing Management Checklist

PRE-LISTING

- [ ] LISTING APPOINTMENT SET
- [ ] PREVIEW COMPARABLES
- [ ] RUN COMPARABLES
- [ ] CREATE CMA
- [ ] EDIT LISTING PRESENTATION
- [ ] PREPARE LISTING PAPERWORK
- [ ] PREPARE LISTING FOLDER FOR CLIENT

CREATE LISTING

- [ ] SCHEDULE PHOTOGRAPHER
- [ ] CREATE VIDEO TOUR
- [ ] INPUT DATA IN MLS
- [ ] SCAN / UPLOAD DOCUMENTS INTO MLS
- [ ] INSTALL YARD SIGN
- [ ] CREATE "JUST LISTED" SOCIAL MEDIA POST
- [ ] CREATE "JUST LISTED" POSTCARDS
- [ ] EMAIL LISTING TO DATABASE

OPEN HOUSE

- [ ] SCHEDULE OPEN HOUSE
- [ ] SCHEDULE BROKERS OPEN HOUSE
- [ ] PREPARE PROPERTY MARKETING MATERIALS
- [ ] PROMOTE OPEN HOUSE TO OTHER AGENTS
- [ ] PROMOTE OPEN HOUSE ON SOCIAL MEDIA

ON THE MARKET

- [ ] MONITOR NEIGHBORHOOD MARKET CHANGES
- [ ] COMMUNICATE CHANGES TO CLIENTS
- [ ] GATHER SHOWING FEEDBACK
- [ ] CREATE SHOWING FEEDBACK REPORT
- [ ] REVIEW PRICING STRATEGY

SETTING CLIENT EXPECTATIONS

- [ ] DISCUSS CLIENTS GOALS
- [ ] IDENTIFY AREAS OF PROPERTY THAT NEED IMPROVING
- [ ] ADDRESS DECLUTTERING, DEPERSONALIZING, REPAIRS
- [ ] DISCUSS PRICING AND TIMING STRATEGY
- [ ] DISCUSS SHOWING PREFERENCES & APPROVALS
- [ ] PRELIMINARY NET SHEET

NOTES

Listing Management Checklist

PRE-LISTING

- [ ] LISTING APPOINTMENT SET
- [ ] PREVIEW COMPARABLES
- [ ] RUN COMPARABLES
- [ ] CREATE CMA
- [ ] EDIT LISTING PRESENTATION
- [ ] PREPARE LISTING PAPERWORK
- [ ] PREPARE LISTING FOLDER FOR CLIENT

CREATE LISTING

- [ ] SCHEDULE PHOTOGRAPHER
- [ ] CREATE VIDEO TOUR
- [ ] INPUT DATA IN MLS
- [ ] SCAN / UPLOAD DOCUMENTS INTO MLS
- [ ] INSTALL YARD SIGN
- [ ] CREATE "JUST LISTED" SOCIAL MEDIA POST
- [ ] CREATE "JUST LISTED" POSTCARDS
- [ ] EMAIL LISTING TO DATABASE

OPEN HOUSE

- [ ] SCHEDULE OPEN HOUSE
- [ ] SCHEDULE BROKERS OPEN HOUSE
- [ ] PREPARE PROPERTY MARKETING MATERIALS
- [ ] PROMOTE OPEN HOUSE TO OTHER AGENTS
- [ ] PROMOTE OPEN HOUSE ON SOCIAL MEDIA

ON THE MARKET

- [ ] MONITOR NEIGHBORHOOD MARKET CHANGES
- [ ] COMMUNICATE CHANGES TO CLIENTS
- [ ] GATHER SHOWING FEEDBACK
- [ ] CREATE SHOWING FEEDBACK REPORT
- [ ] REVIEW PRICING STRATEGY

SETTING CLIENT EXPECTATIONS

- [ ] DISCUSS CLIENTS GOALS
- [ ] IDENTIFY AREAS OF PROPERTY THAT NEED IMPROVING
- [ ] ADDRESS DECLUTTERING, DEPERSONALIZING, REPAIRS
- [ ] DISCUSS PRICING AND TIMING STRATEGY
- [ ] DISCUSS SHOWING PREFERENCES & APPROVALS
- [ ] PRELIMINARY NET SHEET

NOTES

Listing Management Checklist

PRE-LISTING

- [ ] LISTING APPOINTMENT SET
- [ ] PREVIEW COMPARABLES
- [ ] RUN COMPARABLES
- [ ] CREATE CMA
- [ ] EDIT LISTING PRESENTATION
- [ ] PREPARE LISTING PAPERWORK
- [ ] PREPARE LISTING FOLDER FOR CLIENT

CREATE LISTING

- [ ] SCHEDULE PHOTOGRAPHER
- [ ] CREATE VIDEO TOUR
- [ ] INPUT DATA IN MLS
- [ ] SCAN / UPLOAD DOCUMENTS INTO MLS
- [ ] INSTALL YARD SIGN
- [ ] CREATE "JUST LISTED" SOCIAL MEDIA POST
- [ ] CREATE "JUST LISTED" POSTCARDS
- [ ] EMAIL LISTING TO DATABASE

OPEN HOUSE

- [ ] SCHEDULE OPEN HOUSE
- [ ] SCHEDULE BROKERS OPEN HOUSE
- [ ] PREPARE PROPERTY MARKETING MATERIALS
- [ ] PROMOTE OPEN HOUSE TO OTHER AGENTS
- [ ] PROMOTE OPEN HOUSE ON SOCIAL MEDIA

ON THE MARKET

- [ ] MONITOR NEIGHBORHOOD MARKET CHANGES
- [ ] COMMUNICATE CHANGES TO CLIENTS
- [ ] GATHER SHOWING FEEDBACK
- [ ] CREATE SHOWING FEEDBACK REPORT
- [ ] REVIEW PRICING STRATEGY

SETTING CLIENT EXPECTATIONS

- [ ] DISCUSS CLIENTS GOALS
- [ ] IDENTIFY AREAS OF PROPERTY THAT NEED IMPROVING
- [ ] ADDRESS DECLUTTERING, DEPERSONALIZING, REPAIRS
- [ ] DISCUSS PRICING AND TIMING STRATEGY
- [ ] DISCUSS SHOWING PREFERENCES & APPROVALS
- [ ] PRELIMINARY NET SHEET

NOTES

Listing Management Checklist

PRE-LISTING

- [ ] LISTING APPOINTMENT SET
- [ ] PREVIEW COMPARABLES
- [ ] RUN COMPARABLES
- [ ] CREATE CMA
- [ ] EDIT LISTING PRESENTATION
- [ ] PREPARE LISTING PAPERWORK
- [ ] PREPARE LISTING FOLDER FOR CLIENT

CREATE LISTING

- [ ] SCHEDULE PHOTOGRAPHER
- [ ] CREATE VIDEO TOUR
- [ ] INPUT DATA IN MLS
- [ ] SCAN / UPLOAD DOCUMENTS INTO MLS
- [ ] INSTALL YARD SIGN
- [ ] CREATE "JUST LISTED" SOCIAL MEDIA POST
- [ ] CREATE "JUST LISTED" POSTCARDS
- [ ] EMAIL LISTING TO DATABASE

OPEN HOUSE

- [ ] SCHEDULE OPEN HOUSE
- [ ] SCHEDULE BROKERS OPEN HOUSE
- [ ] PREPARE PROPERTY MARKETING MATERIALS
- [ ] PROMOTE OPEN HOUSE TO OTHER AGENTS
- [ ] PROMOTE OPEN HOUSE ON SOCIAL MEDIA

ON THE MARKET

- [ ] MONITOR NEIGHBORHOOD MARKET CHANGES
- [ ] COMMUNICATE CHANGES TO CLIENTS
- [ ] GATHER SHOWING FEEDBACK
- [ ] CREATE SHOWING FEEDBACK REPORT
- [ ] REVIEW PRICING STRATEGY

SETTING CLIENT EXPECTATIONS

- [ ] DISCUSS CLIENTS GOALS
- [ ] IDENTIFY AREAS OF PROPERTY THAT NEED IMPROVING
- [ ] ADDRESS DECLUTTERING, DEPERSONALIZING, REPAIRS
- [ ] DISCUSS PRICING AND TIMING STRATEGY
- [ ] DISCUSS SHOWING PREFERENCES & APPROVALS
- [ ] PRELIMINARY NET SHEET

NOTES

Listing Management Checklist

PRE-LISTING

- [ ] LISTING APPOINTMENT SET
- [ ] PREVIEW COMPARABLES
- [ ] RUN COMPARABLES
- [ ] CREATE CMA
- [ ] EDIT LISTING PRESENTATION
- [ ] PREPARE LISTING PAPERWORK
- [ ] PREPARE LISTING FOLDER FOR CLIENT

CREATE LISTING

- [ ] SCHEDULE PHOTOGRAPHER
- [ ] CREATE VIDEO TOUR
- [ ] INPUT DATA IN MLS
- [ ] SCAN / UPLOAD DOCUMENTS INTO MLS
- [ ] INSTALL YARD SIGN
- [ ] CREATE "JUST LISTED" SOCIAL MEDIA POST
- [ ] CREATE "JUST LISTED" POSTCARDS
- [ ] EMAIL LISTING TO DATABASE

OPEN HOUSE

- [ ] SCHEDULE OPEN HOUSE
- [ ] SCHEDULE BROKERS OPEN HOUSE
- [ ] PREPARE PROPERTY MARKETING MATERIALS
- [ ] PROMOTE OPEN HOUSE TO OTHER AGENTS
- [ ] PROMOTE OPEN HOUSE ON SOCIAL MEDIA

ON THE MARKET

- [ ] MONITOR NEIGHBORHOOD MARKET CHANGES
- [ ] COMMUNICATE CHANGES TO CLIENTS
- [ ] GATHER SHOWING FEEDBACK
- [ ] CREATE SHOWING FEEDBACK REPORT
- [ ] REVIEW PRICING STRATEGY

SETTING CLIENT EXPECTATIONS

- [ ] DISCUSS CLIENTS GOALS
- [ ] IDENTIFY AREAS OF PROPERTY THAT NEED IMPROVING
- [ ] ADDRESS DECLUTTERING, DEPERSONALIZING, REPAIRS
- [ ] DISCUSS PRICING AND TIMING STRATEGY
- [ ] DISCUSS SHOWING PREFERENCES & APPROVALS
- [ ] PRELIMINARY NET SHEET

NOTES

Listing Management Checklist

PRE-LISTING

- [ ] LISTING APPOINTMENT SET
- [ ] PREVIEW COMPARABLES
- [ ] RUN COMPARABLES
- [ ] CREATE CMA
- [ ] EDIT LISTING PRESENTATION
- [ ] PREPARE LISTING PAPERWORK
- [ ] PREPARE LISTING FOLDER FOR CLIENT

CREATE LISTING

- [ ] SCHEDULE PHOTOGRAPHER
- [ ] CREATE VIDEO TOUR
- [ ] INPUT DATA IN MLS
- [ ] SCAN / UPLOAD DOCUMENTS INTO MLS
- [ ] INSTALL YARD SIGN
- [ ] CREATE "JUST LISTED" SOCIAL MEDIA POST
- [ ] CREATE "JUST LISTED" POSTCARDS
- [ ] EMAIL LISTING TO DATABASE

OPEN HOUSE

- [ ] SCHEDULE OPEN HOUSE
- [ ] SCHEDULE BROKERS OPEN HOUSE
- [ ] PREPARE PROPERTY MARKETING MATERIALS
- [ ] PROMOTE OPEN HOUSE TO OTHER AGENTS
- [ ] PROMOTE OPEN HOUSE ON SOCIAL MEDIA

ON THE MARKET

- [ ] MONITOR NEIGHBORHOOD MARKET CHANGES
- [ ] COMMUNICATE CHANGES TO CLIENTS
- [ ] GATHER SHOWING FEEDBACK
- [ ] CREATE SHOWING FEEDBACK REPORT
- [ ] REVIEW PRICING STRATEGY

SETTING CLIENT EXPECTATIONS

- [ ] DISCUSS CLIENTS GOALS
- [ ] IDENTIFY AREAS OF PROPERTY THAT NEED IMPROVING
- [ ] ADDRESS DECLUTTERING, DEPERSONALIZING, REPAIRS
- [ ] DISCUSS PRICING AND TIMING STRATEGY
- [ ] DISCUSS SHOWING PREFERENCES & APPROVALS
- [ ] PRELIMINARY NET SHEET

NOTES

Listing Management Checklist

PRE-LISTING

- [ ] LISTING APPOINTMENT SET
- [ ] PREVIEW COMPARABLES
- [ ] RUN COMPARABLES
- [ ] CREATE CMA
- [ ] EDIT LISTING PRESENTATION
- [ ] PREPARE LISTING PAPERWORK
- [ ] PREPARE LISTING FOLDER FOR CLIENT

CREATE LISTING

- [ ] SCHEDULE PHOTOGRAPHER
- [ ] CREATE VIDEO TOUR
- [ ] INPUT DATA IN MLS
- [ ] SCAN / UPLOAD DOCUMENTS INTO MLS
- [ ] INSTALL YARD SIGN
- [ ] CREATE "JUST LISTED" SOCIAL MEDIA POST
- [ ] CREATE "JUST LISTED" POSTCARDS
- [ ] EMAIL LISTING TO DATABASE

OPEN HOUSE

- [ ] SCHEDULE OPEN HOUSE
- [ ] SCHEDULE BROKERS OPEN HOUSE
- [ ] PREPARE PROPERTY MARKETING MATERIALS
- [ ] PROMOTE OPEN HOUSE TO OTHER AGENTS
- [ ] PROMOTE OPEN HOUSE ON SOCIAL MEDIA

ON THE MARKET

- [ ] MONITOR NEIGHBORHOOD MARKET CHANGES
- [ ] COMMUNICATE CHANGES TO CLIENTS
- [ ] GATHER SHOWING FEEDBACK
- [ ] CREATE SHOWING FEEDBACK REPORT
- [ ] REVIEW PRICING STRATEGY

SETTING CLIENT EXPECTATIONS

- [ ] DISCUSS CLIENTS GOALS
- [ ] IDENTIFY AREAS OF PROPERTY THAT NEED IMPROVING
- [ ] ADDRESS DECLUTTERING, DEPERSONALIZING, REPAIRS
- [ ] DISCUSS PRICING AND TIMING STRATEGY
- [ ] DISCUSS SHOWING PREFERENCES & APPROVALS
- [ ] PRELIMINARY NET SHEET

NOTES

Listing Management Checklist

PRE-LISTING

- LISTING APPOINTMENT SET
- PREVIEW COMPARABLES
- RUN COMPARABLES
- CREATE CMA
- EDIT LISTING PRESENTATION
- PREPARE LISTING PAPERWORK
- PREPARE LISTING FOLDER FOR CLIENT

CREATE LISTING

- SCHEDULE PHOTOGRAPHER
- CREATE VIDEO TOUR
- INPUT DATA IN MLS
- SCAN / UPLOAD DOCUMENTS INTO MLS
- INSTALL YARD SIGN
- CREATE "JUST LISTED" SOCIAL MEDIA POST
- CREATE "JUST LISTED" POSTCARDS
- EMAIL LISTING TO DATABASE

OPEN HOUSE

- SCHEDULE OPEN HOUSE
- SCHEDULE BROKERS OPEN HOUSE
- PREPARE PROPERTY MARKETING MATERIALS
- PROMOTE OPEN HOUSE TO OTHER AGENTS
- PROMOTE OPEN HOUSE ON SOCIAL MEDIA

ON THE MARKET

- MONITOR NEIGHBORHOOD MARKET CHANGES
- COMMUNICATE CHANGES TO CLIENTS
- GATHER SHOWING FEEDBACK
- CREATE SHOWING FEEDBACK REPORT
- REVIEW PRICING STRATEGY

SETTING CLIENT EXPECTATIONS

- DISCUSS CLIENTS GOALS
- IDENTIFY AREAS OF PROPERTY THAT NEED IMPROVING
- ADDRESS DECLUTTERING, DEPERSONALIZING, REPAIRS
- DISCUSS PRICING AND TIMING STRATEGY
- DISCUSS SHOWING PREFERENCES & APPROVALS
- PRELIMINARY NET SHEET

NOTES

Listing Management Checklist

PRE-LISTING

- [ ] LISTING APPOINTMENT SET
- [ ] PREVIEW COMPARABLES
- [ ] RUN COMPARABLES
- [ ] CREATE CMA
- [ ] EDIT LISTING PRESENTATION
- [ ] PREPARE LISTING PAPERWORK
- [ ] PREPARE LISTING FOLDER FOR CLIENT

CREATE LISTING

- [ ] SCHEDULE PHOTOGRAPHER
- [ ] CREATE VIDEO TOUR
- [ ] INPUT DATA IN MLS
- [ ] SCAN / UPLOAD DOCUMENTS INTO MLS
- [ ] INSTALL YARD SIGN
- [ ] CREATE "JUST LISTED" SOCIAL MEDIA POST
- [ ] CREATE "JUST LISTED" POSTCARDS
- [ ] EMAIL LISTING TO DATABASE

OPEN HOUSE

- [ ] SCHEDULE OPEN HOUSE
- [ ] SCHEDULE BROKERS OPEN HOUSE
- [ ] PREPARE PROPERTY MARKETING MATERIALS
- [ ] PROMOTE OPEN HOUSE TO OTHER AGENTS
- [ ] PROMOTE OPEN HOUSE ON SOCIAL MEDIA

ON THE MARKET

- [ ] MONITOR NEIGHBORHOOD MARKET CHANGES
- [ ] COMMUNICATE CHANGES TO CLIENTS
- [ ] GATHER SHOWING FEEDBACK
- [ ] CREATE SHOWING FEEDBACK REPORT
- [ ] REVIEW PRICING STRATEGY

SETTING CLIENT EXPECTATIONS

- [ ] DISCUSS CLIENTS GOALS
- [ ] IDENTIFY AREAS OF PROPERTY THAT NEED IMPROVING
- [ ] ADDRESS DECLUTTERING, DEPERSONALIZING, REPAIRS
- [ ] DISCUSS PRICING AND TIMING STRATEGY
- [ ] DISCUSS SHOWING PREFERENCES & APPROVALS
- [ ] PRELIMINARY NET SHEET

NOTES

It's a slow process

but quitting won't speed it up.

Closing
Trackers

Closing Tracker

CLIENT	ADDRESS	DATE	COMMISSION

Closing Tracker

CLIENT	ADDRESS	DATE	COMMISSION

Closing Tracker

CLIENT	ADDRESS	DATE	COMMISSION

Closing Tracker

CLIENT	ADDRESS	DATE	COMMISSION

You will never always be motivated so you must learn to be disciplined.

Mileage Trackers

Mileage Tracker

DATE	PURPOSE	START ODOMETER	END ODOMETER	TOTAL MILES

Mileage Tracker

DATE	PURPOSE	START ODOMETER	END ODOMETER	TOTAL MILES

Mileage Tracker

DATE	PURPOSE	START ODOMETER	END ODOMETER	TOTAL MILES

Mileage Tracker

DATE	PURPOSE	START ODOMETER	END ODOMETER	TOTAL MILES

Mileage Tracker

DATE	PURPOSE	START ODOMETER	END ODOMETER	TOTAL MILES

Mileage Tracker

DATE	PURPOSE	START ODOMETER	END ODOMETER	TOTAL MILES

Mileage Tracker

DATE	PURPOSE	START ODOMETER	END ODOMETER	TOTAL MILES

Mileage Tracker

DATE	PURPOSE	START ODOMETER	END ODOMETER	TOTAL MILES

Mileage Tracker

DATE	PURPOSE	START ODOMETER	END ODOMETER	TOTAL MILES

Mileage Tracker

DATE	PURPOSE	START ODOMETER	END ODOMETER	TOTAL MILES

Consistency is more important than perfection.

Meeting Notes

Meeting Notes

TOPIC: /   /

BIGGEST TAKEAWAYS

ACTIONS TO TAKE

TOPIC: /   /

BIGGEST TAKEAWAYS

ACTIONS TO TAKE

Meeting Notes

TOPIC: /   /

BIGGEST TAKEAWAYS

ACTIONS TO TAKE

TOPIC: /   /

BIGGEST TAKEAWAYS

ACTIONS TO TAKE

Meeting Notes

TOPIC: /   /

BIGGEST TAKEAWAYS

ACTIONS TO TAKE

TOPIC: /   /

BIGGEST TAKEAWAYS

ACTIONS TO TAKE

Meeting Notes

TOPIC: /   /

BIGGEST TAKEAWAYS

ACTIONS TO TAKE

TOPIC: /   /

BIGGEST TAKEAWAYS

ACTIONS TO TAKE

Meeting Notes

TOPIC: /   /

BIGGEST TAKEAWAYS

ACTIONS TO TAKE

TOPIC: /   /

BIGGEST TAKEAWAYS

ACTIONS TO TAKE

Meeting Notes

TOPIC: /   /

BIGGEST TAKEAWAYS

ACTIONS TO TAKE

TOPIC: /   /

BIGGEST TAKEAWAYS

ACTIONS TO TAKE

Meeting Notes

TOPIC: /   /

BIGGEST TAKEAWAYS

ACTIONS TO TAKE

TOPIC: /   /

BIGGEST TAKEAWAYS

ACTIONS TO TAKE

Meeting Notes

TOPIC: /   /

BIGGEST TAKEAWAYS

ACTIONS TO TAKE

TOPIC: /   /

BIGGEST TAKEAWAYS

ACTIONS TO TAKE

Meeting Notes

TOPIC: /   /

BIGGEST TAKEAWAYS

ACTIONS TO TAKE

TOPIC: /   /

BIGGEST TAKEAWAYS

ACTIONS TO TAKE

Meeting Notes

TOPIC: /   /

BIGGEST TAKEAWAYS

ACTIONS TO TAKE

TOPIC: /   /

BIGGEST TAKEAWAYS

ACTIONS TO TAKE

Meeting Notes

TOPIC: /   /

BIGGEST TAKEAWAYS

ACTIONS TO TAKE

TOPIC: /   /

BIGGEST TAKEAWAYS

ACTIONS TO TAKE

Meeting Notes

TOPIC: /   /

BIGGEST TAKEAWAYS

ACTIONS TO TAKE

TOPIC: /   /

BIGGEST TAKEAWAYS

ACTIONS TO TAKE

Meeting Notes

TOPIC: /   /

BIGGEST TAKEAWAYS

ACTIONS TO TAKE

TOPIC: /   /

BIGGEST TAKEAWAYS

ACTIONS TO TAKE

Meeting Notes

TOPIC: /   /

BIGGEST TAKEAWAYS

ACTIONS TO TAKE

TOPIC: /   /

BIGGEST TAKEAWAYS

ACTIONS TO TAKE

Meeting Notes

TOPIC: /   /

BIGGEST TAKEAWAYS

ACTIONS TO TAKE

TOPIC: /   /

BIGGEST TAKEAWAYS

ACTIONS TO TAKE

Meeting Notes

TOPIC: /   /

BIGGEST TAKEAWAYS

ACTIONS TO TAKE

TOPIC: /   /

BIGGEST TAKEAWAYS

ACTIONS TO TAKE

Meeting Notes

TOPIC: /   /

BIGGEST TAKEAWAYS

ACTIONS TO TAKE

TOPIC: /   /

BIGGEST TAKEAWAYS

ACTIONS TO TAKE

Meeting Notes

TOPIC: /   /

BIGGEST TAKEAWAYS

ACTIONS TO TAKE

TOPIC: /   /

BIGGEST TAKEAWAYS

ACTIONS TO TAKE

Meeting Notes

TOPIC: /   /

BIGGEST TAKEAWAYS

ACTIONS TO TAKE

TOPIC: /   /

BIGGEST TAKEAWAYS

ACTIONS TO TAKE

Meeting Notes

TOPIC: /   /

BIGGEST TAKEAWAYS

ACTIONS TO TAKE

TOPIC: /   /

BIGGEST TAKEAWAYS

ACTIONS TO TAKE

About the author

SAMANTHA FIRST FOUND HER PASSION FOR BEING AN ENTREPRENEUR WHEN SHE OPENED HER FIRST ETSY SHOP IN 2011. SINCE THEN SHE'S CREATED 9 SUCCESSFUL ONLINE BUSINESSES IN E-COMMERCE, SELLING DIGITAL ITEMS, MULTI-LEVEL MARKETING, BRANDING, GRAPHIC DESIGN AND HAS BEEN A LICENSED REAL ESTATE AGENT SINCE 2017.

SHE IS AN ATTRACTION MARKETING EXPERT WITH A MONTHLY REACH OF OVER 450K. HER PASSION FOR CREATING BEAUTIFUL BUSINESSES AND PASSIVE INCOME SOURCES DRIVE HER TO SHARE HER KNOWLEDGE OF BRANDING AND ATTRACTION MARKETING WITH AMBITIOUS WOMEN ENTREPRENEURS.

TODAY SHE FOCUSES MAINLY ON HER REAL ESTATE CAREER WITH HER HUSBAND, ETSY SHOPS SELLING DIGITAL ITEMS FOR FEMALE ENTREPRENEURS & GROWING HER YOUTUBE CHANNEL.

Follow Samantha

@samantha_hauger

youtube.com/c/SamanthaHauger

facebook.com/SamanthaHaugerBlog

pinterest.com/samantha_hauger/

Made in the USA
Las Vegas, NV
07 December 2023

82311255R00177